The Garden Beautiful

You are holding a reproduction of an original work that is in the public domain in the United States of America, and possibly other countries. You may freely copy and distribute this work as no entity (individual or corporate) has a copyright on the body of the work. This book may contain prior copyright references, and library stamps (as most of these works were scanned from library copies). These have been scanned and retained as part of the historical artifact.

This book may have occasional imperfections such as missing or blurred pages, poor pictures, errant marks, etc. that were either part of the original artifact, or were introduced by the scanning process. We believe this work is culturally important, and despite the imperfections, have elected to bring it back into print as part of our continuing commitment to the preservation of printed works worldwide. We appreciate your understanding of the imperfections in the preservation process, and hope you enjoy this valuable book.

THE GARDEN BEAUTIFUL

THE
GARDEN BEAUTIFUL

HOME WOODS, HOME LANDSCAPE

By W. ROBINSON
AUTHOR OF THE 'WILD GARDEN'

> Some trees under no compulsion from men, grow up of themselves, of their own accord, and spread widely over the plains and the winding river banks, like the pliant osier and the limber broom, the poplar, and the willow groves that look so hoary with their grey leaves. Some again spring up from the dropping of seed, like the tall chestnuts, and the forest-monarch which puts forth its royal leaves for Jove, the aesculus, and the oaks—in Greece deemed oracular. With others a forest of suckers shoots up from their roots, as with cherry-trees and elms—nay, the bay of Parnassus rears its infant head under the mighty covert of its mother's shade. These are the modes which Nature first gave to men unasked—to these the whole race of forest-trees and shrubs and sacred groves owe their verdure.—VIRGIL (*Conington*).

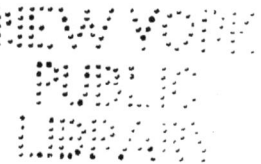

LONDON
JOHN MURRAY ALBEMARLE STREET
1906

Oxford: Horace Hart
Printer to the University

PRÉFACE

This book is for the country house, or any place where there is woodland or land to plant; its object is to get people, after thought of the needs of a true garden, to think more of their woods from aesthetic and other points of view. Its aim is to teach the best of all lessons for garden-lovers —too often absorbed in the exotic, the curious, and the tender—that our own country's trees are the most beautiful we shall ever have, and our native flowers as fair as any. I do not mean any extension of the pleasure-ground, so often a poor 'sticky' thing, little better than the stereotyped flower-garden, but the real woodland. Small gardens are often the most beautiful and the best for the happiness of their owners; but we have to think of the many who have greater opportunities too seldom embraced—woodlands that are not brought into any happy relation with the house and are often not accessible. In the district in which I live there are hundreds of acres of beautiful woods never seen by any but the gamekeeper, woods sheeted with King-

cups, Primroses, and Wood Hyacinths, more beautiful in their effect than any garden.

These woodland gardens rarely depend on the weather, and while Carnations and Roses in the garden may fail through weather and other causes, the woodland flowers are always true to their seasons, and no garden effect can equal theirs in breadth and in succession of beauty over the same ground. With their soft background of underwood it is vain for the gardener to attempt to rival them. During our winters no real flower-gardening is possible in these islands, save in favoured spots near the coast, and even the scared little conifers stuck out in the flower-beds (as before the King's palace in St. James's Park last winter) do not help us. Yet our climate is excellent for the hardy evergreen trees of the north, which give us shelter, warmth, and dignity; and no country of Europe is more favourable to such life than ours. It is not the 'pleasure-ground' but the woodland which enables us to grow fine trees, and their place is the wood and not the pleasure-garden. How seldom 'pinetums' or botanic gardens in England and France contain a well-grown Pine! The whole system of dotting trees on grass is a wrong one; the true way to enjoy their beauty and favour their growth is in woodland planting. Those who have no woods, but have bare lands to plant, can raise woods in ten years if they keep out cows, horses, rabbits, and hares for seven years.

Other reasons for taking to the woods are, that there we at least get away from the vain though harmful talk about 'styles' with which most books on garden design are filled. We also part with the new and foolish teaching of the forestry books, separating tree-culture into two branches—arboriculture and sylviculture. If we go into a real wood anywhere we may soon see that true beauty is there and vigour too. Much wealth has been wasted in our islands in planting Pines in pinetums and pleasure-grounds where they never show their true character nor even grow well, in spite of often costly and needless preparation of soil.

In the free woodland weeding or routine of any kind need not trouble us; and there we may easily naturalize good native plants not already to be found there, or the finer woodland plants of other countries (Narcissus, Snowdrops, blue Windflower) and native plants not found in our district (Royal Fern, the Snowflake, and Lily of the Valley).

The open, airy, and well-considered ways I plead for are not against our woodland work in any way. The finest trees are often found at the sides of rides, their roots occupying all the ground; and such rides are best for hunting, shooting, riding, walking, and every use or pleasure to which woodland can be put.

The words 'Home landscape' in the title lead to the idea that all of the work suggested in the book may be done with benefit to the general effect of the landscape. The hard and ugly lines so often seen about country houses, and which often come from modern ways of fencing and stereotyped plans, have no good reason to be. The artistic eye soon finds them out, and the artist will get out of their way. The only true test of all such things is the artistic one—Do they make for ugliness or for beauty? Breaking into the woods in the way I plead for here gives us many chances of improving the home landscape and opening out views —often airy stretches—into new country, even the rides through a foreground of young woods becoming a fine feature. For the rest, every idea that the book suggests I have proved the good of myself.

W. R.

Gravetye Manor,
  June, 1906.

CONTENTS

CHAPTER I
Garden Design and Recent Writings upon it . PAGE 1

CHAPTER II
Art in relation to Flower Gardening and Garden Design 21

CHAPTER III
Of so-called Styles and some Common Mistakes . 30

CHAPTER IV
Who is to lay out the Garden? 49

CHAPTER V
Flowering Shrubs and Trees, and their Artistic use 53

CHAPTER VI
Climbers and their Artistic use 72

CHAPTER VII
Alpine Flower-, Rock-, and Wall-Gardens . . 86

CHAPTER VIII
The Wild Garden 115

CHAPTER IX
Spring Flowers 126

CONTENTS

CHAPTER X
BORDERS OF HARDY FLOWERS 150

CHAPTER XI
THE NEW ROSE GARDEN 167

CHAPTER XII
THE FLOWER GARDEN IN AUTUMN 182

CHAPTER XIII
THE FLOWER GARDEN IN WINTER 193

CHAPTER XIV
BEAUTY OF FORM IN THE GARDEN 207

CHAPTER XV
MARSH, BOG, AND WATER GARDENS 216

CHAPTER XVI
FRAGRANCE 222

CHAPTER XVII
THE FLOWER GARDEN IN THE HOUSE . . . 229

CHAPTER XVIII
EVERGREEN TREES AND SHRUBS 239

CHAPTER XIX
THE ORCHARD BEAUTIFUL 256

CHAPTER XX
LAWNS AND PLAYGROUNDS 276

CHAPTER XXI
HOME WOODS 281

CONTENTS xi

CHAPTER XXII
The Woodland Garden 303

CHAPTER XXIII
The greater Trees of the Northern Forests . 308

CHAPTER XXIV
Evergreen Covert 327

CHAPTER XXV
Underwoods and what to do with them . . 342

CHAPTER XXVI
Native and European Trees best . . . 349

CHAPTER XXVII
Of Mixed Woods 356

CHAPTER XXVIII
Underplanting 360

CHAPTER XXIX
Forming Woodland Rides 363

CHAPTER XXX
Waste in Planting 370

CHAPTER XXXI
Fencing for Woodland 376

CHAPTER XXXII
English Names for Trees 384

THE GARDEN BEAUTIFUL

CHAPTER I

GARDEN DESIGN AND RECENT WRITINGS UPON IT

OF all things made by man for his pleasure a flower-garden has the least cause to be ugly, barren, or stereotyped, because in it we may have the fairest of the earth's children in a living, ever-changeful state, and not, as in other arts, mere representations of them. And yet we find in nearly every country place, pattern plans, conventional design, and the garden robbed of all life and grace by setting out flowers in geometric ways. A recent writer on garden design tells us that the gardener's knowledge is of no account, and that gardens

should never have been allowed to fall into the hands of the gardener or out of those of the architect; that it is an architectural matter, and should have been schemed at the same time and by the same hand as the house itself.

Formal gardens made in our own day. The chief error he makes is in saying that people, whom he calls 'landscapists', destroyed all the 'formal' gardens in England, and that they had their ruthless way until his coming. An extravagant statement, as must be clear to any one who takes the trouble to look into the thing itself, which many of these writers will not do nor regard the elementary facts of what they write about. Many of the most formal gardens in England have been made in Victorian days : the Crystal Palace, the Royal Horticultural Society's garden at Kensington, Shrubland, Witley Court, Castle Howard, Mentmore, Drayton, Crewe Hall, Alton Towers, and many places in every county. During the whole of that period there was hardly a country seat laid out that was not marred by the idea of a garden as a conventional and patterned thing. So far from formal gardens being abolished, as the Irish peasant said of absentees, 'the country is full of them!' With Castle Howards, Trenthams, and Chatsworths staring at him, it is ludicrous to see a young architect weeping over their loss. Even when there is no money to waste in needless walls and gigantic water-squirts, the idea of the terrace is still carried out—often in plains, and in the shape of green banks piled one above the other, as if they were an artistic treat. There are hundreds of such gardens about the country, and the ugliest and most formally set out and planted gardens ever made in England were formed in Victorian days, when, we are told by writers who do not look into the facts of the thing itself, all these things were lost.

It cannot be too clearly seen that 'formal' gardens of the most deplorable type are things of our own time, as it is only in our own time that the common idea that there is only one way of making a garden has been spread. Hence, in all the newer houses we see the stereotyped garden often made in spite of all the needs of the ground, whereas in old times it was not so, because in those days the stereotyped plans were not in every office and people had to think of the ground itself. Berkeley is not the same as Sutton, and Sutton is quite different from Haddon.

Patterns of flowers and carpet-beds things of our own time. Moreover, on top of all this formality of design of our own day were grafted the most formal and inartistic ways of arranging flowers that ever came into the head of man, ways happily unknown to the Italians or the makers of the earliest terraced gardens. The true Italian gardens were often beautiful with trees in their natural forms, as in the Giusti gardens at Verona; but bedding out, or marshalling the flowers in stiff lines and geometrical patterns, is entirely a thing of our own time, and 'carpet' gardening is simply a further remove in ugliness. The painted gravel gardens of Nesfield and Barry and other broken-brick gardeners were also attempts to get rid of the flowers and get rigid formality instead, as in the Horticultural Society's garden at South Kensington. Part of the garden architect's scheme was to forbid the growth of plants on walls, as at Shrubland, where, for many years, there were strict orders that the walls were not to have a flower or a creeper of any kind upon them. As these pattern gardens were made by persons often ignorant of gardening, and if planted in any human way with flowers would all 'go to pieces', hence the idea arose of setting them out as they appeared on the drawing-board, some of the beds not more than a foot in diameter, blue and yellow paints being used where the broken brick and stone did not give the desired colour!

Loss of old garden ways. With the adoption in most large and show places of the patterned garden, both in design and planting, disappeared almost everywhere the old English garden, that is, one with a variety of form of shrub and flower and even low trees; and now we only find this kind of garden here and there in Cornwall, Ireland, and Scotland, and on the outskirts of country towns. All true plant form was banished because it did not fit into the bad carpet pattern. All this can be seen to-day in the public gardens round London and Paris; even Kew, with the vast improvement of late years, has not emancipated itself from this formal way of flower-planting, as we see there, in front of the palm-house, purple beet marshalled in patterns and the whole laid out in imitation of the worst possible pattern of carpet. But we shall never see beautiful flower gardens again until natural ways of grouping flowers and variety of true form come back to us in the flower-garden.

The Wild Garden does not take the place of the Flower-garden. After the central error above shown there comes a common one of these writers, of supposing that those who seek natural form and beauty in the garden and home-landscape are opposed to the necessary level spaces about a house. I wrote the 'Wild Garden' to save, not to destroy, the flower-garden; to show that we could have all the joy of spring in orchard, meadow or wood, lawn or grove, and to save *the true flower-garden near the house* from being torn up twice a year to effect what is called spring and summer 'bedding'. The idea could be made clear to a child, and it is carried out in many places. Yet there is hardly a cobbler who rushes from his last to write a book on garden design who does not think that I want to bring the wilderness in at the windows, who have given all my days to save the flower-garden from the ridiculous. A young lady who has been reading one of these bad books, seeing the square beds in my little south garden, says: 'Oh! why, *you* have a formal garden!' It is a small square embraced by walls, and I could not have used any other form to get the best use of the space. They are just the kind of beds made in like spaces by the gardeners of Nebuchadnezzar, judging by what evidence remains to us. He no more than I mistook bad carpets for flowers, but enjoyed vine and fig and flower as Heaven sent them. All this wearisome misunderstanding comes from writers not taking the trouble to grasp the simplest elements of what they write about.

The real flower-garden near the house is for the ceaseless care and culture of many and diverse things, often tender and in need of protection, in varied and artificial soils, staking, cleaning, trials of novelties, study of colour effects lasting many weeks, sowing and movings at all seasons. The *wild garden*, on the other hand, is for things that take care of themselves in the soil of the place, things which will endure for generations if we suit the plants to the soil, like Narcissi on a rich orchard bottom, or blue Anemone in a grove on the limestone in Ireland. This garden is a precious aid to the other, inasmuch as it allows of our letting the flower-garden do its best work because relieved of the intolerable and ugly needs of the bedding system in digging up the garden twice a year.

Misuse of terms. Very often terms of gardening are misapplied, confusing the mind of the student, and the air is now full of the 'formal' garden. For ages gardens of simple form have been common without any one calling them 'formal' until our own time of too many words confusing thoughts. Seeing an announcement that there was a paper in the *Studio* on the 'Formal Garden in Scotland', I looked into it, seeking light, and found only plans of the usual approaches necessary for a country house, for kitchen, hall door, or carriage-way. We gardeners of another sort do not get in like the bats through the roof, but have also ways, usually level, to our doors, but we do not call them 'formal gardens'. There are gardens to which the term 'formal' might with some reason be applied. Here are a few words about such by one Percy Bysshe Shelley, whose clear eyes saw beauty if there was any to be seen in earth or sky :—

We saw the palace and gardens of Versailles full of statues, vases, fountains, and colonnades. *In all that belongs essentially to a garden they are extraordinarily deficient.*

A few more by Victor Hugo :—

There fountains gush from the petrified gods, only to stagnate; trees are forced to submit to the grotesque caprices of the shears and line. Natural beauty is everywhere contradicted, inverted, upset, destroyed.

And Robert Southey tells us of one

where the walks were sometimes of lighter or darker gravel, red or yellow sand, and, when such materials were at hand, pulverized coal and shells. The garden itself was a scroll-work cut very narrow, and the interstices filled with sand of different colours to imitate embroidery.

Such gardens may be called formal without too much disregard of language, and yet one might plant every one of them beautifully without in the least altering their outline. *It is only where the plants of a garden are rigidly set out in geometrical design, as in carpet-gardening and bedding-out, that the term 'formal garden' is rightly applied.*

We live in a time when men write about garden design unmeaning words or absolute nonsense; these are men who have had no actual contact with the work. They think garden design is a question that can be settled on a drawing-board, and have not the least idea that in any true sense the art is not possible without knowledge of many beautiful living things, and that the right planting of a country place is of tenfold greater importance than the ground-plan about the house.

In many books on garden design the authors misuse words and confuse ideas. One, writing on the gardens of Hampton Court, is not satisfied with the terms 'garden design', or 'laying out gardens', but uses the word 'gardenage'. Another writes 'lay-out' for 'plan'. Many, not satisfied with the good term, 'landscape gardener', used by Loudon, Repton, and many other excellent men, call themselves 'landscape architects' — a stupid term of French origin implying the union of two absolutely distinct studies, one dealing with varied life in a thousand different kinds and the natural beauty of the earth, and the other with stones and bricks and their putting together. The training for either of these arts is wide apart from the training demanded for the other, and the earnest practice of one leaves no time, even if there were the genius, for the other.

Landscape-gardening. The term 'landscape-planting' is often scoffed at by these writers, yet it is a good one with a clear meaning, which is the grouping and growth of trees in natural forms as opposed to the universal aligning, clipping, and shearing of the Dutch; the natural incidence of light and shade and breadth as the true guide in all artistic planting. The term 'landscape-gardening' is a true and, in the fullest sense, good English one, with a clear and even beautiful meaning, namely, the study of the forms of the earth, and frank acceptance of them as the best of all for purposes of beauty or use of planter or gardener, save where the surface is so steep that one must alter it to work upon it.

We accept the varied slopes of the river bank and the path of the river as not only better than those of a Dutch canal, but a hundred times better; and not only for their beauty, but for the story they tell of the earth herself in ages past. We gratefully take the lessons of Nature in her most beautiful aspects of vegetation—as to breadth, airy spaces, massing and grouping of the woods that fringe the valleys or garland the mountain rocks—as better beyond all that words can express than anything men can invent or ever have invented.

We love and prefer the divinely-settled form of the tree or shrub or flower beyond any possible expression of man's misguided efforts with shears; such as we see illustrated in old Dutch books, where every living thing is clipped to conform to an idea of 'design' that arose in the minds of men to whom all trees were green things to be cut into ugly walls. We repudiate as false and ridiculous the common idea of the pattern book, that these aspirations of ours are in any way 'styles', the inventions of certain men, because we know that they are based on eternal truths of Nature, free as the clouds to any one who climbs the hills and has eyes to see.

The true test of a Flower-garden. The fact that ignorant men, who have never had the chance of learning these lessons, make pudding-like clumps in a vain attempt to diversify the surface of the ground, and other foolish things, does not in the least turn us aside from following the true and only ways to get the best expression possible of beauty from any given morsel of the earth's surface we have to plant. We sympathize with the landscape-painter's work as reflecting for us, though often faintly, the wondrously varied beauty of the earth. We hold that the only true test of our efforts in planting or gardening is the picture. Do we frighten the artist away, or do we bring him to see a garden so free from ugly patterns and ugly colours that, seen in a beautiful light, it would be worth his seeing and perhaps painting? There is not, and there never can be, any other true test.

Even if our aim be right, the direction, as in many other matters, may be vitiated by stupidity, as in gardens where false lines and curves abound, as in the Champs-Elysées in Paris. It is quite right to see the faults of this and to laugh at them; but how about those who plant in true and artistic ways? In Paris there is ceaseless and inartistic and vain throwing up of the ground, and sharp and ugly slopes, which are often against the cultivation of the things planted.

The rejection of clipped forms and book patterns of trees set out like lamp-posts, costly walls where none are wanted, and of all the too facile labours of the drawing-board 'artist' in gardens, first carried out in England, is set down by these writers on garden design as the wicked invention of certain men. No account has been taken of the eternally beautiful lessons of Nature or even the simple facts which should be known to all who write about such things. Thus in 'The Art and Craft of Garden Making' we read:—

> So far as the roads were concerned, Brown built up a theory that, as Nature abhorred a straight line, it was necessary to make roads curl about. Serpentine lines are said to be the lines of Nature, and therefore beyond question the only proper lines.

But nothing is said of the very important fact that

in making paths or roads in diversified country it is often absolutely necessary to follow the line of easiest gradation, and this is often a beautiful bent line. In many cases we are not twenty paces from the level space around a house before we have to think of the lie of the ground in making walks, roads, or paths. We are soon face to face with the fact that the worst thing we can attempt is a straight line. If any one for any reason persists in the attempt the result is ugliness, and, in the case of drives, danger. Ages before Brown was born the roads of England often followed beautiful lines, and it would be just as true to attribute to Brown the invention of the forms of trees, hills, or clouds themselves, as to say that he invented the waved line for path or drive. The statement is of a piece with the other, that the natural and picturesque view of garden design and planting is the mischievous invention of certain men, and not the outcome of the most precious of all gifts, of Nature herself, and of the actual facts of tree and landscape beauty. All who have seen the pictures by the roadsides of many parts of Britain, and the paths over the hills, and, still more so, those who have to form roads or walks in diversified country, will best know the value of such statements.

Variety the true source of beauty in gardens. The

very statement that there is but one way of making a garden is its own refutation; as with this formula before us what becomes of the wondrous variety of the earth and its forms, and of the advantages and needs of change that soil, site, climate, air, and view give us—plains, river valleys, old beach levels, mountains and gentle hills, chalk downs and rich loamy fields, forest and open country?

What is the use of Essex going into Dorset merely to see the same thing done in the home-landscape or the garden? But if Essex were to study his own ground and do the best he could from his own knowledge of the spot, his neighbour might be glad to see his garden. We have too much of the stereotyped style already; in nine cases out of ten we can tell beforehand what we are going to see in a country place in the way of conventional garden design and planting; and clearly that is not art in any right sense of the word, and never can be.

As we go about our country the most depressing sign for all garden lovers (this often in districts of great natural beauty) is the stereotyped garden, probably made from an office book of plans. There is a belief in the virtue of paper plans which is misleading and only suits the wants of professionalism, and prevents the study of the ground itself, the only way to get the best result. Some of the new writers have no heart for the many beautiful things in the shape of trees and shrubs which have come to us during the past generation or two :—

> A very few varieties of English trees are sufficient for all purposes, and we have yew for hedges, fine turf for a carpet, and quite enough flowers of brilliant hue that have always had a place in our gardens without importing curiosities from abroad.

Variety essential. Now if there is any clear fact about gardening it is that its charm often arises from variety, not necessarily botanical variety, but the difference between a Menabilly and the conventional garden essentially lies in a variety of trees, shrubs, and flowers. These writers need to be told that it is impossible to make a beautiful garden without the variety which they say is useless, not having, of course, any idea of the dignity and beauty of the trees of Japan, the Rocky Mountains, and Northern Asia, or America.

One such writer says :—

> It is no use spending money on gardeners and repairs, as it might be much better invested in architectural improvements or waterworks in the pleasure-grounds.

This is a stupid and harmful idea, as the two arts are in no way antagonistic but helpful rather. Take away all true planting and good gardening from our Castle Ashbys, Longleats, or Wiltons and what do we gain? For remember that the ground about a house, even slopes which must be terraced, is often very small in extent compared with the planting we may have to do in the home landscape.

But the ugly buildings that strew the land everywhere—Georgian, carpenter's Gothic, Victorian—if we take away the good planting, the one saving grace about them, there will be nothing left but an ugly pile to laugh at. Good building and good planting go so well together—one helping the other in every way—that it is odd to see any one writing on the subject without seeing that it is so. I cannot suppose that any good architect could fail to see the gain of good planting and good flower-gardening in relation to his work. We have only the greatest satisfaction with a country place when both building and planting are good—a rare thing, unfortunately.

Any way good that best suits the site. To the good gardener all kinds of design are good if not against the site, soil, climate, or labours of his garden—a very important point the last. We frequently see beds a foot in diameter and many other frivolities of paper-plans which prevent the labours of a garden being done with economy or simplicity. In many places where these hard pattern gardens are carried out, they are soon seen to be so absurd that the owners quietly turf the spot over, and hence in many country places we see only grass where there ought to be a real flower-garden. The good gardener is happy adorning old walls or necessary terraces, as at Haddon, as he knows walls are good friends in every way, both as backgrounds and shelters; but he is as happy in a lawn garden, in a rich valley soil, on the banks of a river, on those gentle hill-slopes that ask for no terraces, or in the hundreds of gardens in and near towns and cities of Europe that are enclosed by walls and where there is no room for landscape effect (many of them distinctly beautiful too, as in Mr. Fox's garden at Falmouth); as much at home in a Border castle garden as in the lovely Penjerrick, like a glimpse of a valley in some Pacific isle, or Mount Usher, cooled by mountain streams.

Waterworks garden design. The same architect turns to the waterworks as his chief solace :—

But of all the fascinating sources of effect in garden-making the most fascinating are waterworks. An expensive luxury as a rule, but they well repay the expense.

Well, there is some evidence of the sort of design these afford; some instances terrible in their ugliness (one hideous at Bayreuth). And with all the care that a rich State may take of them, can we say that the effect at Versailles is artistic or delightful? Water tumbling into the blazing streets of Roman cities and nobly designed fountains supplying the people with water was right; but in our cool land artificial fountains are very different, and often a hideous extravagance. Of their ugliness there is evidence in nearly every city in Europe, including our own Trafalgar Square, and that fine (!) work at the head of the Serpentine. We have also our Crystal Palace and Chatsworth, designed as they might be by a theatrical super who had suddenly inherited a millionaire's fortune. What the effect of this is I need hardly say, but with all our British toleration of ugliness I have never heard anybody enthusiastic about their artistic merits. So far as our island countries go, nothing asks for more care and modest art than the introduction into the garden or home-landscape of artificial water. Happily our countries are rich in the charms of natural water too often neglected in its planting.

Talk of the day about art. Among the great peoples of old was one supreme in art, from buildings chiselled as delicately as the petals of the wild rose to the smallest coins in their pockets and bits of baked clay in their graves, and this is clear to all men from what remains of their work gathered from the mud and dust of ages. And from that time of deathless beauty in art comes the voice of one who saw this lovely art in its fulness: *The greatest and fairest things are done by Nature and the lesser by Art* (Plato). There is not a garden in Britain, free from convention and carpet-gardening, from the cottage-gardens nestling beneath the Surrey hills to those fair and varied gardens in Cornwall, which does not tell the same story to all who have eyes to see and hearts to care for the thing itself, and not merely for incoherent talk about it. The only sad thing is that such words must be said again and again; but we live in a time of much printed fog about artistic things—the 'New Art' and the 'New Æsthetic'; 'Evolution,' which explains how everything comes from nothing and goes back again to worse than nothing; the sliding bog of 'realism and idealism' in which the phrasemonger may dance around and say the same false thing ten times over; and, last and not least of all among these imbecilities, the teaching that to form a garden one had better know nothing of the things that should grow in it, from the cedar of Lebanon to the violets of the alpine rocks.

This teaching is as false as any spoken or written

thing can be; there is an absolute difference between living gardens and conventional designs dealing with dead matter, be it brick or stone, glass, iron, or carpets. There is a difference in kind, and while any pupil in an architect's office will get out a drawing for the kind of garden we may see everywhere, the garden beautiful does not arise in that way. It is the difference between life and death we have to think of, and never to the end of time shall we get the garden beautiful formed or planted save by men who know something of the earth and its flowers, shrubs, and trees. I would much rather trust the first simple person, knowing his ground and loving his work, to get a beautiful result than any of those artificers. We have proof of this in the gardens of English people abroad that escape from the too facile plans of the office; far more beautiful gardens arise, as in the Isle of Madeira, where every garden differs from its neighbour and all are beautiful. So it is in a less degree in our islands, where the more we get out of the range of any one conventional idea for the garden the more beauty and freshness and happy incident we see.

CHAPTER II

ART IN RELATION TO FLOWER-GARDENING AND GARDEN DESIGN

THERE is no reason why we should not have true art in the garden, and none why a garden should be ugly, bare, or conventional. The word 'art' being used in its highest sense here, it may perhaps be well to justify its use, and as good a definition of the word as any perhaps is 'power to see and give form to beautiful things', which we see shown in some of its finest forms in Greek sculpture and in the works of the great masters of painting.

But art is of many kinds, and owing to the confusion caused in many minds by the loose 'critical' talk of the day, it is not easy for all to see that true art is based on clear-eyed study and love of nature, rather than on the invention and the 'personality' of the artist of which we hear so much. The work of the true artist is marked by fidelity to nature, and proof of this may be seen in any great art gallery. But people write much about art in magazines and papers, who are blind to its simple law, and we may read essay after essay about it without being brought a whit nearer to the simple truth. On the other hand we get a false idea that it is not by observing, but by inventing and supplementing, that good work is done. The strong man must be there, but his work is to see the whole beauty of the subject, and to help us to see it. To distort it in any way for the sake of making it 'original' is often a way to popularity, but in the end it means bad work. It may be the fashion for a season, owing to some one quality, but it is soon found out; and we have again to turn to the great masters of all ages, who are always distinguished for truth to nature, and show their strength by getting nearer to it.

Realism and Idealism. Beauty in its fulness and subtlety, which is the justification of 'art', writers of the day will not take the trouble to see; they write essays on art in which many long words occur, but in which we do not once meet with the word *truth*. 'Realism' and 'idealism' are words freely misused, and bad pictures are shown us as examples of 'realism', which leave out all the refinement, subtlety, truth of tone, and perhaps even the very light and shade in which all the real things we see are set. There are men so blind to the beauty of actual things that they seek to idealize the eyes of a beautiful child or the clouds of heaven; yet we know that no imagining can come near to the beauty of some things as they are, art itself being often powerless to seize their full beauty. Only a little, indeed, of the beauty that concerns us most—that of the landscape—can be seized for us except by the very greatest masters. Of things visible—flower, tree, landscape, sky, or sea—to see the full and ever-varied beauty is to be saved for ever from any will-o'-the-wisp of the imaginary. But many people do not judge pictures by nature, but by pictures, and therefore miss the subtleties and delicate realities on which all true art depends. Some sneer at those who 'copy nature,' but the answer to such critics is in the work of the great men, be they Greeks, Dutchmen, Italians, French, or English.

Choice Essential. It is part of the work of the artist to select beautiful or memorable things, not the first that come in his way. The Venus of Milo is from a noble type of woman—not a mean Greek. The horses of the Parthenon show the best of eastern breed, full of life and beauty. Great landscape painters like Crome, Corot, and Turner seek not things only because they are natural, but also beautiful; selecting views and waiting for the light that suits the chosen subject best, they give us pictures, working always from faithful study of nature and from stores of knowledge gathered from her; that also is the only true path for the gardener, all true art being based on her eternal laws. All deviation from the truth of nature, whether it be at the hands of Greek, Italian, or other artist, though it may pass for a time, is in the end—it may be ages after the artist is dead—classed as *debased* art.

Why say so much here about art? Because when we see the meaning of true 'art' we cannot endure what is ugly and false in art, and we cannot have the foregrounds of beautiful English scenery daubed with flower gardens like coloured advertisements. Many see the right way from their own sense being true, but others may wish for proof of what is urged here, as to the true source of lasting work in art, in the work of the great artists of all time, and we may be as true artists in the garden and home-landscape as anywhere else.

Artists in planting. There is no good picture which does not give us the beauty of natural things, and why not begin with these and be artists in their growth and grouping? For one reason, among others, that we have the living things around us, and not merely representations of them, as in the other arts.

So far we have spoken of the work of the true artist, which is always marked by respect for nature and by keen study of it; but apart from this we have a great many men who do what is called 'decorative' work, useful, but still not art in the sense of delight in, and study of, things as they are—the whole class of decorators, who make our carpets, tiles, curtains, and who adapt conventional or geometric forms mostly to flat surfaces. Skill in this way may be considerable without any attention whatever being paid to the art that is concerned with life in its fulness.

This it is well to see clearly, as for the flower gardener it matters much on which side he stands. Our gardeners for ages have suffered at the hands of the decorative artist, when applying his 'designs' to the garden, and designs which may be quite right on a flat surface like a carpet or panel have been applied a thousand times to the surface of the reluctant earth. It is this adapting of absurd 'knots' and patterns from old books to any surface where a flower garden has to be made that leads to bad and frivolous design—wrong in plan and hopeless for the life of plants. It is so easy for any one asked for a plan to furnish one of this sort without the slightest knowledge of the life of a garden.

Degradation of flowers. And so for ages the flower-garden was marred by absurdities of this kind as regards plan, though the flowers were in simple and natural ways. But in our own time the same 'decorative' idea has come to be carried out in the planting of the flowers under the name of 'bedding out,' 'carpet bedding,' or 'mosaic culture,' in which the beautiful forms of flowers are degraded to the level of crude colour to make a design, without reference to the natural form or beauty of the plants, clipping being freely done to get the carpets or patterns 'true'. When these tracery gardens were often made by people without any knowledge of the plants of a garden, they were found difficult to plant, hence there were attempts to do without the gardener, and get colour by the use of broken brick, white sand, and painted stone. All such work is wrong and degrading to the art of gardening, and in its extreme expressions is ridiculous.

The term artistic. As I use the word 'artistic,' in a book on the flower-garden, it may be well to say that it is used to mean right and true in relation to all the conditions of the case, and the necessary limitations of all human arts. A lovely Greek coin, a bit of canvas painted by Corot with the morning light on it, a block of stone hewn into the shape of a dying gladiator, the white mountain rocks built into a Parthenon—these are all examples of human art, every one of which can only be fairly judged with due regard to what is possible in the material of each—knowledge which it is essential the artist should possess. Often a garden may be wrong in various ways—as conifers spread in front of many a house; ugly in form, or not in harmony with our native or best garden vegetation, as shown in mountain trees set out on dry plains and not even hardy; so that the word inartistic may help us to describe many such errors. Again, if we are happy enough to find a garden so true and right in its results as to form a picture that an artist would be charmed to study, we may call it an artistic garden, as a short way of saying that it is about as good as it may be, taking everything into account.

Landscape Painting and Gardens. There are few pictures of gardens, because the garden beautiful is rare. Gardens around country houses, instead of forming, as they might, graceful foregrounds to the good landscape, disfigure it all, and drive the artist away in despair. Yet there may be real pictures in gardens; it is not a question of patterns, but one of light and shade, beauty of form, and colour. In times when gardens were made by men who did not know one tree from another, the matter was settled by the shears—it was a question of green walls only. Now we are beginning to see that there is a wholly different and higher order of beauty to be sought for in gardens, and we are at the beginning of a period when we may hope to get much more pleasure and instruction out of this art than ever before.

We have seen in London exhibitions of pictures devoted to gardens, generally of the trifling stippled water-colour order. The painters of these pictures —for the most part ten-minute sketches—have the one main idea that the only garden worth picturing is the shorn one, and pictures of such places are repeated time after time; a clipped line of Arborvitae, with a stuffed peacock by the side of it, is considered good enough for a garden picture. Work of this kind, which is almost mechanical, is so much easier than painting a garden with varied beauty in it.

Artists of real power would paint gardens and home landscapes if there were real pictures to draw; but generally they are so rare that the work does not come into the artist's view at all. Through all the rage of the 'bedding-out' fever, it was impossible for an artist to paint gardens like those which disfigured the land from Blair Athol to the Crystal

Palace. It is difficult to imagine Corot sitting down to paint the Grande Trianon, or the terrace patterns at Versailles, though a poor hamlet in the north of France, with a few willows near, gave him a lovely picture. Once, when trying to persuade Mr. Mark Fisher, the landscape painter, to come into a district remarkable for its natural beauty, he replied: 'There are too many gentlemen's places there to suit my work,' referring to the hardness and ugliness of the effects around most country seats, owing to the iron-bound pudding-clumps of trees, railings, capricious clippings and shearings, bad colours, and absence of fine and true form, with almost certainly an ugly house in the midst of all. We ought to be able to do better than scare away the very men who would enjoy our work most, and delight in painting it, rich as we are in the sources of beauty of tree or flower.

CHAPTER III

OF SO-CALLED STYLES AND SOME COMMON MISTAKES

It is important to get a clear idea of the hollowness of much of the talk about 'styles' in books about laying-out gardens. There are many dissertations on styles, the authors going even to China and to Mexico for illustrations, but almost always parrot repetitions. What is the result to anybody who looks from words to things? That there are two styles: the one the strait-laced, with much wall and stone, fountains and sculpture: the other the natural, which, once free of the house, accepts the ground lines of the earth as the best, and gets plant beauty from flowers and trees arranged in picturesque ways.

There are positions where stonework is necessary; but the best terrace gardens are those built where the nature of the ground demanded them. Nothing is more melancholy than the walls, fountain basins, clipped trees, and long canals of places like the Crystal Palace, not only because they fail to satisfy the desire for beauty, but because they tell of vast wasted effort, and of riches worse than lost. There are, from Versailles to Caserta, a great many ugly gardens in

Europe, but at Sydenham we have the worst example of the waste of enormous means in making hideous a fine piece of ground. This has been called a work of genius, but it is the fruit of a poor ambition to outdo another ugly extravagance—Versailles. As Versailles has numerous tall fountains, the best way of glorifying ourselves was to make some taller ones at Sydenham! Instead of confining the terrace gardening to the upper terrace, by far the greater portion of the ground was devoted to a stony extravagance of design, and nearly in the centre were placed the vast and ugly fountain basins. The contrivances to enable the water to go downstairs: the temples, statues, dead walls, all that costly rubbish, were praised by the papers as the marvellous work of a genius. When a private individual indulges in such fancies he may not injure any but himself, but in this public garden—as an example of all that is admirable—we have, in addition to wasteful outlay, what is hurtful to the public taste : many whose lawns might have been made the most beautiful of gardens have spoiled them for sham terraced gardens, and there is a modern castle in Scotland where the embankments are piled one above another until the whole looks as if Uncle Toby with an army of Corporal Trims had been carrying out his grandest scheme in fortification. The rude stone wall of the hill-husbandman, supporting a narrow slip of soil for olive-trees or vines, became in the garden of the wealthy Roman a well-built one; but, even where the wall is necessary, the beauty of the true Italian garden depends on the life of trees and flowers more than on the plan of the garden, as in the Giusti garden at Verona, whereas in our sham examples of the Italian garden all is flat and lifeless. Most of the more famous Italian gardens were made long ago, when people had not our present splendid wealth of tree and flower, and when the aim was to extend the building in order to get background and alignments for the works of art which that country was so rich in.

Terraced gardens allowing of much building (apart from the house), have been in favour with architects who have designed gardens. The landscape gardener, too often led by custom, falls in with the notion that every house, no matter what its position, should be fortified by terraces, and he busies himself in forming them even on level ground, and large sums are spent on fountains, vases, statues, balustrades, useless walls, and stucco-work out of place. By the use of such materials many a noble lawn is cut up; and often the 'architectural' gardening is pushed so far into the park as to curtail and injure the view.

The best effect is got not by carrying architectural features into the level town garden, but by the contrast between the garden vegetation and its built surroundings — not the sham picturesque, with rocks, cascades, and undulations of the ground, but the simple dignity of trees and the charm of turf. Elaborate terraced gardens in the wrong place often prevent the formation of beautiful lawns, though a good lawn is the happiest thing in a garden. For many years past there has been so much cutting up, geometric and stonework, that it is rare to find a good lawn, and many a site so cut up would be vastly improved if changed into a large, nobly fringed lawn. A poorly built house with a fine open lawn has often a better effect than a fine one with a rectilineal garden and terraces in front of it, though there are cases where walls would be the way to a good result.

A beautiful house in a fair landscape is the most delightful scene on the cultivated earth, all the more so if there be an artistic garden. The union between the house beautiful and the ground near it—a happy marriage it should be—is worthy of more thought than it has had in the past, and the best way of effecting that union artistically should interest men more and more as our cities grow larger and our lovely English landscape shrinks back from them. We have never yet got from the garden and the home landscape half the beauty we might get by abolishing the patterns which disfigure so many gardens. Formality is often essential to the plan of a garden but never to the arrangement of its flowers or shrubs, and to array these in rigid lines, circles, or patterns can only be ugly wherever it may be.

After we have settled the essential approaches and levels around a house, the natural form or lines of the earth itself are in nearly all cases the best to follow, and where it is disfigured by ugly or needless banks, lines, or angles it is often well to face any labour to get the ground back into its natural grade. In the true Italian garden *on the hills* we have to alter the natural lines of the earth, or 'terrace it', because we cannot otherwise cultivate the ground or stand at ease upon it; in such ground the formal is right, as the lawn in a garden in the Thames valley is. For the lawn is the heart of the true English garden, as essential to it as the terrace to the gardens on the steep hills, and English lawns have been too often destroyed for plans ruinous both to the garden and the home landscape. Sometimes on level ground the terrace walls cut off the landscape from the house, and, on the other hand, the house from the landscape!

We may get every charm of a garden and every

use of a country place without sacrificing the picturesque or beautiful; there is no reason, either in the working or design of gardens, why there should be a false line in them; every charm of the flower garden may be secured by avoiding the knots and scrolls which subordinate all the plants and flowers of a garden, all its joy and life, to a conventional design. The true way is the opposite. With only the simplest plans to ensure good working, we should see the flowers and feel the beauty of plant forms, and secure every scrap of turf wanted for play or lawn, and for every enjoyment of a garden.

Time and Gardens. Time's effect on gardens is one of the main considerations. Fortress-town and castle moat are now without use, where in old days gardens were set within the walls. To keep all that remains of such gardens should be our first care— never to imitate them now. Many are far more beautiful than the modern gardens, which by a stupid perversity have been kept bare of plants or flower life. At one time it was rash to make a garden away from protecting walls; but when the danger from civil war was past, then arose the beautiful Elizabethan house, free from all moat or trace of war. In those days the extension of the decorative work of the house into the garden had some novelty to carry it off, while the kinds of evergreens were very much fewer than now. Hence if the old gardeners wanted an evergreen hedge or bush of a certain height, they clipped a Yew tree to the form and size they wanted. We have no evidence, however, that anything like the flat monotony often seen in our own time existed then. To-day the ever-growing city, pushing its hard face over our once beautiful land, should make us wish more and more to keep such beauty of the earth as may be still possible to us; and the railway embankments, where once were the beautiful suburbs of London, cry to us to save all we can save of the natural beauty of the earth.

Architecture and Flower Gardening. The architect is a good gardener when he makes a beautiful house. Whatever is to be done or considered afterwards, one is always helped and encouraged by its presence; while, on the other hand, scarcely any amount of skill in gardening softens the presence of an ugly building. No one has more reason to rejoice at the presence of good architecture than the gardener and planter, and all stonework near the house, even in the garden, should be dealt with by the architect. But when architecture goes beyond this limit, and seeks to replace what should be a living garden by an elaborate tracery on the ground, then error and waste are at work. The proof of this is at Versailles, at the Crystal Palace in great part, in the gardens in Vienna, and at Caserta, near Naples. One may not so freely mention private places as public ones, but many ugly and extravagant things have been done in trying to adapt a mode of garden design essential in a country like Italy, where people often lived for health's sake on the tops of the hills, to gardens in the plains and valleys of England. I know a terrace in England built right against the house, so as to exclude the light from, and make useless, what were once the reception rooms. That deplorable result came about by endeavouring to adapt Italian modes to English conditions, and was the work of Sir Charles Barry. To any one deeply interested in the question, one of the best places from which to consider it is the upper terrace at Versailles, looking from the fine buildings there to the country beyond, and seeing how graceless and inert the whole vast design is, and how the clipped and often dying, because mutilated, Yews thrust their ugly forms into the landscape beyond and rob it of all grace. To those who tell me this sort of work is necessary to 'harmonize' with the architecture I say there are better ways, and that to rob fine buildings of all repose by a complex geometrical pattern in the foreground is often the worst way.

Cost and care of stonework in gardens. Where stone or stucco gardening is done on a large scale, its cost and maintenance are monstrous. The repair of elaborate stonework in gardens is a hopeless task, as any one may see at Versailles and at the Crystal Palace. Is it in the interest of architecture that noble means should be so wasted? As the cost and difficulties of the finest work in building increase, the more the need to keep it to its true and essential uses, especially in face of the fact that half the houses in England will need to be rebuilt if our architecture is to prove worthy of its aims. I delight in walls for my Roses and build walls, provided they have any true use as dividing, protecting, or supporting lines. To take advantage of these and sunny sheltered corners in and about our old or new houses, and make delightful little gardens in and near them, as at Drayton or Powis, is quite a different thing from cutting off the landscape with vast flat 'patterns' and scroll-work, as on the terrace at Windsor and in many gardens made in our own day.

'Design' not formal only. I find it stated by writers on this subject that 'design' can only concern formality—an error, as the artistic grouping and giving

picturesque effect to groups and groves of Oak, Cedar, or Fir evinces higher design than putting trees in lines. There is more true design in Richmond Park and other noble parks in England, where the trees are grouped in picturesque ways and allowed to take natural forms, than in a French wood with straight lines cut through it, which the first carpenter could design as well as anybody else. In our own day a wholly different order of things has arisen, because we have thousands of beautiful things coming to us from all parts of the temperate and northern world, and those who know them will not accept a book pattern design instead of our infinitely varied garden flora. The trees of North America and Asia form a garden in themselves, and it is impossible to lay out gardens of any size or dignity without a knowledge of those and all other hardy trees, not only in a cultivated but in a wild state. If anything demands special study, it is that of garden design with our present materials. If that art is to be mastered, the work of a life must be given to it —more than that, a life's devotion—and no less is the sacrifice his own art requires of the architect.

There is no such thing as a style fitted for every situation; only one who knows and studies the ground well will ever make the best of a garden, and any 'style' may be right where the site fits it. A garden on the slopes about Naples is impossible without much stonework to support the earth, while about London or Paris there is usually no such need. These considerations never enter into the minds of men who plant an Italian garden in one of our river valleys, where in nine cases out of ten an open lawn is often the best thing before the house, as at Bristol House, Roehampton; Greenlands, Henley-on-Thames; and many gardens in the Thames valley. There are right and wrong ways where we cannot have a lawn garden: Haddon, simple and charming, on the one hand, and Chatsworth on the other; Knole and Ightham and Rockingham without a yard of stonework not absolutely needed for the house and its approaches, and on the other hand places with a fortune spent in display of costly stonework, only effective in robbing the foreground of all repose.

The idea that the old style of building in England was always accompanied by elaborate terrace gardening is erroneous. The Elizabethan house had often an ample lawn in front or plenty of grass near, and such houses are quite as good in effect as the old houses and castles where simple terracing was necessary and right, owing to the ground, such as Berkeley, Powis, and Rockingham.

The idea that trees must be clipped to make them 'harmonize' with architecture is a mere survival. In the old days of garden design, when in any northern country there were few trees in gardens, these trees were slashed into any shape that met the designer's views; but now that many beautiful trees and shrubs are coming to us from many countries, the aim of true gardening is, so far from mutilating them, to develop their natural forms. In by far the greater number of beautiful places in England, from Knole to Haddon, and from the fine west-country houses to the old border castles, there are many of the fairest gardens where the trees are never touched with shears. Sutton Place, near Guildford, built in 1521, is one of the most beautiful old houses in the home counties, and its architecture is none the less delightful because the trees near show their true forms. It is also an example of a fine old house around which there is no terraced gardening.

It would be as hopeless to design a building without knowing anything of its uses or inhabitants as to design a garden without full knowledge of its nobler ornaments—trees and the many things that go to make our garden flora vary so much in form, habits, and hardiness according to soils, situations, and districts. Errors of the most serious kind arise from dealing with such things without knowledge, and any attempt to keep the gardener out of the garden must fail, as it did in our own day in the case of the broken brick and stone flower beds at South Kensington. Except for what is mostly a very small area near the house, the architect and garden-designer deal with distinct subjects and wholly distinct materials. They should work in harmony, but not seek to do that for which their training and knowledge have not fitted them.

Of various pretended 'garden ornaments'. By common consent the British statue is rarely a thing to be proud of, and a witty French writer, M. Harduin, has lately been protesting against *statuomanie*, and says justly that a statue in a garden is no good substitute for tree, or grass, or flower effect: and assuming that statues have any reason to be, it is unnecessary to dot them over parks and gardens while there are buildings, embankments, and streets.

In a northern country a statue of high merit as a work of art deserves to be protected by a building. The effect of frost and rain in our climate on statuary is very destructive. The scattering of numerous statues of little or no artistic merit, which we see in some Italian gardens, gives a bad effect, and the statues in the public gardens of Paris and London are destructive of all repose. A place used for the exhibition of sculpture out of doors ought not to be called a garden. Statues in public gardens are often of artificial material, and those who use a garden as a place for exhibiting such 'works of art' do not think of the garden as the best of places to show the work of nature at its best.

The earliest recollection I have of a large garden was one strewn with the remains of statues, but as my evidence might not be thought impartial, let me call as a witness M. Victor Cherbuliez :—

'It was one of those classical gardens planned by men who were proud of being able to give lessons to Nature in good behaviour; to teach her geometry and the fine art of irreproachable lines; but Nature is for geometers an unwilling pupil, and if she submits to their tyranny does so with an ill grace, and will be revenged. ... The fountain no longer held water, and the dolphins, which in days gone by had spouted it from their throats, looked as if asking each other to what purpose they were in this world. But the statues had suffered most; moss and a green damp had invaded them, as if a kind of plague or a leprosy covered them with sores; and as if pitiless Time had inflicted on them mutilations and insults, one had lost an arm, another a leg, and almost all had lost their noses. There was in the fountain a Neptune whose face was badly damaged, leaving nothing but his beard, and he had lost half his trident; and further on a headless Jupiter with the rainwater standing in his hollow neck.'

As to the artistic value of much of our sculpture,

Lord Rosebery, in his speech at Edinburgh in 1896, said:—

'If those restless spirits that possessed the Gadarene swine were to enter into the statues of Edinburgh, and if the whole stony and brazen troop were to hurry and hustle and huddle headlong down the steepest place near Edinburgh into the deepest part of the Firth of Forth, art would sustain no serious loss.'

Yet this is the sort of 'art' that some wish us to expose in the garden, where there are rarely the means to do even as good work as we see in cities. If the politician and the journalist ask to be delivered from the statues with which the squares and streets of our cities are adorned, our duty as lovers of nature in the garden is clear. At its best there is nothing more precious than sculpture; in its debased forms it is perhaps the least valuable of almost any form of art. The Greek sculpture in the Vatican, the Louvre, or the British Museum is the work of great artists, and those who love it will not be led astray by goddesses in lead or nymphs in cement. If we wish to see the results of sculpture in architectural work we have but to look at the public buildings in London, where it is used apparently as a foil to any beauty such buildings possess. By looking at buildings, then, we may the better judge how far we may go in our gardens with such things.

Real artists in sculpture are not concerned with

garden design, and sculpture is not the business of the builder or the landscape gardener. A garden is a place for beautiful life, not death. It is not that we despise other arts than our own; they may charm and even help us, as a landscape painting will sometimes. Even a drawing of a tree or flower may be a lesson in form and beauty; but debased 'art' is more harmful in the garden than anywhere else, because it is at war with some of the loveliest things in nature.

The same may be said of any showy fountain basins or excess of vases, which often spoil large gardens. Only things of the best design should be tolerated, and these to a modest degree and rightly placed.

The interest taken of late in gardening has led some not closely connected with the art to push a form of business which has little relation to true gardening, namely, the collection of miscellaneous rubbish and varied lumber gathered up at sales and hunted for in Italy, where we see so much that is bad as well as good in that way, to be sold at auction sales under the name of 'garden ornaments', which of all things made by man have the least right to that name. Not one in ten of these things has any claim to beauty of design or material, and among them are ridiculous 'rustications' and New Road castings. It is a bad look out for gardens of any real interest if they are to be disfigured by such things. When people have to live with such 'ornaments' they soon find out their true value. Some take the form of garden benches, often a want in gardens, but for our country these Italian seats are not so good as a hard well-made oak seat, or one of stone with light oak boards placed over it. Worse still are the ornaments that take plastic shape, as if good the climate is against them, and if bad they had better be buried out of sight. For garden lovers the only true ornament is living nature, with its changes of season in tree, shrub and flower; all other things should be subsidiary. Nothing needs more care than introducing into gardens various forms of statuary, and giving such things a predominance in a garden is to make it take a lower place in the eyes of all those who seek a garden's true sources of beauty.

These deplorable ornaments are always worst when seen with natural surroundings, as in some town and public gardens in northern countries—a wretched cement vase stood in a group of natural masses of rock, a fountain in several tiers with a fringe of natural rock around it, a painted figure in a bed of roses and so on. How can such absurdities be justified? It is the innate toleration of ugliness by our people, encouraged in our own day too by hideous drawings in the comic and popular papers: by the advertisements on walls everywhere: by the ugly everyday dress of men and women.

A fault in garden making. There is a common practice of raising mounds with the idea of getting certain effects, but as generally carried out it is against all good work in landscape gardening. It is assumed by the mound-makers that the level ground is not right for their purpose, and so heaps of earth are thrown up here and there to change the natural form of the ground. Any one going through St. James's Park will be able to judge for himself whether anything is gained by this heaping up of the surface. At least two things are lost. In the first place, those who make these mounds have rarely any eye for natural gradation, and therefore false lines and stiff banks occur here and there and are very unsightly. In the second place, piling mounds of earth around trees is surely destructive of one of the most beautiful aspects of tree life—the stem rising from the earth, often with a wide-spreading bole. In St. James's Park and the other places where this needless work has been done, the base of the tree is often hidden. Where trees are allowed to grow naturally one can see the beautiful way in which their stems are built, a form of beauty which should never be concealed by needless earthwork. Such treatment of the ground surface is common in France, and some of its worst effects may be seen in the Champs-Elysées, which is full of false lines, stiff banks, and beds at impossible angles, ill-concealed by the beauty of the trees and the good planting. In valleys like those of the Thames and the Seine we only lose by altering the natural lie of the ground. No planting of flower or shrub is one whit advanced by the creation of artificial mounds in a valley where the soil is generally good. The 'art' of present-day landscape-gardeners too often consists largely in this chopping and changing of surface, often at great expense and with anything but gain in real effect; and nowhere is the ugliness of these distortions more seen than in public parks and gardens. It is true that where the ground is naturally broken, a slight change in surface may sometimes open up hidden beauty and give a better effect; but to create mounds for the mere sake of avoiding a flat surface is a false idea of art. Whenever it is necessary, in grading for walks or for any other purpose, to alter existing surfaces, care should be taken to avoid this earthing up of tree-stems, which not only hides one of their finest features, but is often fatal to certain kinds of trees.

CHAPTER IV

WHO IS TO LAY OUT THE GARDEN?

COTTAGE, farm, and manor gardeners are fortunate in that the need for making the most of their space prevents any 'office'-plans being used, so that the simple lines they are thus compelled to adopt are themselves a source of beauty. It is when we get to places of some size that the question arises: Who is to lay out the garden? I say that he who knows the ground best can always do best in the planting of a country place, but there are various reasons why many feel unequal to facing the problem unaided, and in the present state of things are very likely to get into trouble even when help is sought. There is no organized profession to help, any one may call himself a landscape gardener; a navvy who has had some experience of walk and road making; a jobbing gardener, and others without any training undertake the work, and many nurserymen advertise themselves as landscape gardeners, their own work being the wholly different one of growing trees and shrubs and plants into the best state for planting. There are even a few architects who offer to lay out gardens; and in France landscape gardeners retort by taking lessons in architecture, and where they can they build the house as well as lay out the grounds. In America, where the profession of landscape gardener is taking organized shape, landscape gardeners are debarred from undertaking other work than their own.

A man of genius arises now and then, like Robert Marnoch and F. L. Olmstead, and there are some good landscape gardeners in practice. But how are we to know a good one? By this among other signs, that he will study the ground thoroughly first, and bring no plan in his pocket. He will work on the ground itself and be able to mark on the ground what his views are as regards the lines near the house and the flower-garden. Plans are feeble substitutes for the thing itself, but the custom of plan and paper is so fixed that it is not easy to get this truth accepted. One day I was considering the site for a flower-garden; there was a beautiful lake below us, with other rare advantages to be brought into relation with the proposed flower-garden, but the owner insisted on my going into the house to see a plan of the ground, which showed nothing but a few bare lines. Plans are for men who work in offices; the man who would make the best of his ground can do better without any plan but such as he marks out on the ground itself.

Let it be remembered by those who care for the beauty of a country place, that the planning out of the ground about a house is but a very small part of the work. It is only when we get clear of the parts near the house that the larger questions of planting, breadth, and variety really arise, and here no good work is possible without knowledge of the trees of our own country and the hardy trees and shrubs of northern lands. There can be no true work in landscape gardening save by one who knows these by heart, and there is no royal road to that save a life's study. We are not like the old Dutch, who had only one or two native trees to hack into green walls; we are rich with the trees of three continents, and what we want are naturalists and artists, not mere artificers who work with dead materials.

For all important ground work there should be a professional man who should have nothing to do with the nursery trade beyond controlling it, should receive no commissions from any one but his employer, and who should have the same discretion to reject unsuitable material as an architect has.

The relation of nurserymen to garden design is a delicate one. A nurseryman's business is a wholly different and very useful one, and if he does his own work well he has not the time or the knowledge to act as a professional garden designer, and in his case where is the control which should be exercised in all extensive work by some one independent of the tradesman? No, the nursery should be the source of our good supplies, but not of design, or we shall never get very far away from the mixed muddle now generally characteristic of planting, arranged at first on the model of the show-border in a nursery, on which Pines of giant race are set out with bushes and form a verdant border pleasing no doubt to the nursery mind, but when carried out in private places ending in hideous failure.

The lesson of all this is, that although there is nothing so good as wise professional advice when we can get it, the best results and the most distinct on the whole, are for those who study their own ground. In our colonies and in certain islands where there are no office-plans handy, people have to think for themselves and the result is more beautiful than can be got in any settled country, the gardens being quite distinct one from the other; and so it should always be.

CHAPTER V

FLOWERING SHRUBS AND TREES, AND THEIR ARTISTIC USE

THERE is no branch of our art concerned with flower-beauty which gives so good a return for the cost as that of flowering shrubs and trees. Often neglected in many places they do not get a tithe of the care and space they deserve, while much tiresome trouble may be given to plants that bloom for a few months only.

Spring comes to us wreathed in Honeysuckle, and summer brings the Wild Rose and the May bloom, and these are but messengers of a host of lovely shrubs and low trees of the hills and plains of northern and temperate regions, and also of the high mountains of countries like India, where there are vast alpine regions with shrubs as hardy as our own, as we see in the case of the white Clematis that adorns many an English cottage wall with its fair white bloom. If we think of the pictures formed in thousands of places in England, Scotland, and Ireland, by the May alone, we may get an idea of the precious beauty of the many American, Asiatic, and European kinds, some of which flower later than our own and make the May-bloom season longer. Nothing is lovelier among flowering trees than a group of the various Thorns, beautiful also in fruit, and the foliage of some kinds is finely coloured in autumn. The Thorns are but one branch of the most important order of flowering trees, embracing the Apples (a garden in their varied flowers alone); Pears, wild and cultivated; Crabs, pretty in bloom and bright in fruit; Quinces, Medlars, Snowy Mespilus, Almonds, Double Cherries, Japan Quinces, Plums (including Sloe and Bullace), and a number of less important families. Among these, the larger and more important branches of this great order of plants, there is some likeness in habit and size, which allows of similar use.

Double Peaches are among the most precious trees of this order, but for some reason we rarely see them in any but a poor state in England. In France they are sometimes lovely in the very mass of colour from healthy growth, and there is such noble variety among these trees that there is room for distinct effects. A point in favour of trees like Thorns, Crabs, Almonds, and Cherries is that, in their maturity, in groups, they stand free on the turf —free, too, from all care; and it is easy to see how important this is for all who care for English tree-fringed lawns—more beautiful than any other kind of tree garden. It is not only the flowers on the trees we have to think of, but also their uses in the house, gathered when the buds are ready to open on the branchlets and long twigs and placed in vases to open. This way will prolong the blooming time, or save the flowers from hard frost, and in a cold spring it will advance the bloom a little, the warmth of the house giving a few weeks' gain in time of opening. Among the kinds of shrubs that may be cut to bloom in the house there are many of the same race, from the Sloe to the beautiful kinds of Apple.

Flowering Evergreens. While such trees as the Almond or Crab will usually be in the more distant parts of the garden picture, the variety of flowering shrubs is so great that we may choose from among them for the most precious of flower-garden groups. Take a flower garden, often with the beds in winter as bare as oilcloth, and think what beautiful groups of flowering evergreens we might plant in them! Mountain Laurels (Kalmia), Japan and American Andromeda, Azaleas, choice Evergreen Barberries, Evergreen Daphne, Desfontainea, in the south; the taller hardy Heaths, Escallonia, Ledum, alpine and wild forms of Rhododendron, Sweet Gale, Star bush, and various Laurustinus, leaving out not a few which thrive only in the warmer districts. Charming gardens might be made of such bushes, not lumped together, but in open groups with the more beautiful American hardy flowers between them, such as the Wood Lily and Mocassin flower, many rare Lilies, and beautiful bulb flowers of all seasons. The light and shade and variety in such beds of choice evergreens and flowers mingled are charming, and the plan would be permanent, as it would tend to abolish the never-ending digging in the flower garden. Beds of flowering shrubs in the flower garden are not always so well suited for small gardens; but in bold ones, often naked in winter, they would make them sightly even at that season, and much easier to deal with in early summer. Rhododendrons of the hybrid sorts are too much used, and, as they are nearly always grafted, the common stock that bears them in the end kills the plant it should support, and so we too often see the common pontic kind. Yet there are many beautiful things among these hybrids. The good colours are well worth picking out from them, and the aim of the planter should be to show the habit and form of the plant. This does not mean that they may not be grouped or massed just as before, but openings of all sizes should be left among them for light and shade, and for handsome herbaceous plants that die down in the winter, thus allowing the full light for half the year to evergreens.

Arbutus, etc. In the south and west the various Arbutus are charming for lawns and ravines, and for sheltering the flower garden, as is also the sweet Bay or true Laurel, but the common Cherry Laurel and the Portugal should not be planted near anything precious. The hardy Azaleas are, for their great number and variety, perhaps the most precious flowering shrubs we have; they are fine in form of bush, even when they get little freedom, and superb in colour—the foliage in autumn, too, richly tinted. The Hydrangeas are noble plants in warm valleys, and on soils where they are not too often cut down by the winter; not only the common one of the markets, which, in soils where it turns blue, is so effective in the garden, but a variety of good kinds, among which should always be the oak-leaved Hydrangea, as old plants of it are so handsome. As these plants cannot be grown everywhere, this is a good reason why they should be made much of where the climate suits them. And there are few garden sights more interesting than groups of Hydrangeas well grown.

Broom and Furze. The Brooms have many effective plants and none more so than the common and the Spanish Brooms, which should be massed on banks, or where they will come into the picture, and some of the smaller Brooms are excellent for rockgardens. The Furze in all its forms is just as precious, as it blooms so early; it will grow almost anywhere, and it brightens up a landscape as no other plant does. We have only to place it in any rough places to enjoy it without care. Native shrubs should not be neglected; the wild single Guelder Rose is as pretty a shrub as any from across the sea, while all the hardy kinds may give us good and bold effects grouped with or near such bushes as Deutzias, Weigelas, Mock Oranges—all plants of high value and much variety.

Hardy Heaths. From an artistic point of view nothing is better than groups of our hardy Heaths in any open place where room can be found for them, including White Heather and all other strong varieties of Heather, as well as all other kinds of hardy Heaths. After planting they give little trouble, and they are good in colour even in winter, being generally happiest out of the garden proper, where any other wild plants may be allowed to grow among them. No doubt, the choicest and smallest of these Heaths deserve careful garden culture, but for effect the forms of our common Heather, the Cornish and Irish Heath, are the best, and in bold masses not primly kept, but, once well rooted, allowed to mingle with any pretty wild plants. We might even assist this idea by sowing or planting other things, such as Foxgloves, Harebells, or the small Furze, among the Heaths. When Heaths are grown in this way their bloom is charming from the first days of spring, when the little rosy Heath of the mountains of Central Europe begins to open, until the mild winter ones, when the delicately tinted Portuguese Heath (*E. codonodes*) blooms in the south and west of England.

We take little notice of such minor things as the Fire-bush, so lovely in Cornwall, and pretty also in other seashore districts, as it may not be enjoyed in the country generally, and also leave out some others, like the Witch Hazels, the Winter Sweet, and the Allspice bushes, which, though pretty near at hand, do not give us those definite effects in the garden landscape which it is well to seek if we wish to avoid the fatal jumble of the common shrubbery. The Escallonias, though very precious in seashore gardens and in the south on warm soils, are elsewhere apt to go into mourning after hard winters. So many of our island gardens are near the sea that we must not undervalue these shrubs, but a constant source of waste is the planting of things not really hardy in districts where they perish in hard winters, such as the Arbutus about London and in the midlands.

Fuchsias. Even where things seem hardy, some of them, like Fuchsias, never give the effects we get from them in the west of Ireland, in Wales, and in warm coast gardens, whatever care we take. Such facts should not discourage, because they only emphasize the lesson that the true way in a garden is for each to do his best with what soil and climate allow, and in that way arrive at the most important artistic gain of all, i.e. that each garden has its own distinct charms.

Magnolias. Such lovely things as the Snowdrop tree, the Stuartias, and bush Magnolias, may be grouped together. The Magnolias have recently become more numerous, and it is easy to have a Magnolia garden, at least in favoured places. The tree Magnolias should come among the taller flowering trees—the Horse Chestnuts, Buckeyes, Tulip trees, Laburnums, Catalpa, and Yellow Wood, in the distant parts of our flower grove. The Alpine Laburnum, so very beautiful in bloom, becomes a tall slender tree if not overcrowded, and the flowering Ash (*Ornus*) must not be forgotten among the taller flowering trees. For the Paulownia, so beautiful in France and Italy in spring, our climate is not warm enough to secure a good bloom, save in the most favoured places in the south.

Some shrubs—such as the flowering Currant, Tamarix, and Ceanothus—of modest charm as to their flowers, give very pretty effects in well-placed groups; but none more charming than the wild Roses in summer, the Sweet Briar being taken as representing our native wild Roses; the Glossy Rose (*R. lucida*), the American wild Roses; the many-flowered Rose (*Polyantha*), and the Japanese (*R. rugosa*). These and others I have planted in hedgerows and rough fences, and have never planted anything that has given a more beautiful return.

The Judas Tree is neglected in England, and rarely planted in an effective way. In the Parc Monceau in Paris there is a beautiful grove of it in which trees of various ages form one family party, so to say, showing some differences in colour and earliness. Such slight but often valuable differences arise when we raise trees from seed and do not slavishly follow the habit of grafting one thing on another. This is one of the gains of following a more natural mode of increasing trees than is usual in nurseries, as those raised from seed have a chance of interesting variations, whereas grafting from the same identical form excludes all chance of it. It is curious that a tree so effective in bloom, and so distinct in habit as the Judas Tree is, should be so little planted with us, and, when planted, so often left to the scant mercy of the shrubbery border. All such trees have their own ways and wants, and should not be crowded up in the common way of planting. I have never seen anything with greater pleasure than a bush of Citrus Trifoliata in the School Garden at Versailles—a sheet of large and beautiful flowers in April, and it grows and blooms well in England.

Lilacs. If the Japanese had Lilacs as varied as their Cherries and Plums they would have a Lilac festival, as where these lovely shrubs are well done they give beautiful effects in the home landscape, as well as charm in the hand and fragrance. To no family has grafting been more injurious than to the Lilac: often grafted on Privet for the sake of cheapness and ease of increase, it has proved an alliance they resent by dying. So it has been in many gardens where Lilacs have been planted but rarely show their fine value, though so many superb varieties have been raised of recent years. In our country the best results from Lilacs are often seen about farm-houses and in small gardens, where the Persian Lilac on its own roots, and perhaps a few common kinds also, are grown. The degradation of the Lilac is seen at its worst in London squares like Lincoln's Inn Fields and St. James's Square, where it runs wild but cut underneath to allow of the useless and ugly digging. When it sows itself in the open the bush takes a pretty habit, but this way of pruning distorts its natural shape and is ruinous in all ways.

What we have to secure is the full value of the varieties that now exist, with their long racemes beautiful in colour when well grown, and to effect this the first thing is to insist that none shall be grafted on the Privet. The best way to increase Lilacs is by cuttings or layers, or by grafting on vigorous plants of the Common Lilac. Some growers say that they will not grow so well on their own roots, but this is not the case. By sowing seeds of the finer varieties one may get strong plants and perhaps some charming new kinds. As to arrangement, the best is to group our Lilacs in the sunlight: they are too often put away among mixed shrubs where they degenerate owing to crowding. No plants more deserve a clear space in the open sun, where they can ripen their wood free from the encroachments of coarser neighbours.

Lilacs are too often neglected in the matter of pruning, though few shrubs are better worth the care, without which they become a tangled mass of shoots and we do not get the fine full thyrses of bloom that are seen in French gardens. Fading flowers should be removed, and the small and weak shoots also if the plants are too 'stalky', the aim being to secure healthy and open growth during summer. Cutting back in winter is wrong, because the flowers are produced on the wood of the previous year, and cutting back to a stiff ugly outline does not deserve the name of pruning. To prune is to help the natural shape of the bush and let the light into it, so that it can concentrate its energy on a number of strong flowering-shoots.

We read sometimes that the Lilac will do in any soil, and so it may in some districts where the soil is warm and good, as in much of Ireland, where the Rouen Lilac, commonly called the Persian, makes such lovely trees. In certain heavy soils Lilacs are slow in growth and do not ripen their wood well or flower so freely as in soils of an open nature. If we are not fortunate to possess this open soil we must make it if the Lilacs are to do well.

Cold places in valleys are not so good for them, especially where heavy soil occurs, because being early the bloom is often caught by late frosts. Therefore, as well as warm soil we should try and secure positions not too low down and somewhat sheltered. Coming from a sunnier land than our own—Transylvania and the regions near—very cold soils are against success.

Lilacs grow freely from seed, if sown as soon as ripe. Cuttings are best made from the young wood in early summer, struck in sand on a hot-bed where they root in six to eight weeks. Layering should be done in early autumn, or suckers may be taken in spring and root readily. When once we have the Lilac on its own roots, increase from suckers is easier than the nurseryman's way, though some kinds sucker less freely than others. Grafting on the common Lilac, though far better than on the fatal and ugly Privet, is not so good as 'own roots', for there is always the chance of finding flowers of a choice variety mixed up with those of the common kind. Beside this, where the flower-garden has any such collection of shrubs and flowers as is now possible, the gardener has no time for watching and removing suckers, which in a rational system of propagation do not trouble him.

The best kinds. Though some of the old varieties were beautiful—even the Common Lilac when well-grown—to have a good Lilac-time it is essential to have the newer varieties raised in France and remarkable for their size, and range of colour. The best are :—

Singles: White—*Marie Legraye, Princess Alexandra, Frau Dammann, Madame Moser, alba pyramidalis*; Pink—*Dr. Regel, Eckenholm, Fürst Lichtenstein, Schermerhornii, Jacques Callot,* and *Lovanensis*; Dark flowers—*Dr. Lindley, Ludwig Späth, Aline Mocqueris, Toussaint L'Ouverture, Volcan, Philémon, Président Massart.*

Doubles: White—*Madame Lemoine, Madame Casimir Périer, Obélisque, Madame Abel Châtenay*; Lavender and blue—*Alphonse Lavallée, Président Grévy, Lamarck, Léon Simon, Monument Carnot, Condorcet, Doyen Keteleer, Guizot, Marc Micheli*; Dark shades—*Charles Joly, Colbert, Georges Bellair, La Tour d'Auvergne, Souvenir de Louis Thibaut, Maréchal de Bassompierre*; Rosy-lilac—*Madame Jules Finger, Rosea grandiflora,* and *Émile Lemoine.*

If one-tenth the trouble wasted on 'carpet-bedding' plants and other fleeting rubbish had been spent on flowering shrubs, our gardens would be all the better for it. There are no plants so much neglected as flowering shrubs, and even when planted they are rarely well grown, owing to the traditions of what is called the 'shrubbery'. The common way is to dig the shrubbery every winter, and this is often carried out as a matter of form without giving the soil any manure, while much harm is done by mutilating the roots of the shrubs. The labour and time wasted in this way, if devoted to the proper culture of a portion of the ground each year, would make many a garden delightful. Many shrubs, as fair as any flower requiring the shelter of glass, have been introduced into this country; but for the most part they have been destroyed by muddle planting.

The common idea of shrubbery planting is so fatally rooted in the popular mind that it is almost hopeless to expect much change for the better. The true way is to depart wholly from it as a mass of *mixed* shrubs, and give to each family or plant a separate place, free from the all-devouring Privet and Laurel, and each part of the shrubbery its own character by grouping, instead of mixing, which ends in the death of the choice kinds. We do not allow stove and green-house plants to be choked in this way, yet no plants are more worthy of a distinct place and of care than hardy shrubs. Low flowering trees, like Hawthorns, group admirably on the turf, but the finer kinds of flowering shrubs should be planted in beds. The shrubbery need no longer be a dark dreary mass, but light and shade may play in it, its varied life be well shown, and the habits and forms of each thing be seen. Shrubs of great beauty or rarity deserve to be well grown. Any one who thinks how much less trouble is given by hardy shrubs than by pot plants will not begrudge attention to outdoor things, and some may even consider a garden of beautiful shrubs as a conservatory in the open air, no kind of flower gardening being more delightful or enduring.

It is not only flowers that suffer from being stuck in lines and patterns; our beautiful flowering shrubs are injured in the same way. The Rhododendron and the Azalea, and what are commonly called American plants, are often put in such close masses that their forms cannot be seen. We may get the flowers to some extent, but they are not so enjoyable as when the plants are allowed to show their individual forms. There is not the slightest reason why we should not have all the force of colour too, because it is quite possible to have a number of beautiful flowering shrubs together without putting them in the serried masses in which they are usually seen.

The Camellia as a garden shrub. The cultivation

ARTISTIC USE OF FLOWERING SHRUBS

of the Camellia in pots having gone a little out of use, and as indoors it did not always do well unless planted out in large houses, we have come to this, that in many places we see it well grown neither indoors nor out. If neglected or forgotten in the house and not seen out of doors we lose the charm of one of the handsomest shrubs of temperate climes, both for the effect of its foliage and its brilliant flowers. There are many places over half our country at least where the Camellia can be grown well as a shrub. In some parts of the south, and near the sea generally, success is so marked that the plants grow as freely as Hollies. They would thrive much farther north if they had a fair chance. In all valleys the plants suffer more from cold in winter, so that in gardens where there is some diversity of surface, and on the sides of hills, their growth would be the safer. A mistake has been made in the adoption of the double to the exclusion of the single kinds, and especially in its outdoor aspect, we doubt if the double flower is an improvement. The single Camellias are more beautiful in colour and varied depth of flower surface, and there is no doubt that many beautiful single kinds which would have graced our gardens, have been thrown away in the past in the chase after double varieties. In a cool climate like our own the double flower does not open so well out of doors, and everything points to the superiority of the single Camellia in its pure and decided colours. Hitherto, in planting out, most people have only taken the warmest positions, so that while the wood ripened well, the flower was exposed too soon to the deceptions of our early February suns and suffered all the more. A northern exposure will often suit it, and those who plant the Camellia should do so in a variety of aspects, and even favour the northern and eastern ones. As to soil, we have known the plant to grow in the coarsest rubbish, and it is not difficult anywhere if we avoid lime.

Sir F. T. Barry has well shown in his garden at St. Leonard's Hill, Windsor, that it is not only in the favoured southern counties that success with the Camellias may be hoped for, and in various notes to *The Garden* and other journals has told of his success; he has many plants thriving out of doors in all aspects and they flower beautifully in spring and early summer and even ripen fertile seeds, from which plants have been raised. This being so, it should surely be easy for growers in favoured districts to raise and offer stocks of well-grown plants; failing these, supplies may be looked for where the Camellia is commonly grown as a shrub, as in Italy, Western

France, Madeira, and Japan. In the Isle of Wight and coasts near, the success is most marked, the bushes flowering as profusely as they do in Madeira on the hills. At Osborne they do remarkably well; but of all spirited planters of the Camellia the late Lord Falmouth was the chief. Having confidence in the growth of the Camellia at Tregothnan he collected plants from many sources, with a most interesting and beautiful result.

CHAPTER VI

CLIMBERS AND THEIR ARTISTIC USE

The splendid squadrons of the Pine, with crests proud in alpine storm and massed in serried armies along the northern mountains, the Oak kings of a thousand winters in the forest plain, are lovely gifts of the earth mother, but more precious still to the gardener are the most fragile of all woody things that garland bush and tree with beautiful forms, the Clematis, Jasmine and Honeysuckle. It is delightful to be able to turn our often ugly inheritance from the builder into gardens by the aid of these; but it is well to take a wider view of these climbing and rambling bushes and their places in the garden and in the pleasure ground. It is well to remember that many climbers may be grown well without such laborious training as nailing them to walls. The tendency is to overpruning of the climbers on walls, and the more freely things are trained the better.

It should not be forgotten that many of these plants grow by themselves like the Honeysuckles, which, while pleasant to see on walls, are not less so on banks, or even on the level ground. Pretty fences and dividing screens may also be easily formed by hardy climbers. The wild kinds of Clematis are charming, and, apart from their use in the flower garden, they should be encouraged for trees and banks.

The Ivy of our northern woods has broken into numbers of beautiful varieties often distinct in form and even in colour; they deserve far more attention for evergreen bowers, evergreen fences, and dividing lines, apart from their growth on walls and trees. The bush forms of these may make broken hedge-like garlands 2 ft. to 3 ft. high round little isolated flower gardens. Almost equally beautiful plants in form of leaf are the Green Briers (Smilax), some of which are hardy in England, but seen in few gardens, and rarely treated in an artistic way, though excellent for walls and rocks.

Of the beauty of the Jasmine of all creepers there is least need to speak, yet how rarely one sees the old white Jasmine made good use of in large gardens. It should be in bold wreaths or masses where it thrives, and so also the winter Jasmine, which is a precious thing for our country, should not be put in as a plant or two in bad conditions, but treated as a fine distinct thing in masses round cottages and outhouses. The finest of hardy climbers, the Wistaria, is much more frequently and rightly planted in France than in our gardens, though it thrives in the Thames valley as well as in the Seine valley. It should, in addition to its use on walls and houses, be made into bold covered ways and bowers and trained up trees, and even along stout wooden fences.

Vigorous climbers on trees. It is not only that stout climbers are more beautiful, and show their form better growing amongst trees, but it is the best way that many of them can be grown with safety owing to their vigour. The way the common Ivy wreaths the trees in rich woods, and the wild Clematis throws ropes up trees on the chalk hills, shows what the larger hardy climbers do over trees or rough or open copses, or even now and then in hedgerows. Some vigorous climbers would in time ascend the tallest trees, and there is nothing more beautiful than a veil of Clematis montana running over a tall tree. Besides the well-known climbers, there are species of Clematis which have never come into general cultivation, but which are beautiful for such uses, though not at all showy. The same may be said of the Honeysuckles, wild Vines, and various other families with which much of the northern tree and shrub world is garlanded. We see wild Roses rambling over trees, and among our garden pictures few are more lovely than the taller wild Roses of other lands planted among shrubs and low trees. By means of these and the hardiest of garden climbing Roses beautiful pictures might be formed in our pleasure grounds.

Climbers of classic beauty or rarity are often found a home for on walls, and in our country some variety of wall surface is a great gain. In the milder districts of the country and in favoured spots round the coast some of the finest exotics, such as Lapageria, and some greenhouse plants of great beauty, like Clianthus, which in the midland and northern counties can only be enjoyed in a greenhouse, may be grown on walls in the open air. Some of the fine plants of Chili also may be grown on walls of various aspects. *Abelia, Lardizabala, Berberidopsis* and *Rhynchospermum* are among the plants sometimes so grown, and there is a wide range as to selection. Many who have visited our best gardens will probably have stored away in their memories some of the pictures they have seen given by noble wall plants well grown in this way—as, for example, the New Zealand Edwardsia at Linton, so fine in form and colour, and the handsome Fremontia. Hard winters settle the fate of many beautiful things among these, but, happily, some of the loveliest things are hardy, like the Winter Sweet, *Bignonia, Magnolia,* and sometimes the fine colour of the Pomegranate buds is seen among them.

Fragile Climbers on shrubs. Apart from the vigorous climbers that we may trust in shrubberies, woods, and on rough banks, and which, when fairly started, take care of themselves, there are fragile things which deserve to be used in rather a new way as far as most gardens are concerned, namely, for throwing a delicate lacework of flowers over the evergreen and other choice shrubs and low trees grown in our gardens. Often stiff, unbroken masses of Rhododendrons and evergreen flowering shrubs will be more varied if delicate flakes of Clematis (white, lavender, or claret-red) or the bright arrows of the Flame Nasturtium come among them here and there in autumn. The great showy hybrid Clematises of our gardens are not so good for this use as the more elegant wild Clematises of North America, Europe, and North Africa. These are so fragile in growth that many of them may be trusted among groups of choice shrubs like Azaleas, throwing veils over the bushes here and there. Two lovely twining shrubs must never be left out in any scheme of this kind, the Atragene or Alpine Clematis of the mountains of Europe, hardy as the Oak, and tender in colour as the dove, and in all the warmer districts the winter-flowering Clematis of the islands of the Mediterranean and North African coasts, where with the Smilax it garlands thousands of acres of jackal-haunted scrub.

Roses as climbers. Many of the more vigorous wild Roses of the northern world are almost climbing plants, and some of them grow 20 ft. high up trees. In gardens many varieties might be mentioned which in past years were a great source of beauty and gave a very showy effect when well used, and in our own time, and within the past generation or two, since the raising of Gloire de Dijon, a noble series of climbing Roses, wholly distinct from the old climbing kinds, has been raised in France, the most precious kinds that have ever adorned the Rose-garden.

The old Climbers and Garland Roses were almost too vigorous for the garden, and their bloom did not last long enough to justify their getting a place there; but now, with the great climbing Tea Roses, we may count on a bloom for months. Hence we have in these Roses, where they thrive, the best, the most precious of all ornaments for walls of houses, trellis work and pergola. In southern parts of the country we even get fine results from these Roses on the north side of walls, where some Roses flower better than on the south side. Also we can grow them in the open on trellises or away from walls; but in the northern parts of the country, where these great climbing Tea Roses may not thrive so well, walls come in to help us more and more by their shelter and warmth, and the encouragement they give to early bloom.

Apart from these great Roses of garden origin, which will long be among the most precious, some wild Roses are of the highest importance in warm districts and good soils, particularly the Indian *R. Brunonis* and the many-flowered Roses (*R. polyantha*) of Japan; but with the need of so much wall space for the garden Roses these wild Roses will usually be best in the shrubbery or some place apart, where they may be let alone, and no good can arise from choice garden ground being given to wild Roses which are even more vigorous than our own wild Dog Rose.

Vines, for their beauty of form. Going back some thousands of years to the earliest sculptured remains of some of the oldest peoples, we see evidence that the Grape Vine was in common use, and it is no doubt older than the monuments of Assyria. Among the Kabyle villages of North Africa I passed many

Vines of great age trailing over very old Olive trees in the little orchard fields. In such countries there was the value of the fruit, but even in ours, where the Grape rarely ripens out of doors, the charm of the plant is so great that we see many cottages in Surrey and Norfolk set deep in Vine leaves. The Grape Vine, however, is but one of a large family, and, though we may not see in our country its garlands from tree to tree purple with fruit, we may see much of its fine forms of leaf. The wild Vines are too vigorous for use on walls, though excellent for banks and trees and for any place outside the flower garden, clambering up forest trees, spreading into masses of fine foliage on the ground, and sending out long arms in search of the nearest trees—handsome climbers, hardy, vigorous, and soon covering dry banks, rocks, and trees.

To the Vines (*Vitis*) have now been joined by the botanists Virginian Creepers (*Ampelopsis*), and between the two groups it need not be said what noble things they offer for garlanding trees, walls, bowers, rocks, and banks. It cannot be said that we neglect these Virginian and Japanese creepers, but the Vines are so far seldom well used with us.

Pergolas. Though our summer is often not sunny, there are seasons when shaded walks may be enjoyed, and numbers of free-growing climbing plants give an abundant and lovely choice of living drapery for them. In Italy and warm countries one often sees in gardens the pergola serving the twofold purpose of supporting Grape Vines and giving pleasant coolness during the summer heat. These pergolas are often rude trellis-work structures of wood, sometimes supported by stone posts where these are at hand. In the gardens in the neighbourhood of Rome, Naples, and Florence there are beautiful examples of pergolas—stately structures, the supports of which are massive columns of stone covered and festooned with Banksian Roses, Wistaria, Clematis, Honeysuckles, Passion Flowers, scarlet Trumpet Flowers, and other climbers which give cool shade in the hot days. But such pergolas seldom occurred outside the gardens of the great villas, and near humbler dwellings they were usually simple structures made for the purpose of supporting the Grape Vine.

These creeper-clad covered ways should usually lead to somewhere and be over a frequented walk, and should not cut off any line of view nor be placed near big trees, especially such trees as the Elm, whose hungry roots would travel a long way to feed upon the good soil that the climbers should be planted in. A simple structure is the best. The supports, failing the Italian way of making posts of stone, should be oak stems, about 6 to 9 inches in diameter, let into the ground 30 inches. On no account let the 'rustic' carpenter adorn it with the fantastic branchings he is so fond of, as all such begin to rot as soon as put up.

Trees supporting Climbers. Instead of trusting to wire and posts or the many artificial ways for supporting Climbers, why should we not use living trees to carry the Vine or Climber, as the Italians and people of South Europe do? Weeping trees of graceful leaf and form might be used in this way with fine effect. Abroad they take for this purpose any kind of tree which happens to be near and keep it within bounds, and those who know our garden flora may select trees which, while beautiful themselves, will not be much trouble to keep in bounds, like the weeping Cherry, weeping Aspen, some Willows even, and any light-leaved weeping tree would be worth a place for its own sake as well as for what it might carry.

Light arches over walks. When a quiet walk leads from one part of the garden to another and is spanned at intervals with slender light arches clothed with Honeysuckle, Clematis, or Jasmine, it gives an added grace to the walk. This also is a good way of framing, so to say, a flower border, the light arches springing up from the line of the trellis, which should be used to cut off the borders from the kitchen garden.

Annual and Herbaceous Climbers. However rich we may be in shrubby climbers, we must not forget that we have the climbing things among annual and like plants to help us, especially in the smaller class of gardens. Hedges of Sweet Peas there are few things to equal; the fragile annual Convolvuli in many colours are pretty for low trellises, the vigorous herbaceous Bindweeds for rough places outside the flower garden. Most showy of all annual climbers are the many Gourds, which, treated in a bold way, give fine effects when trained over outhouses, sheds, or on strong stakes as columns. The showy annual climbing Tropaeolums, as well as the brilliant herbaceous and tuberous rooted kinds, are most precious; nor must we forget the Hop as a vigorous and graceful herbaceous climber, of much value where well placed. Among these climbers we may place the Passion Flower. Because so often short-lived in the cold and more inland parts of our islands, it is best for sheltered and sea-coast places, and is not quite hardy even there in our coldest seasons; still, if its base be sheltered with some dry Fern, it will spring up again.

Covered ways of fruit trees. This way of growing fruit trees and shading walks is not often seen, though few things would be prettier or more useful in gardens if fruit trees of high quality were chosen. Although in our gardens the shaded walk is not so necessary as it is in Italy and Southern France, in hot seasons shade is welcome in Britain; and, as in many gardens we have four times as many walks as are needed, there is plenty of room for covering some of them with fruit trees which would give us flowers in spring, fruit in autumn, and light shade. The substance of which walks are made is often good for fruit, and those who know the Apricot district of Oxfordshire and the neighbouring counties may see how well fruit trees do in hard walks. It is not only in fruit gardens that their shade might be welcome, but in flower gardens, if we ever get out of the common notion of a flower garden, which insists on everything being seen at one glance and the whole as flat and hard as oilcloth.

Plashed alleys. In some old gardens there was a way of 'plashing' trees over walks—trees like the Lime, which grew so vigorously that they had to be cut back with an equal vigour, this leading in the end to ugliness in the excessive mutilation of the trees. One result of the frequent cutting was a vigorous summer growth of shoots, which cast a dense shade and dripped in wet weather. The purpose of such walks would be well fulfilled by training fruit trees over them, as they are trees which much more readily submit to training, and give the light and airy shade which is best in our country. The fruit trellis, whatever it is formed of, need not be confined to fruit trees only, but here and there wreaths of Clematis or other elegant climbers might vary the lines.

Evergreens as Climbers. Those who live in sheltered valleys, or among pleasant hills above the line of hard frosts, may be so rich in evergreens that they will keep their walls for the fairest of true climbers. But in cold, exposed, and inland parts people are often glad to have good evergreens on walls, even bushes not naturally climbers in habit, such as Garrya, the evergreen Barberries, *Camellias, Azara, Escallonia, Cotoneaster*. The Laurustinus, too, is charming on many cottage walls in winter, and may escape there when it would suffer in the open; the Myrtle is happy on walls in southern districts, and even the Poet's Laurel may be glad of the shelter of a wall in the north. The evergreen Magnolia, which in warmer Europe is a standard tree, must in our country usually be grown on walls, even in the south, and there is no finer picture than a good tree of Magnolia on a house. The beautiful Ceanothus of the Californian hills often keep company with these evergreens on walls; but even in the warmer soils of the home counties they are tender, and their delicate sprays of flowers are much less frequently seen with us than in France and, although we cannot resist trying them on sunny walls, on chalky and sandy soils they have better chances.

Apart from true shrubs used as evergreens so frequently in Britain, we have some natural evergreen climbing plants for walls, foremost being our native Ivy, in all its beautiful forms and varied uses for walls, houses, borders, screens, and even summer-houses and shelters. How much better to make bowers of Ivy rather than of rotten timber, straw, or heath! If we make a strong and enduring framework, and then plant the Ivy well, we soon get a living roof, which, with little care, will last for many years and always look well.

CHAPTER VII

ALPINE FLOWER- ROCK- AND WALL GARDENS

It was a common idea, not confined to the public, but propagated by writers whenever they had to figure or describe alpine flowers, that the exquisite flowers of alpine plants could not be grown in gardens in the lowland regions. So far from its being true, however, there are but few alpine flowers that ever cheered the traveller's eye that cannot be grown in these islands.

Alpine plants grow naturally on high mountains, whether they spring from sub-tropical plains or green northern pastures. Above the cultivated land these flowers begin to occur on moorland and in the fringes of the hill woods; they are seen in multitudes in the broad pastures with which many mountains are robed, enamelling their green, and also where neither grass nor tall herbs exist. Where mountains are crumbled into slopes of shattered rock by the contending forces of heat and cold, even there, amidst the glaciers, they spring from the ruined ground, as if the earth-mother had sent up her loveliest children to plead with the spirits of destruction.

They fringe the fields of snow and ice of the mountains, and at such elevations often have scarcely time to flower before they are again buried deep in snow. Enormous areas of the earth, inhabited by alpine plants, are every year covered by a deep bed of snow, and where tree or shrub cannot live from the intense cold, a deep mass of down-like snow falls upon them, like a great cloud-borne quilt, under which they rest safe from alternations of frost and biting winds with moist and spring-like days as in our green winters.

But these conditions are not always essential for their growth in a cool northern country like ours. The reason that alpine plants abound in high regions is because no taller vegetation can exist there; were these places inhabited by trees and shrubs, we should find fewer alpine plants among them; on the other hand, were no stronger vegetation found at a lower elevation, these plants would often appear there. Also, as there are few hard and fast lines in nature, many plants found on the high Alps are also met with in rocky or bare ground at much lower elevations. Gentiana verna, for example, often flowers very late in summer when the snow thaws on a very high mountain; yet it is also found on much lower mountains, and occurs in England and Ireland. In the close struggle upon the plains and low tree-clad hills, the smaller species are often overrun by trees, trailers, bushes, and vigorous herbs, but, where in far northern and high mountain regions these fail from the earth, the lovely alpine flowers prevail.

Alpine plants possess the charm of endless variety, and include things widely different :—tiny orchids, tree-like moss, and ferns that peep from crevices of alpine cliffs, often so small that they seem to cling to the rocks for shelter, not daring to throw forth their fronds with airy grace; bulbous plants, from Lilies to Bluebells; evergreen shrubs, perfect in leaf and blossom and fruit, yet so small that a finger glass would make a house for them; dwarfest creeping plants, spreading over the brows of rocks, draping them with lovely colour; Rockfoils and Stonecrops no bigger than mosses, and, like them, mantling the earth with green carpets in winter, and embracing nearly every type of the plant-life of northern lands.

In the culture of these plants, the first thing to be remembered is that much difference exists among them as regards size and vigour. We have, on the one hand, a number of plants that merely require to be sown or planted in the roughest way to flourish—Arabis and Aubrietia, for example; and, on the other, there are some kinds, like Gentians and the Primulas of the high Alps, which are rarely seen in good health in gardens and it is as to these that advice is chiefly required. Nearly all the misfortunes which these little plants have met with in our gardens are due to a false conception of what a rock-garden ought to be, and of what the alpine plant requires. It is too often thought that they will do best if merely raised on tiny heaps of stones and brick rubbish, such as we frequently see dignified with the name of 'rockwork'. Mountains are often 'bare', and cliffs devoid of soil; but we must not suppose that the choice jewellery of plant-life scattered over the ribs of the mountain lives upon little more than the air and the melting snow. Where else can we find such a depth of stony soil as on the ridges of shattered stone and grit flanking some great glacier, stained with tufts of crimson Rockfoil? Can we gauge the depth of that chink from which peep tufts of the beautiful little Androsace helvetica, which for ages has gathered the crumbling grit, into which the roots enter so far that we cannot dig them out? And if we find plants growing from mere cracks without soil, even then the roots simply search farther into the heart of the flaky rock, so that they are safer from drought than on the level ground.

We meet on the Alps plants not more than an inch high firmly rooted in crevices of slaty rock, and by knocking away the sides from bits of projecting rock, and laying the roots quite bare, we may find them radiating in all directions against a flat rock, some of the largest perhaps more than a yard long. Even smaller plants descend quite as deep, though it is rare to find the texture and position of the rock such as will admit of tracing them. It is true we occasionally find in fields of flat hard rock hollows in which moss and leaves have gathered, and where, in a depression of the surface, without an outlet of any kind, alpine plants grow freely; but in droughts they are just as liable to suffer from want of water as they would be in our plains. On level or sloping spots of ground in the Alps the earth is of great depth, and, if it is not all earth in the common sense of the word, it is more suitable to the plants than what we usually understand by that term. Stones of all sizes broken up with the soil, sand, and grit prevent evaporation; the roots lap round them, follow them down, and in such positions they never suffer from want of moisture. It must be remembered that the continual degradation of the rocks effected by frost, snow, and heavy rains in summer, serves to 'earth up', so to speak, many alpine plants.

In numbers of gardens an attempt at 'rockwork' has been made; but the result is often ridiculous, not because it is puny when compared with Nature's work, but because it is generally so arranged that rock-plants cannot exist upon it. The idea of rockwork first arose from a desire to imitate those natural croppings-out of rocks which are often half covered with dwarf mountain plants. The conditions which surround these are rarely taken into account by those who make rock-gardens. In moist districts, where rains keep porous stone in a humid state, this straight-sided rockwork may support a few plants, but in the larger portion of the British Isles it is useless and ugly. It is not alone because they love the mountain air that the Gentians and such plants prefer it, but also because the great elevation is unsuitable to coarser vegetation, and the alpine plants have it all to themselves. Take a patch of Silene acaulis, by which the summits of some of our highest mountains are sheeted over, and plant it 2,000 feet lower down in suitable soil, keeping it moist and free from weeds, and it will grow well; but leave it to Nature, and the strong herbs will soon cover it, excluding the light and killing it.

Although hundreds of kinds of alpine flowers may be grown without a particle of rock near them, yet the slight elevation given by rocky banks is congenial to some of the rarest kinds. The effect of a well-made rock-garden is pretty in garden scenery. It furnishes a home for many native and other plants which may not safely be put in among tall flowers in borders; and it is important that the most essential principles to be borne in mind when making it should be stated. The usual mistake is that of not providing a feeding-place for the roots of the plants. On ordinary rockwork even the coarsest British weeds cannot find a resting-place, because there is no body of soil for the roots to find nourishment sufficient to keep the plant fresh in all weathers.

Position for the Rock-garden. The rock-garden should never be near walls; never very near a house; never, if possible, within view of formal surroundings of any kind, and it should be in an open situation. No efforts should be spared to make all the surroundings, and every point visible from the rock-garden, graceful and natural as they can be made. The part of the gardens around the rock-garden should be picturesque, if possible, and, in any case, be quiet and airy, with as few jarring points as may be. No tree should be in the rock-garden; hence a site should not be selected from which it would be necessary to remove favourite trees. The roots of trees would find their way into the masses of good soil for the alpine flowers, and soon exhaust them. Besides, as these flowers are usually found on treeless-wastes, it is best not to place them in shaded places.

As regards the stone to be used, sandstone or millstone grit would perhaps be the best; but it is seldom that a choice can be made, and almost any kind of stone will do, from Kentish rag to limestone: soft and slatey kinds and others liable to crumble away should be avoided, as also should magnesian limestone. The stone of the neighbourhood should be adopted for economy's sake, if for no other reason. Wherever the natural rock crops out, it is sheer waste to create artificial rockwork instead of embellishing that which naturally occurs. In many cases nothing would be necessary but to clear the ground, and add here and there a few loads of good soil, with broken stones to prevent evaporation, the natural crevices and crests being planted where possible. Cliffs or banks of chalk, as well as all kinds of rock, should be taken advantage of in this way. Many plants, like the dwarf Harebells and Rock Roses, thrive in such places. No burrs, clinkers, vitrified matter, portions of old arches and pillars, broken-nosed statues, or other rubbish, should ever be seen in a garden of alpine flowers. Never let any part of the rock-garden appear as if it had been shot out of a cart. The rocks should all have their bases buried in the ground, and the seams should not be visible. Wherever a vertical or oblique seam occurs, it should be crammed with earth and the plants put in with the earth will quickly hide the seam. Horizontal fissures should be avoided as much as possible. No vacuum should exist beneath the surface of the soil or surface-stones, and the broken stone and grit should be so disposed that there are no hollows. Myriads of alpine plants have been destroyed from the want of observing this precaution, the open crevices and loose soil allowing the dry air to destroy the alpine plants in a very short time, and so one often sees what was meant for a 'rock-garden' covered with weeds and brambles and forgotten!

In all cases where elevations of any kind are desired, the true way is to obtain them by a mass of soil suitable to the plants, putting a 'rock' in here and there as the work proceeds; frequently it would be desirable to make these mounds of earth without any strata. The wrong and usual way is to get the elevation by piling up ugly masses of stones, vitrified bricks, and other rubbish.

No formal walks. No walk with regularly trimmed edges should come near the rock-garden; but this need not prevent the presence of good walks through or near it, as by allowing the edges of the walk to be broken and stony, and by encouraging Stonecrops, Rockfoils, and other little plants to crawl into the walk at will, a pretty margin will result. There is no surface of this kind that may not be thus adorned. Violets, Ferns, Forget-me-nots, will do in the shadier parts, and the Stonecrops and many others will thrive in the full sun. The whole of the surface of the alpine garden should be covered with plants as far as possible, except a few projecting points. In moist districts, Erinus and the Balearic Sandwort will grow on the face of the rocks; and even upright faces of rock will grow a variety of plants. Regular steps should never be in or near the rock-garden. Steps may be made quite picturesque, and even beautiful, with Violets and other small plants jutting from every crevice; and no cement should be used. Where the simplest type of rock-garden only is attempted, and where there are no steps or rude walks in the rock-garden, the very fringes of the gravel walks may be graced by such plants as the dwarfer Stonecrops. The alpine Toadflax is never more beautiful than when self-sown in a gravel walk. A rock-garden so made that its miniature cliffs overhang is useless for alpine vegetation, and all but such wall-loving plants as Corydalis lutea soon die on it. The tendency to make it with overhanging 'peaks' is often seen in the cement rock-gardens now common.

Soil. The great majority of alpine plants thrive best in deep soil. In it they can root deeply, and when once rooted they will not suffer from drought, from which they would quickly perish if planted in the usual way. Three feet deep is not too much for most kinds, and in nearly all cases it is a good plan to have plenty of broken sandstone or grit mixed with the soil. Any free loam, with plenty of sand and broken grit, will suit most alpine plants. But peat is required by some, as, for example, various small and brilliant rock-plants like the Menziesia, Trillium, Cypripedium, Spigelia, and a number of other mountain and bog-plants. Hence, though the body of the soil may be of loam, it is well to have a few masses of peat here and there. This is better than forming all the ground of good loam, and then digging holes for the reception of small masses of peat. The soil of some portions might also be chalky or calcareous, for the sake of plants that are known to thrive best on such soils, like the Milkworts, the Bee Orchis, and Rhododendron Chamaecistus. Any other varieties of soil required by particular kinds can be given as they are planted.

It is not well to associate a small lakelet or pond

ALPINE FLOWER- ROCK- AND WALL GARDENS

with the rock-garden, as is frequently done. If a picturesque piece of water can be seen from the rock-garden, well and good; but water should not, as a rule, be closely associated with it. Hence, in places of limited extent, water should not be thought of.

Planting. In every kind of rock-garden, it should be remembered that *all* the surface should be planted. Not alone on slopes, or favourable ledges, or chinks, should we see this exquisite plant-life, as many rare mountain species will thrive on the less trodden parts of footways; others, like the two-flowered Violet, seem to thrive best in the fissures between steps; many dwarf succulents delight in gravel and the hardest soil. In cultivating the very rarest and smallest alpine plants, the stony, or partially stony, surface is to be preferred. Full exposure is necessary for very minute plants, and stones are useful in preventing evaporation and protecting them in other ways. Few have much idea of the number of alpine plants that may be grown on fully exposed ordinary ground. But some kinds require care, and there are usually new kinds coming in, which, even if vigorous, should be kept apart for a time. Therefore, where the culture of alpine plants is entered into with zest, there ought to be a sort of nursery spot on which to grow the most delicate and rare kinds. It should be fully exposed, and sufficiently elevated to secure perfect drainage.

Ill-formed Rock-gardens. The increased interest in rock-gardening of recent years has led to much work of this kind being done throughout the country, and without good results artistically. The rock-gardens are not right in structure nor good for growing plants. If they were good for the life of plants one might pass over their other defects, but when made, as they often are, of cement, and even of natural stone, so that the plants grow with great difficulty, owing chiefly to the stones overhanging so as to leave dry and dusty recesses, the result is altogether bad. No doubt rocks do in nature often have such recesses, but they very often come out of the ground in ways that the flowers and moss grow well on them.

In the present state of the art of garden design, rock-gardens are formed mainly by nurserymen; these are not as a rule men who, by the very nature of their business, can give much attention to the study of rocks in natural situations, or learn how the different strata crop out in the ways most happy for vegetation, without which study we think no good work in this way is possible. The work we see now is often done better than the ugly masses of scoria and various rubbish of the earlier 'rock works', but it is still a very long way from what is artistic. Simplicity is rarely thought of, or of the rock coming out of the ground in any pretty way, of which we may see numerous examples in upland moors in England, even without going to the mountains or the Alps. On the contrary, we see pretentious rickety piles of stone on stone, with pebbles between to keep the big ones up, and forty stones where seven would be enough. A characteristic of these elaborate failures is a rocky depression, often an ugly one, in the ground. This is by no means the most likely thing in Nature to give the prettiest effects. If alpine and rock plants wanted shelter, we could see some meaning in these depressions, but the conditions that suit such plants are quite the opposite, and a rock-garden should be for the most part made on a fully exposed rocky knoll.

The fact that such bad work is usual is no proof that we cannot get nearer to the truth, and there is a good opening for one who would devote himself to going on the hills and seeing the ways in which rocks and flowers meet. He would have to study not only the more imposing aspects of that charming subject, but also the simpler ones, because in gardens in all that concerns the rocks we can get only simple effects, and on a small scale. One of the commonest mistakes is piling stone upon stone in such a way that there is no room for grouping anything. If one were to take five or six of the stones one sees in a rock-garden, and simply lay them with the prettiest and most mossy sides showing out of the bank in the right kind of earth, one would get a better place for plants than a rock-garden, made it may be of hundreds of tons of stone, could give, because then we should have room to group and mass them, without which no good effect is possible.

The common 'rockery', like the common mixed border, is an incoherent muddle, and can scarcely be anything else so long as the present plan is followed. The plants hate it. We should seek gardens of alpine flowers, with here and there a mossy stone showing modestly among them—not limiting one's efforts to any one idea, but beginning at least with simplicity of effect. Then groups and carpets of rock plants would be easy to form, and their culture would be easier in every way.

Refuse brick 'Rockeries'. Whoever started using the refuse of the brickyard to form the rock-garden was no friend of the garden, as alpine flowers do not thrive on masses of vitrified brick rubbish. And these brick rubbish horrors are put up with overhanging brows so that a drop of moisture cannot get to the plants, and a dry wind can sweep through them as easily as through a grill. If the practice were confined to cottages near brickfields it would not much astonish us; but in Dulwich Park several thousand tons of it have been put about under the pretence of making rock-gardens, and also at Waterlow Park, Highgate, which was once a pretty and varied piece of ground. If the County Council waste money in this way, we cannot perhaps wonder so much at the owners of villas doing it, but in any case it is ugly and disgraceful in a garden, though we see it freely used in many large country gardens. No ignoble materials should be seen in any rock-garden, in which even stumps of trees are out of place. With some people any broken-nosed statue or other stony or vitrified rubbish is used in what should be the most beautiful and natural of all gardens—the alpine garden. If we have not rock in its natural position, or cannot secure some pieces of natural rock to use even on a small scale, it is far better to grow the rock plants in simple ways, even on the level earth on which many of them thrive. When these villainous banks of brick-yard refuse were first erected, anything more hideous in a public garden was not to be seen, but by piling on them common shrubs, evergreens, Tobacco, Stonecrops, China Asters, Begonias, Chrysanthemums, Beetroot, Heath, Elder, and higgledy-piggledy verdure of this nature, a sort of brick-rubbish salad was the result, and the effect of the brick was less seen. It is not only the ugliness of this that is bad; it is also an injustice to the gardener, to expect him to get any good results at all seasons from the kind of thing a Brentford cobbler who lives near a brickyard makes a little 'rockwork' of in his garden.

Misplaced artificial rock. Artificial rock is formed now and then in districts where the natural rock is beautiful, as in the country round Tunbridge Wells; though why anybody should bring the artificial rock-maker into a garden or park where there is already fine natural beautiful rock it is not easy to see. Also, in certain districts, it is a mistake to place this artificial rock under conditions where rock of any kind does not occur in nature. It would be much better, as far as alpine and rock plants are concerned, to dispense with much of this ugly artificial rockwork, and take advantage of the fact that many of these plants grow perfectly well on raised borders and on fully exposed low banks.

Alpine plants in groups. Many vigorous alpine flowers will do perfectly well on level ground in our cool climate, if they are not overrun by coarser plants. Where there are natural rocks or good artificial ones it is best to plant them properly; but people who are particular would often be better without artificial 'rockwork' if they wished to grow these plants in simpler ways. There is not the slightest occasion to have what is called 'rockwork' for these flowers. I do not speak only of things like the beautiful Gentianella, which for many years has been grown in our gardens, but of the Rockfoils, the Stonecrops, and the true alpine plants in great numbers. Then, for the sake of securing the benefits of the refreshing rains, it would often be best, in the south of England at least, to avoid the dusty pockets hitherto built for rock flowers. In proof of what may be done in this way there is a little alpine garden, made in quite a level place in the worst possible soil for growing the plant, the hot Bagshot sand, where the soil is always fit for working after heavy rain, but in hot summer is almost like ashes. By making the soil rather deep, and by burying a few stones among the plants to prevent dryness, this flower, which naturally thrives in loamy soil, grew well, and the plan suits many alpine plants.

The next point is the great superiority of natural grouping over the botanical or labelled style of little single specimens of a great number of plants. In a few yards of border, in the ordinary way, there would be fifty or more kinds, but nothing pretty for those who have ever seen the beautiful mountain gardens. Many rightly contend that, in a sense, Nature includes all, and that therefore the term 'natural' may be misapplied, but is a perfectly just one when used in the sense of Nature's way of arranging flowers, as opposed to the lines, circles, and other set patterns so commonly followed by man. Through bold and natural grouping we may get fine colour without a trace of formality. But most gardeners find it difficult to group in this natural way, because so used to setting things out in formal lines. But a little attention to natural objects will help us to get away from set patterns, and let things intermingle here and there and run into each other to form groups such as we may see among the rocks by alpine paths. After a little time the plants themselves begin to help us, and an excellent way is, if a number of plants are set out too formally—as in most cases they are—to pull up a number here and there, replanting them on the outer fringes of the groups or elsewhere.

Wall-gardens. Those who have observed alpine plants must have noticed in what arid places many flourish, and what fine plants may spring from a chink in a boulder. They are often stunted and small in such crevices, but longer-lived than when growing upon the ground. Now, numbers of alpine plants perish, if planted in the ordinary soil of our gardens, from over-moisture and want of rest in winter; but if placed where their roots are dry in winter, they may be kept in health. Many plants from countries a little farther south than our own, and from alpine regions, will find on walls, rocks, and ruins that dwarf, sturdy growth which makes them at home in our climate. There are many alpine plants now cultivated with difficulty in frames that may be grown on walls with ease. The Cheddar Pink, for example, grows on walls at Oxford much better than I have ever known it do on rockwork or on level ground. A few seeds of this plant, sown in an earthy chink and covered with a dust of fine soil, soon grow, living for years on the wall and increasing.

In garden formation, especially in sloping or diversified ground, what is called a dry wall is often useful, and may answer the purpose of supporting a bank or dividing off a garden quite as well as masonry. Where the stones can be got easily, men used to the work will often make gently 'battered' walls which, while fulfilling their object in supporting banks, will make homes for many plants which would not live one winter on a level surface in the same place. In my own garden I built one such wall with large blocks of sandstone laid on their natural 'bed,' the front of the stones almost as rough as they come out, and chopped nearly level between, so that they lay firm and well. No mortar was used, and as each stone was laid slender rooted alpine and rock plants were placed between the courses with a sprinkling of sand or fine earth enough to slightly cover the roots and aid them in getting through the stones to the back, where, as the wall was raised, the space behind it was packed with gritty earth. This the plants soon found out and rooted firmly in. Even on old walls made with mortar, rock-plants and small native ferns very often establish themselves, but the 'dry' walls are more congenial to rock-plants, and one may have any number of beautiful alpine plants in perfect health on them.

One charm of this kind of wall-garden is that little attention is required afterwards. Even on the best rock-gardens things get overrun by others, and weeds come in; but on a well-planted wall we may leave plants for years untouched beyond pulling out any interloping plant or weed that may happen to get in. So little soil is put with the plants that there

ALPINE FLOWER- ROCK- AND WALL GARDENS 107

is little chance of weeds. If the stones were stuffed with much earth weeds would get in, and it is best to have the merest dusting of soil with the roots, so as not to separate the stones, but let each one rest firmly on the one beneath it.

Among the things which do well in this way almost the whole of the beautiful rock and alpine flowers may be trusted, such things as Arabis, Aubrietia, and Iberis being among the easiest to grow; but as these can be grown without walls it is hardly worth while to put them there, pretty as some of the newer forms of the Aubrietia are. Between these stones is the very place for mountain Pinks, which thrive better there than on level ground, and the dwarf alpine Harebells; while the alpine Wallflowers and creeping rock-plants, like the Toad Flax (Linaria), and the Spanish Erinus, are quite at home there. The Gentianella does very well on the cool sides of such walls, and we get a different result according to the aspect. All our little pretty wall ferns, now becoming so rare where hawkers abound, do perfectly on such rough walls, and the alpine Phloxes may be used, though they are not so much in need of the comfort of a wall as the European alpine plants. The Rocky Mountain dwarf Phloxes, being very hardy and enduring, flourish in our gardens on level ground. The advantage of the wall is that we can grow things that would perish on level ground, owing to excitement of growth in winter or other causes. The Rockfoils are charming on a wall, particularly the silvery kinds, and the little stone covering sandwort (A. balearica) will run everywhere over such a wall. Stonecrops and Houseleeks would do too, but are easily grown in any open spot of ground. In many cases the rare and somewhat delicate alpines, if care be taken in planting, would do far better on such a wall than as they are usually cultivated. Plants like the Thymes are free in such conditions, also the alpine Violas, and any such pretty rock-creepers as the blue Bindweed of North Africa, and all the forms of the sweet Violet.

There is in fact no limit to the beauty of rock and alpine flowers we may enjoy on the rough wall so often and most easily made about gardens in rocky and hilly districts, dressed or expensive stone not being needed. In my own garden there are three wholly different kinds of walls thick set with plants; and the easiest way to the enjoyment of the most interesting and charming of the mountain flowers of the north is by the aid of walls.

Colour in the Rock-garden. Although in their native lands there is no colour more beautiful than that of rock-plants, their full value is seldom shown in gardens. The common way of making what is called a rockery prevents all breadth of grouping; the puerile idea that a rock-garden is made by standing stones on end is against all effective planting; you cannot get plants into natural colonies in that way, and the 'pockets' prevent them from taking anything like their usually pretty spreading habit. The great majority of Alpine plants do not want 'pockets'; they want to be raised above the level in order to escape the surface water; they enjoy having their roots behind stones, but they no more object to a flat surface or gentle slopes than grass does, as may be seen upon the Alps in all directions. If people would put their rocks in simple ways instead of exposing their sides like milestones, it would be much easier to group well and get the full effect of the colour of the mountain flowers. Another mistake long rooted in our habits and which spoils all the mixed borders in the land, is the common way of placing dots instead of easy groups, putting cultivation or good effect out of court. Hence, although we may secure much of the individual beauty of the plant seen close at hand, we do not get the true colour effect, which is the most subtle charm.

Beauty of grouping. No other plants specially put out for their show of colour give such brilliant effects, and owners of rock-gardens might get far more enjoyment from them if they adopted simpler ways of grouping. I do not say that only one kind of plant should be used in a given spot, for two kinds sometimes intermingle with pretty effect, as they often do in their native haunts, but the great thing is to get broad groups of each plant, whether it be Alpine Heath, or the Purple Rock Cress which flowers for three months in the spring, or such plants as the common Woodruff, which group themselves if we let them. Ten kinds well used are more effective than a hundred as commonly set out. The plants that may be used are numerous, and their colours refined and beautiful in the highest sense. Beside the true rock-plants there are many dwarf shrubs like Helianthemums, some of the smaller Roses, and mountain shrubs generally, that lend themselves to fine effect in colour. It is not only beauty that we get, but also helpful simplicity in cultivation; for, clearly, if we have to make changes when a plant gets tired of the ground or for any other reason, it is far easier to deal with visible masses than with scattered dots. Another point is, that with the feeble dotting system in use, the weeds take possession of the bare ground, whereas many of these mountain plants, if allowed to spread into groups, unite to keep the enemy out. In every way, therefore, the rock-garden is much more easy to manage where the dotting system is set aside. There remains the question of getting enough plants to secure this effect, and happily most things in common use are readily increased by cutting or division. Rockfoils, for example, which are so useful, are easily increased to any extent by division; the little American Phloxes also. The Aubrietias come freely from seed or cuttings. It is only the rareties which may be difficult of increase; most things of free growth, as rock-plants, are of quick increase by simple means.

Coarse plants. Coarse plants are too often seen, flowerless, too vigorous, or without beauty of colour; these should be removed to the herbaceous borders and the Wild Garden or elsewhere—not only because of their ugliness, but as being apt to exhaust the ground near fragile plants, robbing them of moisture and light, or actually overgrowing and killing them —a common sight on neglected rock-gardens. Plants growing upon *moraines* or cliffs are not overfed, but at least they have not to fight with the vigorous herbs one too often sees on rock-gardens. These also help to mar the colour of the rock-garden, breaking up masses and giving a very un-alpine look to the scene.

Repetition fatal to good effect. The repetition of the same thing all over the rock-garden is the surest way to destroy harmonious and right colour. If we are fond of Yellow Alyssum, or any other showy plant, let it be on a bank or wall in a bold way in one place; or, if it is a plant we are very fond of, we may even have two or three groups of it in different aspects, but if scattered all along the same line of view the result is fatal to any harmony of colour. Again, harsh contrasts should be avoided, seeking rather gentle and harmonious effect. The grouping and massing should never be stiff; masses might run one into the other here and there, and need not always be confined to plants of one sort. Things of like stature and character might at times be allowed to run together, any hard and fast rule being against good work in gardening as in art. The making and keeping up of a good rock-garden is a costly thing, and the least return that can be expected by those willing to incur the cost is to get the full colour value from the plants.

Grass. Often, even in well-formed rock-gardens, there are grass paths which are troublesome to keep and less good in their effect than stone. Also, in some of our best rock-gardens, there are often isolated rocks surrounded by grass, whereas they ought always to rise out of a bed of Thyme, creeping Speedwells, dwarf Heaths, Daphnes, or Milkworts. Some of the most charming scenes in those parts of the Alps richest in plants are where single stones rise, perhaps, only a couple of feet out of ground which is densely covered with dwarf Daphne or Alpine Anemone. If fearful of trampling upon such plants (which we need not always be, seeing how the Thyme upon our heaths will bear trampling), the simplest way is to put a few old flag-stones down as a path, not more than a foot apart; these permit of passage in all weathers without injuring the plants. Spaces wasted in many rock-gardens upon grass or gravel might, if well-carpeted, give good colour, and may at least be planted with Thyme, Stonecrop, Rockfoil, tiny Peppermint, and Sandworts. The objection to grass is that it is not nearly so good in effect as the rock-flowers, and it has constantly to be cut at the cost of needless labour.

Since writing the above a wall covered with *Erinus* has come into view, and not for the first time. Its modest colour is most effective when held together in this way, and there could hardly be a better example of the fine colour value that lies half-hidden in these mountain flowers. As a dot this plant is without effect; on the wall it is beautiful hundreds of yards away, as well as in every nearer point of view.

The full value of many of the prettiest rock and alpine plants is rarely felt, even by growers of these plants, owing to the absence of all broad and natural grouping. Rightly used, half the number of kinds of plants would give far better effects than the ill-planted collection we so often see. Good cultivation, seed saving and other ways of increase, freedom from vigorous weeds and other enemies, would all be more easy to attain through bold and artistic grouping.

CHAPTER VIII

THE WILD GARDEN

In a rational system of flower-gardening one of the first things to do is to get a clear idea of the aim of the 'Wild Garden'. When I began to plead the cause of the innumerable hardy flowers against the few tender ones put out in a formal way, the answer sometimes was, 'We cannot go back to the mixed border'—that is to say, to the old way of arranging flowers in borders. Thinking, then, much of the vast world of plant beauty shut out of our gardens by the 'system' in vogue, I was led to consider the ways in which it might be brought into them, and of the 'Wild Garden' as a home for numbers of beautiful hardy plants from other countries, which might be naturalized with very little trouble in our gardens, fields, and woods—a world of plant beauty in places bare or useless. We could grow thus not only flowers often more lovely than those commonly seen in what is called the flower garden, but also many which, by any other plan, we should have little chance of seeing.

The term 'Wild Garden' is applied to the placing of perfectly hardy plants where they will take care of themselves. It does not necessarily mean the picturesque garden, for a garden may be picturesque and yet in every part the result of ceaseless care. What it does mean is best explained by the winter Aconite flowering under a grove of naked trees in February; by the Snowflake, abundant in meadows by the Thames; and by the blue Apennine Anemone in a British wood. Multiply these instances by adding many plants from countries as cold as our own, and one may get an idea of the Wild Garden. Some have thought of it as a garden allowed to run wild, or with annuals sown promiscuously, whereas it does not meddle with the flower garden proper at all.

In the smaller class of gardens there is little room for the Wild Garden, but in the larger gardens there is often ample room on the outer fringes of the lawn, in grove, park, copse, or by woodland walks or drives, where beautiful effects may be created by its means.

Reasons for the Wild Garden. Among reasons for it are the following :—1. Many hardy flowers will thrive better in rough places than ever they did in the old border. 2. Among plant, fern and flower and climber, grass, and trailing shrub, they will look infinitely better than in stiff plots or borders. 3. No ugly effects will result from decay and the swift passage of the seasons. In a semi-wild state the beauty of a plant will tell in flowering time, and when out of bloom it will be succeeded by other kinds. It will enable us to grow many plants that have never yet obtained a place in our 'trim gardens'—multitudes that are not showy enough to be considered worthy of a place in a flower garden. 4. Among the plants often thought unfit for garden cultivation are some like the American Asters and Golden Rods, which overrun the choicer border-flowers when planted among them. Such plants are happy in rough places, where their blossoms might be seen in due season. To these might be added plants like the winter Heliotrope, and many others which are apt to spread so rapidly as to become a nuisance. 5. In this way we may settle the question of spring flowers, and the spring garden, as well as of hardy flowers generally; and many parts of the grounds may be made alive with spring flowers, without any interfering with the flower garden. The blue stars of the wild Anemones will be seen to greater advantage in half-shady places, under trees, or in the meadow grass, than in any flower garden, and those but one of many spring flowers for the Wild Garden.

Narcissi in the Wild Garden. Perhaps an example

or two of what has already been done with Daffodils and Snowdrops may serve to show the way, and there is no more charming flower to begin with than the Narcissus, which, while fair in form as any Orchid of the tropics, is as much at home in our climate as the Kingcups in the marsh and the Primroses in the wood. And when the wild Narcissus comes with these, in the woods and orchards of Northern France and Southern England it has also for companions the Violet and the Cowslip, hardiest children of the north, blooming in and near the still leafless woods. And thus it is not only a garden flower we have here, but one which may give beauty to our woods and fields and meadows as well as to the pleasure grounds.

There is plenty of room to grow them other than in the garden proper, and this is not only in country seats, but in orchards and cool meadows. To chance growth in such places we owe it already that many Narcissi or Daffodils, which were lost to gardens in the period when hardy plants were set aside for bedding plants, have been preserved to us which at first probably in many cases were thrown out with the garden refuse. In many places in Ireland and the west of England, Narcissi lost to gardens have been found in old orchards and meadows.

There is scarcely a garden in the kingdom not disfigured by vain attempts to grow trees, shrubs, and flowers not really hardy, and it would often be wiser to devote attention to things that are quite hardy in our country, like most Narcissi to which the hardest winters make no difference. Besides, we know from their distribution in Nature how fearless they are in this respect. Three months after our native kind has flowered in the weald of Sussex and in the woods or orchards of Normandy, many of its allies are in the mountain valleys of Europe waiting till the summer sun melts the deep snow and sets them free. On the cool mountain marshes and pastures, where the snow lies deep, the plant has abundance of moisture, which is one reason why it succeeds better in our cool soils. Light, sandy or chalky soils in the south of England are useless, and Narcissus culture on a large scale should not be attempted on such soils.

Years ago I planted many thousands of Narcissi in the grass, and they have thriven, bloomed regularly, the flowers large and handsome. In open, rich, heavy bottoms, along hedgerows and banks, in open loamy fields, in every position they have been tried. They are delightful seen near at hand, and effective in the picture : the leaves disappear before mowing time, and do not interfere with the use of the ground. The harrowing and rolling of the fields in the spring hurts the leaves a little, but near wood walks, grass walks, open copses and lawns which abound in so many country places, the plants are free from this.

The kinds we may naturalize with advantage are almost without limit, but generally it is better to take the great groups of Star Narcissi, the Poet's, and the wild Daffodil, of which there are so many handsome varieties. These are hardy in our soils; and, as we have to do in a bold way, we had best plant kinds that are easy to get in quantity. There is hardly any limit except rarity, and for the most part we must put our rare kinds in good garden ground till they increase, although in some cases Narcissi that will not thrive in a garden will do so in the grass of an orchard.

The fine distant effect of Narcissi in groups in the grass is distinct from their effect in gardens, and it is most charming to see them reflect, as it were, the glory of the spring sun. It is not only their effect near at hand that charms us, but as we walk about we may see them in the distance in the varying lights, sometimes through and beyond the leafless woods or copses. There is nothing we have to fear in this charming work save the common error—overdoing. To scatter Narcissi equally over the grass everywhere is to destroy all repose, relief, and all chance of seeing them in the ways in which they often arrange themselves, while it is almost as easy to plant in pretty ways as in ugly ways. There are hints to be gathered in the way wild plants arrange themselves, and even in the sky. Often a small passing cloud will suggest a very good form for a group, in being closer and more solid towards its centre, as groups of Narcissi in the grass should be. The regular garden way of setting things out is necessary in the garden, but it will not help us to the pictures we can get from Narcissi in the turf. It is always well to keep open turf here and there among the groups, and in a lawn or a meadow we should leave a large breadth quite free of flowers.

Snowdrops in the Wild Garden. In congenial soils the snowdrop often becomes naturalized and often forms pretty pictures. The common single and double forms are still the best for naturalization. There are finer varieties, but not any grow and increase so well in our gardens as do these northern kinds. The best of the eastern Snowdrops are very bold and beautiful, they are unsurpassed for vigour of leafage and size of bloom if carefully cultivated, but they do not grow and increase on the grass as do G. nivalis and all its forms.

For solid green leafage and size and substance of flower, G. Ikariae when well grown is, as I believe, the finest of all Snowdrops, but it is from Asia Minor, and does not really love our soil and climate, nor is it likely to naturalize itself with us as G. nivalis has done. The best of all the really hardy and truly northern Snowdrops is a fine form of G. nivalis, leaning to the broad-leaved or G. caucasicus group, which was found in the Crimea in 1856 and introduced from the Tchernaya valley to Straffan. It is called G. nivalis grandis, or the Straffan Snowdrop, and to see it at its best is a great pleasure, the flowers large and pure in colour, and borne on stalks a foot or more in length.

Snowdrops thrive in deep free soils and half shade, and their flowers wither and brown quickly on dry, light soils in full sunshine. In damp woods, copses, and hedgerows they seem most at home.

How to Plant. I usually plant Narcissi in grass by turning back the sod, making two cuts with the spade at right angles, and then pressing up and back the sod, laying it back on a hinge as it were, putting in a few bulbs, mostly round the sides of the hole, turning the sod back and treading firmly upon it. It is largely a question of convenience and the ground one has to plant. If one could improve the subsoil it would be better for some soils, no doubt, but if the work is done in a bold way and there is much other planting going on, one has not time to plant things carefully in grass. Sometimes in breaking new ground or carrying out changes one gets a chance of throwing in some bulbs before the surface is levelled up. When the men are making sod banks for the only true field fence—a live one—is a very good time to put in Sweet Briars in the bank. In certain soils, seeds of Foxglove, Evening Primrose, and stout biennials, may be sown betimes. Fragile bulbs will want more care and less depth than the bolder Narcissi. Many ways of planting are good, though far more important than any is thought as to the wants of the thing we plant, not only as to soil, but as regards association with the things that will grow about it in grass, in hedgerows and rough places.

All planting in the grass should be in natural groups or colonies growing to and fro as they like after planting. Lessons in grouping are to be learned in the woods, copses, heaths, and meadows, by those who look about them as they go. Many will find it difficult to avoid formal masses at first, but the difficulty may be got over by studying the natural groupings of wild flowers. Once established, the plants soon begin to group themselves in pretty ways.

The Secret of the Soil. The important thing is to find out what things really do in the soil, without which much headway cannot be made in wild gardening. Many people err in planting things notoriously tender in our country, but rash planting apart, plants perfectly hardy may disappear owing to some dislike of the soil. They flower feebly at first and afterwards gradually wane in spite of all our efforts. I have made attempts to establish spring Snowflakes in grass, none of which succeeded, owing to the cool soil, yet one of the Snowflakes in the Thames Valley grows with the vigour of a wild plant. I have put thousands of Snowdrops in places where I could hardly see a flower a few years later, yet in some places it establishes itself in friable soil by streamlets, and in many other situations. So it is with the Crocus. I find it difficult to naturalize, taking but slowly and gradually diminishing, and yet it in many places covers the ground. What will do or will not do is often a question of experience, the point is to take the lesson when we see a thing doing well. People often complain of the texture of the grass as a cause of failure, yet I have thousands of the Tenby Daffodil for ten years in rich and rank masses of Cocksfoot and other coarse grasses in coverts—never mown nor the old grass taken away at any time, and the

Narcissus gets better year by year. So it is a question of finding out the thing the soil will grow, and we shall perhaps arrive at that knowledge only after various discouragements. Some things are so omnivorous that they will grow anywhere, but the more beautiful races of bulb and other early flowers will only thrive and stay with us where they like the soil.

Hardy Flowers beneath Trees. Where the branches of trees, both evergreen and summer-leafing, sweep the turf in pleasure-grounds many pretty spring-flowering bulbs may be naturalized beneath the branches, and will thrive without attention. It is chiefly under deciduous trees that this can be done; but even in the case of pines and evergreens some graceful plants may be dotted beneath the outermost points of their lower branches. We know that numbers of our spring flowers and hardy bulbs mature their foliage and go to rest early in the year. In spring they require light and sun, which they obtain abundantly under the summer-leafing tree; they have time to flower and grow under it before the foliage of the tree appears; then, as the summer heats approach, they are overshadowed, and go to rest; but in the fall they soon reappear and cover the ground with beauty.

CHAPTER IX

SPRING FLOWERS

In our islands, swept by the winds of iceless seas, spring wakes early in the year, when the plains of the north and the mountains of the south and centre are cold in snow. In our green springs the flowers of northern and alpine countries open long before they do in their native homes; hence the inartistic error of any system of flower-gardening which leaves out the myriad flowers of spring. It is no longer a question of gardens being bare of the right plants; nurseries and gardens where there are many good plants are not rare, but to make effective use of these much thought is seldom given. Gardens are often rich in plants but poor in beauty, many being stuffed with things but ugly in effect.

If we are to make good use of our spring garden flora we should avoid much annual culture, though it is not well to get rid of it altogether, as many plants depend for their beauty on rich ground and frequent cultivation. But many grow well without these, and the most delightful spring gardens can only be where we grow many spring-blooming things that demand no annual care, from Globe-flowers to Hawthorns.

A common kind of 'spring gardening' consists of bedding out Forget-me-nots, Pansies, Daisies, Catchflies, and Hyacinths; but this way is only one of many, and the meanest, most costly, and inartistic. It began when we had few good spring flowers; now we have many.

The fashion of leaving beds of Roses and choice shrubs bare of all but one subject should be given up. The half bare Rose and choice shrub beds should be a home for the prettiest spring flowers—Pansies, Violets, early Irises, Daffodils, Scillas, and many other dwarf plants in colonies between the Roses or shrubs. Double Primroses are happy and flower well in such beds. The slight shade such plants receive in summer from the other tenants of the bed assists them. Where Rhododendrons are planted in an open way (these precious bushes never ought to be jammed together), a spring garden of another kind may be made, as the peat-loving plants (there are many fair ones among them) will be quite at home there. The White Wood Lily of the American woods (*Trillium*), the Virginian Lungwort, the Canadian Bloodroot (*Sanguinaria*), the various

Dog's-tooth Violets, double Primroses, and many early-flowering bulbous plants enjoy the partial shade and shelter.

In the kitchen garden, in its usual free and rich soil, having simple beds of favourite spring flowers, such as Polyanthuses, Bunch Primroses in their coloured forms, self-coloured Auriculas, and Pansies of various kinds, is a good way of enjoying such plants, and more easily managed than the 'bedding out' of spring flowers. That may follow the fashion of the hour, and with such plants as Forget-me-nots, Daisies, Silene, Pansy, Violet, Hyacinth, Anemone, and Tulip, showy effects may be formed; but, without any of these pattern beds under the windows, fair gardens of spring flowers may be made in every place, and the problem of the design for the few set beds of the 'spring parterre' will not be so serious a matter as in the past, there being so many aids in other ways.

Rock and Alpine Plants. There are so many hardy plants among these that flower in spring (many alpine plants blooming as soon as the snow goes), that there is not room to name them all in an essay devoted to the more effective groups and their best garden use. We must omit any detailed notice of plants like Adonis, Cyclamen, Draba,

Erodium, and the smaller Rockfoils and Stonecrops, Dicentra, Fumaria, Orobus, Ramondia, Silene, and many other flowers of the rocks and hills, which though beautiful individually do not tell so well in the picture as many here named.

Rock Cresses and Wallflowers. Among rock plants the first place belongs to certain mountain plants of the northern world, which, in our country, come into bloom before the early shrubs and trees, and among the first bold plants to cheer us in spring are those of the Wallflower order—the yellow Alyssum, effective and easy to grow, the white Arabis, even more grown in Northern France than in England (it well deserves to be spread about in sheets and effective groups), and the beautiful purple Rock Cresses (*Aubrietia*), lovely plants of the mountains of Greece and the countries near, which have developed a number of varieties even more beautiful in colour than the wild kinds. Nothing for gardens can be more precious than these plants, the long spring bloom being effective in almost every kind of flower gardening—banks, walls, edgings, borders of evergreen, rock plants, or carpets beneath sparsely set shrubs. The white evergreen Candytufts are also effective plants in clear sheets for borders, edgings to beds, tops of walls, and the rougher flanks of the rock-garden. These are among the plants that have been set out in hard lines in flower gardens, but it is easy to have better effects from them in groups and even in broken lines and masses, or as carpets beneath bushes, thus giving softer and more beautiful, if less definite, effects. Happy always on castle wall and rocks, the Wallflower is most welcome in the garden, where, on warm soils and in genial climates, it does well, but hard winters injure it often in cold and inland districts, and it is almost like a tender plant in such conditions. Yet it must ever be one of the flowers best worth growing in sheltered and warm gardens; and even in cold places one may have a few under the eaves of cottages and on dry south borders. It is where large masses of it are grouped in the open and are stricken—as the greens of the garden are stricken—in cold winters, that we have to regret having given it labour and a place which might have been better devoted to things hardy everywhere. The various old double Wallflowers are somewhat tender too and rarely seen to advantage save in favoured soils, which is all the more reason for making the most of them where the soil and air favour them. Certain allies of the Wallflower, mountain plants for the most part, such as the alpine Wallflower, also give good effects where well done and grouped on dry banks or warm borders.

The Windflowers are a noble group among the most beautiful of the northern and eastern flowers, some being easily naturalized (like the blue Italian and Greek Anemones), while the showy Poppy Anemones are easily grown where the soils are light and warm, and in genial warm districts; but they require some care, and are among the plants we must cultivate and even protect on cold soils in hard winters. The same is true of the brilliant Asiatic Ranunculus and all its varied forms—Persian, Turkish, and French, as they may be called, all forms of one wild North African buttercup. Unhappily they are too tender to endure our winters in the open air, but they should be abundantly grown on the warm limestone and other soils which suit them about our coasts and in Ireland. There is no more effective way of growing these than in simple 4-foot beds in the kitchen or reserve garden. The Wood Anemone is so often seen in the woods that there is rarely need to grow it; but some of its varieties are essential, most beautiful being A. Robinsoniana, a flower of lovely blue colour, and a distinct gain in the spring garden grown in almost any way. The Hepatica is a lovely little Anemone where the soil is free, though slow in some soils, and where it grows well all its varieties should be encouraged, in borders and margins of beds of American bushes as well as in the rock-garden. The Snowdrop Windflower (*A. sylvestris*) is most graceful in bud and bloom, but a little capricious in not blooming well on all soils, unlike our Wood Windflowers, which are as constant as the Kingcups. The Pasque-flower is lovely on the chalk downs and fields of Normandy and parts of England in spring, but never quite so pretty in a garden. It would be worth naturalizing in chalky fields and woods or banks.

Columbine, Marsh Marigold, Clematis, Lenten Rose, and Globe-flower. Columbines are very beautiful in the early part of the year, and if we had nothing but the common kind (Aquilegia vulgaris) and its forms, they would be precious; but there are many others which thrive in free soils, some of which are very graceful in form and charming in colour. The Kingcup or Marsh Marigold, so fine in wet meadows and by the riverside, should be brought into gardens wherever there is water, as it is a most effective plant when well grown, and there are several forms, double and single. The Clematis, the larger kinds, are mostly for the summer, but some (C. montana, C. alpina, C. cirrhosa) are at their best in the spring; they should be made abundant use of on house walls and over banks, trees and shrubs. The Winter Aconite (earliest of spring flowers) naturalizes itself in some soils, but on others dwindles and dies out, and it should not be grown in the garden, but in shrubberies, copses, or woods, where the soil suits it. Some kinds of hardy Ranunculus, the herbaceous double kinds, are good in colour, and in bold groups pretty; but taller and bolder and finer in effect are the Globe-flowers, easily naturalized in moist, grassy places or by water, and also free and telling among stout herbaceous plants. The most distinct addition to the spring garden of recent years is the Oriental Hellebore in its many beautiful varieties, of which some have been raised in gardens. They are handsome and stately plants, with large flowers, often delicately marked. With the usual amount of garden shelter and fairly good soil they grow bold and free, and have a stately habit and fine foliage, as well as beautiful flowers excellent for cutting. They are most effective, sturdy, impressive plants for opening the flower year with, often blooming abundantly at the dawn of spring, and have the essential merit of not requiring annual culture, tufts remaining in vigour in the same spot for many years.

Dog's-tooth Violets, Snowdrop, Snowflake, Crocus, Scilla, Fritillary, and Hyacinth. The European Dog's-tooth Violet is pretty in the budding grass, where it is free in growth and bloom. The Fritillary is one of the most welcome flowers for grass, and is best in moist meadows; the rarer kinds do well in good garden soil, those with pale yellow bells being beautiful. Every plant such as these, which we can so easily grow at home in grassy places, makes our cares about the spring garden so much the less, and allows of keeping all the precious beds of the flower garden itself for the plants that require some care and rich soil always.

The Hyacinth, which is often set in such stiff masses in our public gardens, gives prettier effects more naturally grouped, but it is not nearly so important for the open air as many flowers more easy to grow and better in effect, though some of the more slender wild species, like H. amethystinus, are beautiful and deserve a good place. The Snowdrop is of even greater value of late years, owing to new forms of it, some of which have been brought from Asia Minor and others raised in gardens. In some soils it is quite free and becomes easily naturalized, in others it dwindles away, and the same is true of the vernal Snowflake (*Leucojum vernum*), a beautiful plant. The larger Snowflakes are more free in ordinary soils, and easily naturalized in river-bank soil. The Crocus, the most brilliant of spring flowers, does not lend itself to growing naturally in every soil, but on some it is quite at home, especially those of a chalky nature, and will naturalize itself under trees, while in many garden soils it is delightful for edgings and in many ways.

To the Scilla we owe much, from the wild plant of our woods to the vivid Siberian kind; some kinds are essential in the garden, and some, like the Spanish Scilla (*S. campanulata*), may be naturalized in free soils. Allies of these lovely early flowers have come of recent years to our gardens—the beautiful Chionodoxa from Asia Minor, of about the same stature and effect as the prettiest of the Scillas, and some of them even more precious for colour. These are among the plants which may be planted with best results in bold groups on the surface of beds planted with permanent flowers, such as Roses—where Rose beds are not surfaced with manure, as all Rose-growers unwisely advise.

Iris, Grape Hyacinth, Narcissus, and Tulip. In warm soils some of the more beautiful of the flowers of spring are the early Irises, but in gardens generally the most beautiful of Irises come in late spring with the German Iris, which is so free and hardy throughout our country. Orchid-houses themselves cannot give any such array as these when in bloom, and they are often deserving of a little garden to themselves, where there is room for it, while they are useful in many ways in borders and as groups. About the same time come the precious Spanish Iris in many colours, lovely as Orchids, and very easily grown, and the English Iris. The Grape Hyacinths are pretty and early plants of Southern Europe, beautiful in colour. They increase rapidly, and some kinds do very well in the grass in free and peaty soils; but the rarer ones are best on warm borders and groups in the rock-garden. The Narcissus is worth growing in every way; the rarer kinds in prepared borders or beds and the many that are plentiful in almost any cool soil in the grass. In our country, where there are so many cool and rich soils allowing of the Narcissus being naturalized and grown admirably in many ways, it is, perhaps, the most precious of all our spring flowers. But the Tulip is the most gorgeous in colour of all the flowers of spring, and for its effectiveness is better worthy of special culture than most. Indeed, the florists' kinds and the various rare garden Tulips must be well grown to show their full size and beauty.

Replanting now and then is almost essential with a Tulip garden if we are to keep the bulbs free from disease; the wood Tulip and certain wild species may be naturalized, and then are as beautiful, if not so large, as the cultivated bulbs. The Tulip deserves a far better place among spring flowers than it has had, as, apart from the two great groups of early and late Tulips hitherto cultivated in European gardens, a number of handsome wild kinds are being introduced from Central Asia and other countries, many of them having early flowers of great beauty and fine colour, and if they will only take kindly to our climate the Tulip garden will soon leave all hothouse brilliancy a long way in the rear.

Paeony, Poppy, and Lupin. Paeonies are nobly effective in many ways. Where single or other kinds are plentiful they may be well used as broad groups in new plantations, among shrubs and low trees, and as to the choice double kinds, no plants better deserve a little garden or border to themselves, while the tree kinds make superb groups on the lawn and are safer from frost on high ground. The great scarlet Poppies are showy in spring, and best grown among trees and in the wild garden, and with them may be named the Welsh Poppy, a very effective plant in spring as well as summer, and often sowing itself in all sorts of places. The various garden forms of the opium Poppy and of the field Poppy, both double and single, are very showy where any space is given to annual flowers.

The common perennial Lupin is a very showy, pretty plant grown in a free way in groups and masses, and may sometimes be naturalized; associated with Poppies and free-growing Columbines in the wild garden, it is very effective.

Primrose, Tulip, Cowslip, Polyanthus, and Auricula. Primroses are a lovely host for the garden, especially the garden varieties of the common Primrose, Cowslip, and Oxlip. Few things deserve a better place, or are more worthy of good culture in visible groups and colonies or rich garden borders. Apart from the lovely races of garden forms raised from the Primrose, the Cowslip, and the Oxlip, and also the Alpine Auriculas, double Primroses should not be forgotten, as in all moist districts and in peaty and free soil they give such tender and beautiful colour in groups, borders, or slightly shaded among dwarf shrubs. Primroses and Polyanthus of native origin are well backed up by the beautiful Indian Primrose (*Primula rosea*), which thrives apace in cool soils in the north of England and in Scotland, and which, when grown in bold groups, is very good in effect, as are the purplish Indian Primroses under like conditions.

Rockfoil, Gentian, and Alpine Phlox. The large-leaved Indian Rockfoils (Saxifraga) are in many soils very easily grown, and are showy spring flowers in bold groups, especially some of the improved varieties. Although it is only in places where there is rocky ground or large rock-gardens that one can get the beauty of the smaller Mountain Rockfoils (*Saxifraga*), we cannot omit to notice their beauty—both the white, yellow, and crimson-flowered kind—when seen in masses. The same may be said of Gentians; beautiful as they are in the mountains, few gardens have positions where we can get their fine effect, always excepting the old Gentianella (*G. acaulis*), which in old Scotch and English gardens used to make such handsome broad edgings, and which is easily grown in a cool soil, and gives, perhaps, the noblest effect of blue flowers that one can enjoy in our latitudes in spring. The tall Phloxes are plants of the summer, but there is a group of American dwarf alpine Phloxes of the mountains which are among the hardiest and most cheery flowers of spring, thriving on any dry banks and in the drier parts of rock-gardens, forming mossy edgings in the flower garden, and breaking into a foam of flowers early in spring.

Pansies. The Viola family is most precious, not only in the many forms of the sweet Violet, which will always deserve garden cultivation, but also in the numerous varieties of the Pansy, which flower so effectively in the spring. The best of all, perhaps, are the Tufted Pansies, which are delightfully simple in colour—white, pale blue, or lavender, and various other delicate shades. Almost perennial in character, they can be increased and kept true, and they give us distinct and delicate colour in masses as wide as we wish, instead of the old 'variegated' effect of Pansies. Though the separate flowers of these were often handsome, the effect of the Tufted Pansies with their pure and delicate colours is more valuable, and these also, while pretty in groups and patches, will, where there is space, often be worth growing in little nursery beds.

Forget-me-nots are among the most welcome flowers of spring. Before the common one, most beautiful of all—the marsh Forget-me-not—comes, there are the wood Forget-me-not (*M. sylvatica*) and M. dissitiflora and M. alpestris, all precious early flowers. Allied to the ever-welcome Forget-me-not is the common Omphalodes, or creeping Forget-me-not, valuable for its freedom in growth in half-shady or rough places in almost any soil—one of the most precious of the early flowers which take care of themselves if we take a little trouble to put them in likely places. Among

Annual flowers that bloom in Spring, where the soil is favourable excellent results are often obtained by sowing Sweet Peas in autumn. Where this is done, and they escape the winter, they give welcome hedges of flowers in the early year. So, too, the Cornflower, a lovely spring flower, and perhaps the finest blue we have among annual plants. But to have it good and early it should be always sown in Autumn, and for effect it should be in broad masses, sometimes among shrubs or in recently broken ground which we desire to cover. Some of the Californian annuals are handsome and vigorous when sown in autumn, always provided they escape the winter. The White Godetia is very fine in this way. In all chalky, sandy, and warm soils the Stocks for spring bloom are handsome and fragrant, but it is a waste of time to attempt to grow them on cold soils. It would be taking too narrow a view to omit from our thoughts of spring gardens the many beautiful flowering

Shrubs and trees that bloom in Spring, as some of the finest effects come from the early trees and shrubs. Among the most stately are the Chestnuts, particularly the red kinds, fine in all stages, but especially when old. The snowy Mespilus is a hardy, low-sized tree, blooming regularly, and well deserves a place in the pleasure garden or the fringes of shrubberies. The Almonds, more than any shrubs, perhaps, in our country and in France, light up the earliest days of spring, and, like most southern trees, are best in warm valley soils, growing more slowly in cool heavy soils. They should be in groups in order to tell in the home landscape. The double Peaches are lovely in France, but rarely so with us, owing, perhaps, to some defect of the stock used. Perhaps of all the hardy shrubs ever brought to our country the Azaleas are the most precious for effect. They are mostly wild on the mountains of America, and many forms have been raised in gardens which are of the highest value. Many places do not as yet show the great beauty of the different groups of hardy Azalea, particularly the late kinds raised of recent years. A neglected tree with us is the Judas-tree, which is very handsome in groups, as it ought always to be grown, and not as a starved single tree. The various double Cherries are noble flowering trees, showy as well as delicate in bloom, and the Japanese kinds do quite as well as the old French and English double

Cherries, though the trees are apt to perish from grafting. The American Fringe-tree (*Chionanthus*) is pretty, but some American flowering trees do not ripen their wood well enough in England generally to give us the handsome effects seen in their own country. Hawthorns are a host in themselves; those of our own country make natural spring gardens of hills and rocky places, and should teach us to give a place to the many other species to be found in the mountains of Europe and America, which vary the bloom and prolong the season of early flowering trees. There are many varieties of our native hawthorn—red, pink, double, and weeping. The old Laburnum has for many years been a joy with its golden rain, and of late we are doubly well off with improved forms, with long chains of golden flowers. These will become noble flowering trees as they get old; hence the importance of grouping Laburnum trees to get the varieties together.

Among the early charms in the spring garden are the slender wands of the Forsythia, hardy Chinese bushes, pale yellow, delightful in effect when grown in picturesque ways; effective also on walls or grouped in the open air on banks. Another plant of refined beauty, but too little planted, is the Snowdrop tree (*Halesia*). Unlike other American trees, it ripens its wood in our country, and often flowers well. The mountain Laurel of America (*Kalmia*) is one of the most beautiful things ever brought to our country, and as a late spring flower is precious, thriving both in the open and in half shady places.

Broom and Furze. There is no more showy plant, or one more beautiful in effect in masses, than the common Broom and all its allies that are hardy enough, even the little Spanish Furze giving fine colour. The common Broom should be encouraged on bluffs and sandy or gravelly places, so as to save us the trouble of growing it in gardens, for in effect there is nothing better. The same may be said of the Furze, which is such a beautiful plant in England and the coast regions of France; and the double Furze deserves to be massed in the garden in picturesque groups. In country seats, especially those which command views, its value in the foreground is very great, and it is so easily raised from seed that fine effects are very easily secured, though it may be cut down now and then in hard winters.

Rhododendron and Magnolia. The glory of spring in our pleasure grounds, the Rhododendrons, are so over-mastering in their effect on people's minds that they very often lead to neglect of other things. It would be difficult to overrate their charms, but we should avoid the too early and tender kinds. Many of the kinds raised from R. ponticum and the Indian Rhododendron, while they thrive in mild districts in the south of England and west of France near the sea, are not hardy in the country generally. Some of these tender hybrids flower early, but we get little good from that. The essential thing, when we give space to a hardy shrub, is that we should get its bloom in perfection, and therefore we should choose the broad-leaved hardy kinds, which are mostly raised from the very hardy North American R. catawbiense, and be a little particular in grouping the prettiest colours, never using a grafted plant. For many years the Yulan Magnolia has, when well grown, been one of the finest trees in English southern gardens, and nothing is more effective than the Lily-tree in gardens like Syon and others in the Thames valley; while of late years we have seen precious additions to this, the noblest family of flowering trees. Some of these, like M. stellata, have proved to be valuable; all are worth a trial, and as to the kinds we are sure of, the great thing is to group them. Even in the case of the common Lily-tree (*M. Yulan*) it makes a great difference whether there are four or five trees or one.

Amongst the most beautiful of the smaller alpine

bushes ever brought to our country is the Alpine Forest Heath, which is cheery and bright for weeks in spring. It is one of the plants that never fails us, and only requires to be grown in bold ways to be effective—in groups and masses fully exposed to the sun. Other Heaths, like the Mediterranean Heath, are also beautiful in some favoured parts of the country, but not so hardy generally as the little Alpine Forest Heath, which has the greatest endurance and most perfect hardiness, as becomes a native of the Alps of Europe.

Pyrus japonica, a handsome old shrub often planted on cottage garden walls, may in many soils be used with good effect in groups and hedges. The evergreen Barberries in various forms are beautiful early shrubs, with soft yellow flowers, and excellent when grouped in some quantity. Two very important families are the Deutzias and Syringas, which are varied and beautiful, mostly in white masses. They should never be buried in the common shrubbery, but grouped in good masses of each family. The flowering Currant (*Ribes*) of the mountains of N.W. America is in all its forms a very cheery and early bush, which tells well in the home landscape if rightly placed. Perhaps the most welcome and important of all early trees and shrubs is the Lilac, which in Britain is often grown in a few kinds only, when there are many in France. Beautiful in almost any position, Lilacs are most effective when planted together, so as to allow the full sun to ripen their wood; the danger of thick planting can be avoided by putting Irises or other hardy flowers over the ground between the shrubs, which should never be crowded.

Crab Bloom. Apart from the many orchard trees grown for their fruit, we have in our own day to welcome some of their allies—lovely in flower, if often poor in fruit. Our country has never been without some of this kind of beauty, as the Crab itself is as handsome a flowering tree as many of the Apples which are descended from it in all the countries in Europe, from Russia to Spain. In our gardens there were for many years the old Chinese double Pyrus, a handsome tree, which became popular, and the American Crab, which never became so; but of late years we have been enriched by the Japan Crab, a lovely tree for some weeks in spring, and other handsome kinds, including Parkman's Crab, which comes to us under more than one name, and a red form of the Japanese flowering Crab before mentioned. All these trees are as hardy as our native Crab, and differ much in colour and sometimes also in form. It is difficult to describe how much beauty they give where well grown and well placed; they are not the kind of things we lose owing to change of fashion, and in planting them it is well to put them in groups where they will tell. Apart from these more or less wild species there are numbers of hybrid Crabs—raised between the Siberian and some common Apples of America and our country—that are beautiful also in flower, and remarkable too for beauty of fruit, so that a beautiful grove of flowering trees might be formed of Crabs alone. With these many fine things, and the various Honeysuckles, we are carried bravely down to the time of Rose and Lily—summer flowers, though Roses often come on warm walls in spring.

Spring Flowers in sun and shade and North and South Aspects. It is worth while thinking of the difference in the blooming of spring flowers in various aspects, as differences in that way will often give us a longer season of bloom with some of our most precious things. Daffodils do better in half-shade than in full sunshine, and Scillas and other bulbs are like the Daffodils in liking half-shady spots; so also Crown Imperials, which, like the Scillas, bleach badly if fully exposed to the sun. We may see the Wood Hyacinth pass out of bloom on the southern slopes of a hill, and in fresh and fair bloom on its northern slopes. Flowering shrubs, creepers on walls, and all early plants are influenced in the same way. Such facts may be taken advantage of in many ways, especially with the nobler flowers that we make much use of. If different aspects are worth securing for hardy flowers generally, they are doubly so for those of the spring, when we often have storms of snow and sleet that may destroy an early bloom. If fortunate enough to have the same plant on the north side of the hill or wall, we have still a chance of a second bloom, and a difference of two or three weeks in the blooming of a plant.

CHAPTER X

BORDERS OF HARDY FLOWERS

OF the flowers that are worthy of a place in gardens, the number and variety is almost without limit, and the question is, how the garden-lover is to enjoy as many of these treasures as his conditions allow. A simple border has always been the first expression of flower-gardening, and, as there is no arrangement of flowers more graceful, varied, or capable of giving more delight, and none so easily adapted to almost every kind of garden, some ideas as to the various kinds of borders of hardy flowers deserve our first consideration.

Cost and Endurance. The difference in cost of growing hardy or tender flowers should be thought of. The sacrifice of flower-gardens to plants that perish every year has often left them poor of all the nobler plants. We must take into account the hot-houses, the propagation of plants by thousands at certain seasons, the planting out in June, the digging up and storing in autumn, the care in the winter.

Perhaps the most striking effects from individual

plants ever seen in England were those of the Japanese Lilies grown for years in the open air by Mr. M'Intosh among his Rhododendrons at Weybridge Heath. Not only Lilies, but many noble flowers may be grown in the same simple way. A few years ago we saw only dense masses of Rhododendrons; now the idea of growing this shrub with the finer hardy plants has spread. It means more room to show the form of the shrubs, and more light and shade; mutual relief of shrub and plant; colonies and groups of lovely plants among the shrubs. Good preparation and some knowledge of plants are needed, but there is no necessity whatever for any system that may not be called permanent.

There are numbers of things which, given thorough preparation at first, it would be wise to leave alone for some years at a time—as, for example, groups or beds of the various Tritomas, Irises, Lilies, Paeonies, the free-flowering Yuccas, Narcissi —these and many more, either grouped with others or in families. When these exhaust the ground or become too crowded, by all means move them and replant, but this is a very different thing from moving all plants in the flower-garden twice a year.

It would be better if gardeners always did what

they could with the flower-garden unaided by the hothouse; but meanwhile the wise man will reduce the expense of glass, labour, fire, repairs, paint, pipes, and boilers to something like reasonable proportions. In presence of the wealth of our hardy garden flora, the promise of which is such as men never expected a few years ago, no one need doubt of making a fair flower-garden from hardy plants alone. Choose some beautiful class of plants and select a place that will suit them, even as to their effect in the garden landscape. Let the beds be planted as permanently and as well as possible, so that there will remain little to do for years. All plants may not lend themselves to this permanent plan, but such as do not may be grown apart, for instance, the Poppies, Anemones, Turban and Persian Ranunculus, Carnations, Stocks, Asters, and the finer annuals. But a great many delightful plants can be planted permanently, and be either allowed to arrange themselves, to group with others, or to grow among peat-loving shrubs, which in many places are jammed into pudding-shaped masses void of form or grace, or light and shade.

Avoid the conventional pattern plans, and adopt simple beds and borders, in positions suited to the plants they are to grow. These can best be filled permanently, because the planter is free to deal with them in a bolder and more artistic way than if he had to consider their relation to a number of small beds. The delight of flowers is much more keenly felt as one sees them relieved, sees them at different times, and to more advantage than the flowers stereotyped under the window. Roses grouped well together, and not trained as standards, would lend themselves admirably to culture with other things—Moss Roses growing out of a carpet of double Primroses, and Tea Roses with Carnations. Then many groups can be made with the aid of the finer perennials, such as the Delphiniums and Phloxes, by choosing things that would go well together. Other plants, such as Yuccas, of which there are now various beautiful kinds, are often best by themselves; and noble groups they form, whether in flower or not. The kinds of Yucca that flower very freely, such as Y. recurva and Y. flaccida, lend themselves to grouping with Flame Flowers (*Tritoma*) and the bolder autumn plants.

No plan which involves expensive yearly efforts on the same piece of ground can ever be satisfactory. All garden plants require attention, but not annual attention. The true way is quite different—the devotion of the skill and effort to fresh beds and effects each year. It does not exclude summer bedding, but it includes lovely and varied aspects of vegetation far beyond that attainable in summer bedding. It also helps to make the skill of the gardener effective of lasting good instead of being thrown away in annual displays. There can be no gardening without care; but there is a vast difference between some of these beds and borders and those with flowers which disappear with the frosts of October, and leave us nothing but bare earth.

The main charm of bedding plants—that of lasting in bloom a long time—is really a drawback. It is the stereotyped kind of garden which we have to fight against; we want beautiful and changeful gardens, and should therefore have the flowers of each season. Too short a bloom is a misfortune, but so is too long a bloom, and numbers of hardy plants bloom quite as long as can be desired.

Nothing used in bedding out is comparable for colour, form, or fragrance with many families of hardy plants—Irises, Lilies, Delphiniums, Evening Primroses, Paeonies, Carnations, Narcissi, and a host of others. Are we to put aside or into the background all this glorious beauty for the sake of a few things that merely give us flat colour? No one who knows even to a slight extent the plants of the northern and temperate world can admit that this sort of gardening should have the first place. Nothing among 'carpet' plants is equal to Windflowers in many kinds, flowering in spring, summer, and autumn; Torch Lilies, superb in autumn; Columbines; Harebells; Delphiniums; Day Lilies; Everlasting Peas; Evening Primroses; Paeonies; Phloxes; Ranunculus, double and single, and the many fine species; all the noble autumn-blooming, Daisy-like flowers; Scabious; plumy Spiraeas; Globe Flowers; Lilies, in noble variety; Polyanthus; Primroses; Auriculas; Wallflowers; Meadow Saffrons; Crocuses, of the spring and autumn; Scillas; Gladioli; Snowflakes; Grape Hyacinths; Narcissi, in lovely variety; Tulips, the old florists' kinds, and many wild species; Yuccas; Carnations and Pinks; Dielytras; Cornflowers; Foxgloves; Stocks; Starworts; great Scarlet and other Poppies; Christmas Roses, both of the winter and spring; Forget-me-nots; Pansies and many of the rock-plants of the mountains of Europe—from the Alps to the hills of Greece, cushioned with Aubrietia, and sky-blue Windflowers—all hardy as the Docks by the frozen brooks.

Flower borders to shrubberies. What is called the 'mixed border' is often made on the edge of a shrubbery, the roots of which leave little food or even light for the flowers. The face of a shrubbery should be broken and varied; the shrubs should not form a hard line, but here and there they should come full to the edge and finish it. The variety of positions and places afforded by the front of a shrubbery so arranged is tempting, but it is generally best to use plants which do not depend on high culture, which, in fact, fight their way near shrubs: and there are a great many such—Evergreen Candytufts, the large-leaved Rockfoils, Acanthus, Day Lilies, Solomon's Seal, Starworts, Leopard's Banes, Moon Daisies, and hardy native Ferns.

A scattered, dotty, mixed border along the face of a shrubbery gives a poor effect, but a good effect may be secured by grouping the plants in the open spaces between the shrubs, making a careful selection of plants, each occupying a bold space. Nothing can be better than such a border when made; but it requires knowledge of plants, and that desire to consider plants in relation to their surroundings which is never shown by those who make mixed borders the same all the way along. The presence of tree and shrub life is a great advantage to those who know how to use it. Here is a group of shrubs over which we can throw a delicate veil of some pretty creeper that would look stiff and wretched against a wall; there a shady recess beneath a flowering tree: instead of planting it up with shrubs in the common way, cover the ground with Woodruff, which will form a pretty carpet and flowers very early in the year, and through the Woodruff a few British Ferns; in front of this use only low plants, and we shall thus get a pretty little vista, with shade and a pleasant relief. Next we come to a bare patch on the margin. Cover it with a strong Evergreen Candytuft, and let this form the edge. Allow a group of Japan Quince to come right into the grass edge and break the margin; then a large group of broad-leaved Saxifrage, receding under the near bushes and trees; and so proceed, making groups and colonies, considering every aid from shrub or tree, and never using a plant of which we do not know and enjoy the effect.

This plan is capable of much variety, whether we are dealing with an established and grown shrubbery, or a choice plantation of flowering evergreens. In the last case, owing to the soil and the neat habit of the bushes, we have excellent possibilities for good culture. One can have the finest things among them—if the bushes are not jammed together. The ordinary way of planting shrubs is such that they grow together in one solid leafy mass, and it is not possible to have flowers between them or to see the true form of the bushes. In growing fine things —Lilies or Cardinal Flowers, or tall Evening Primroses—among open bushes we may form a delightful garden, we secure sufficient space for the bushes to show their forms, and we get light and shade among them. In such plantations one might have in the back parts colonies of lovely things which it might not be well to show in the front of the border, or which required shade and shelter that the front will not afford.

Borders by grass walks in shade or sun. Not only in the flower-garden, but also away from it there are many places better fitted for growing the more beautiful things which do not require continual attention. Unhappily, the common shrubbery has robbed many grass walks of all charm. The great trees, which take care of themselves, are often fine, but the common mixed plantation of evergreens means death to the variety and beauty of flower we may have by grass walks in sun or shade. The shrubs are frequently planted in mixtures, the most free-growing so thickly set as soon to cover the whole ground, Cherry Laurel, Portugal Laurel, Privet, and such common things frequently killing all the choicer shrubs and forming dark heavy walls of leaves. Some of these evergreen shrubs being very hungry things, overrun the ground, rob the trees, and frequently, as in the case of the Portugal Laurels, give a dark, monotonous effect while keeping the walls wet, airless, and lifeless.

Light and shade and the charm of colour are impossible in such cases with these heavy, dank evergreens, often cut back, but once one is free of their slavery what delightful places there are for growing all hardy flowers in broad masses, from the handsome Oriental Hellebores of the early spring to the delicate lavenders of the Starworts in October. Not only hardy flowers, but graceful climbers like the wild Clematis, and lovely corners of light and shade may be made instead of the walls of sombre evergreens. If we want the ground green with dwarf plants, we have no end of delightful plants at hand in the Ivies, and evergreens like Cotoneaster. There is no need for the labour and ugliness of clipping. I have seen places with acres of detestable clipped Laurels, weary and so ugly! With all these grubbed and burnt, what places they would make for such beautiful things as the giant Fennels with their more than Fern-like grace, and all our strong, hardy Ferns which want no rocks, with Solomon's Seal and

Foxgloves among them. Such walks may pass from open spaces into half-shady ones or through groves of old Fir or other trees, and so give us picturesque variety apart from their planting with flowers.

Flower borders against walls and houses. In many situations near houses, and especially old houses, there are delightful opportunities for a very beautiful kind of flower border. The stone forms a fine background, and there are no thieving tree-roots. Here we have conditions exactly opposite to those in the shrubbery; here we can have the best soil, and keep it for our favourites; we can have Delphiniums, Lilies, Paeonies, Irises, and all choice plants well grown. Walls may be adorned with climbers of graceful growth, climbing Rose, Wistaria, Vine, or Clematis, which will help out our beautiful mixed border. These must to some extent be trained, although they may be allowed a certain degree of unrestrained grace even on a wall. In this kind of border we have, as a rule, no background of shrubs, and therefore we must get the choicest variety of plant-life into the border itself, and we must try to have a constant succession of interest. In winter this kind of border may look bare from the windows, but the variety of good hardy plants is so great that we can make it almost evergreen by using evergreen rock-plants. Where walls are broken with pillars, a still better effect may be obtained by training Vines and Wistaria along the top and over the pillars or the buttresses.

The Flower border in the Fruit or Kitchen garden. We have here a frequent kind of mixed border often badly made, but which might be excellent. A good way is to secure from eight to ten feet of rich soil on each side of the walk, and separate it from the main garden by a trellis of some kind from seven to nine feet high. This trellis may be made of strong iron wire, or, better still, of simple rough wooden branches. Any rough permanent trellis will do, on which to grow climbing **Roses** and Clematis and all the choicer but not rampant climbers. Rose and Jasmine can be grown in their natural uncontrolled grace along the wires or rough branches, or up and across a rough wooden trellis. Fix the main branches to the supports, and leave the rest to the winds; a fine type of flower border can be formed in this way, as we have the graceful climbing plants in contrast with the flowers in the border.

Borders may be made in various ways; but for this purpose choose only good plants and throw away weedy kinds, as there is no scarcity of the best. Put, at first, rare kinds in lines across four nursery beds, so that a stock of plants may be at hand. The choicest borders should not be made where they can be robbed by the roots of trees. The soil must be good and rich, and at least two and a half feet deep, so that, in a dry season, the roots can seek their supplies far below the surface. Plant in naturally disposed groups, never repeating the same plant along the border at intervals, as is so often done with favourite plants. Do not graduate the plants in height from the front to the back, but sometimes let a bold plant come to the edge; and let a little carpet of a dwarf plant pass in here and there to the back, so as to give a varied surface. Have no patience with bare ground, and cover the border with dwarf plants, not put them along the front only. Let Hepaticas and double and other Primroses, and Saxifrages, and Golden Moneywort and Stonecrops, and Forget-me-nots, and dwarf Phloxes, and many like plants cover the ground among the tall plants betimes—at the back as well as the front. The little ground plants will form broad patches and colonies by themselves occasionally, and should be let pass into and under other plants. A white Lily will be all the better for having a colony of creeping Forget-me-nots over it in the winter, and the variety that may be thus obtained is almost infinite.

Thoroughly prepared at first, the border might remain for years without any digging in the usual sense. When a plant is old and rather too thick, never hesitate to replant it on a wet day in the middle of August, any more than in the middle of winter. Take it up and put a fresh bold group in fresh ground; the young plants will have plenty of roots by the winter, and in the following spring will flower much more strongly than if they had been transplanted in spring or in winter. Do not pay much attention to labelling; if a plant is not worth knowing, it is not worth growing; let each good thing be so bold and so well grown as to make its presence felt.

One of the prettiest garden borders I ever knew was against a small house. Instead of the walk coming near the windows, a bed of choice shrubs, varying from 9 feet to 15 feet in width, was against the house. Nothing in this border grew high enough to intercept the view from the windows on the ground floor, from which were seen the flowers of the border and a green lawn beyond. Among the shrubs were tall Evening Primroses, and Lilies, and Meadow Sweets, and tall blue Larkspurs, which, after the early shrubs had flowered, bloom above them. The ground was always furnished and the effect good, even in winter.

Evergreen borders of hardy flowers. The plants

of the older kind of mixed border were—like the grasses of the meadows of the northern world—stricken to the earth by winter, and the border was not nearly so pretty then as the withered grass of the plain or copse. But since the revival of interest in hardy and alpine flowers, and the many introductions of recent years, we have a great number of beautiful plants which in winter enable us to make evergreen borders. The great white blanket which covers the north and many mountain ranges in winter, protects also for months many alpine plants which do not lose their leaves in winter, such as Rockfoils, Stonecrops, Primroses, Gentians, and Christmas Roses. The most delicate of alpine plants exposed to our winter suffer from excitement of growth, to which they are not subject in their own home, but many others do not mind our winters much, and it is easy by good choice of plants to make excellent borders wholly or in greater part of evergreen hardy flowers.

They are not only good as evergreens, but also delightful in colour, many being beautiful in flower in spring and having also the charm of assuming their most refreshing green just when other plants are dying in autumn. Together with these rock and herbaceous plants we may group a great many shrublets that come almost between the true shrub and the alpine flower—little woody evergreen creeping things like the dwarf Partridge Berry, Canadian Cornel, hardy Heaths, and Sand Myrtles, often good in colour when grouped.

Among these various plants we have plenty for evergreen borders. Many might object to the bare earth of the ordinary border of herbaceous plants near the house or in other favourite spots, but with borders of evergreen plants the effect may be charming and natural throughout the year.

Of garden pictures, there are few prettier than Crocus, Snowdrops, or Scilla, coming through the green, moss-like carpets in these evergreen borders, far prettier to those who love quiet and natural colour than more showy effects would be. Narrow evergreen borders are often the best things that can be placed at the foot of important walls, as the way of allowing grass to go right up to the walls is a foolish one and often leads to injury to the wall trees. A narrow border (18 inches will do), cut off with a natural stone edging from the grass or walk, is best; even a border of this size may have many lovely things, from early Cyclamen to the rarer Meadow Saffrons in the autumn. Besides the flowers already named, we have Violets, Yuccas, Periwinkles, Carnations, Pinks, white Rock Cress, Barrenworts charming in foliage, purple Rock Cresses, Omphalodes, Iris, Acanthus, Indian and other Strawberries, Houseleeks, Thymes, Forget-me-nots, Sandworts, Gentianella, Lavender, Rosemary, hardy Rock Roses, and many native and other hardy evergreen Ferns in all their fine variety; Bamboos, Ruscus and Dwarf Savin, these are an essential aid in the making of evergreen borders.

CHAPTER XI

THE NEW ROSE GARDEN

WITHOUT a complete change in our ideas about Roses, as regards their culture and the choice of kinds, beautiful flower-gardening is out of the question. The nobler flowers have been rejected as unfit for the flower garden in our own day, and first among them the Rose. Since the time when people went in for patterned colour many flowers were set aside, like the Rose, the Carnation, and the Lily, that did not lend themselves to flat colour ; and thus we see ugly, bare, and at the same time costly gardens round country houses. Therefore I devote this chapter to the Rose, too long left out of her right place.

There is great loss to the flower garden from the usual way of growing the Rose as a thing apart, and its absence at present from most flower gardens. It is surprising to see how poor and hard many places are to which the beauty of the Rose might add delight, and the only compensation for all this is what is called the rosery, which in large places is often an ugly thing with plants that usually only blossom for a few weeks in summer. This idea of the Rose garden arose when we had a much smaller number of Roses, and a greater number of these were kinds that flowered in summer mainly. The old standard Rose had something to do with this separate growth of Roses, it being laid down in the books that the standards did not 'associate' with other shrubs, and so it came about that all the standards grafted were placed in the rosery and there held up their buds to the frost! The nomenclature, too, in use among Rose-growers, by which Roses that flower the shortest time were given the name of Hybrid Perpetuals, has had something to do with the absence of the Rose from the flower garden. Shows, too, have had a bad effect on the Rose in the garden, where it is many times more important. The whole aim of the man who shows Roses, and who is too often followed as a leader, was to get a certain number of large flowers grown on the Dog Rose, Manetti, or any stock which enabled him to get this at the least cost; so, if we go to any Rose-showing friend, we shall probably find his plants for show grown in the kitchen garden with a deep bed of manure on the surface of the beds, and the rose bushes as pretty as so many broomsticks. This idea of the Rose as a show flower leads to the cultivation of Roses that have not a high value as garden flowers, and Roses that do not open their flowers well in our country in the open air, and are not really worth growing, are grown because they happen to produce flowers now and then that look well on a show bench. So altogether the influence of the shows has been against the Rose as a garden flower, and a cause why large gardens are quite bare of the grace of the queen of flowers.

The rose not a 'decorative' plant! It is instructive to study the influence of Rose books upon the Rose as well as that of the Rose exhibitions, as they brought about an idea that the Rose was not a 'decorative' plant. It was laid down that the Rose did not associate properly with other flowers, and it was therefore better to put it in a place by itself, and, though this false idea had less influence in the cottage garden, it did harm in all large gardens. In a recent book on the Rose, by Mr. Foster-Melliar, we read:

> I look upon the plant in most cases only as a means whereby I may obtain glorious Roses. I do not consider the Rose pre-eminent as a decorative plant; several simpler flowers, much less beautiful in themselves, have, to my mind, greater value for general effect in the garden, and even the blooms are, I imagine, more difficult to arrange in water for artistic decoration than lighter, simpler, and less noble flowers.
>
> It must be remembered that the Rose is not like a bedding plant, which will keep up continual masses of colour throughout

the summer, but that the flush of flowers is not for more than a month at most, after which many sorts, even of the Teas, will be off bloom for a while, and the general effect will be spoiled.

The author is only embodying here the practice and views of the Rose exhibitors which most unfortunately ruled the practice of gardeners, and it is very natural many should take the prize-takers as a guide. There was some reason in the older practice, because until recent years the roses most grown were summer flowering, that is to say, like our wild roses, they had a fixed and short time of bloom, which usually did not last more than a few weeks; but in our days, and within the last fifty years, there have been raised, mainly by crossing with the Bengal Rose and some others, a number of beautiful Roses which flower for much longer periods. There are, for example, the monthly Roses and the lovely Tea Roses, which also come in some way from the Indian Rose, and which, when well grown, will flower throughout the whole summer and autumn; not every kind, perhaps, but in a collection of the best there is scarcely a week in which we have not a variety of beautiful flowers. So that, while our forefathers might have been excused for taking the view that Roses are only fit to plant in a place apart, there is no need for the modern grower to do so, who is not tied to the show bench as his one ideal and aim, and nothing could be more untrue and harmful than this ideal from a garden point of view.

The rose to come back to the flower garden. The Rose is not only 'decorative' but is the queen of all decorative plants, not in one sort of position or garden, but in many—not in one race or sort, but in many, from Anna Olivier, Edith Gifford, and Tea Roses of that noble type in the heart of the choicest flower-garden, to the wild Rose that tosses its long arms from the hedgerows in the rich soils of midland England, and the climbing Roses in their many forms, from the somewhat tender Banksian Rose to climbing Roses of British origin. And fine as the old climbing Roses were, we have now a far nobler race—finer indeed than one ever expected to see—of climbing Teas which, in addition to the highest beauty, have the great quality of flowering, like Bouquet d'Or, throughout the fine summer and late into the autumn. Of these there are various climbing Roses that open well on walls, and give masses of beauty, the like of which no other plant whatever gives in our country. See, too, the monthly Roses in cottage gardens in the west and cool coast country, beautiful through the summer and far into the cool autumn, and consider the fine China Roses, such as Laurette Messimy, raised in our own day, all decorative in the highest sense of that poor word.

The outcome of it all is that the Rose must go back to the flower garden—its true place, not only for its own sake, but to save the garden from ugliness and hardness, and give it fragrance and dignity of leaf and flower. The idea that we cannot have prolonged bloom from Roses is not true, because the finer monthly and Tea Roses flower longer than any bedding plants, even without the advantage of fresh soil every year which bedding plants enjoy. And they must come back, not only in beds but in the old ways—over bower and trellis and as bushes where they are hardy enough to stand our winters, so as to break up flat surfaces, and give us light and shade where all is usually so level and hard. But the Rose must not come back in ugly ways, in roses stuck—and mostly starving—on the tops of sticks or standards, or set in raw beds of manure, and pruned hard and set thin so as to develop large blooms; but, as the bloom is beautiful in all stages and sizes, Roses should be seen closely massed, feathering to the ground, the queen of the flower garden in all ways.

The standard rose. A taking novelty at first, few

things have had a worse influence on gardening than the standard Rose in all forms. Grown throughout Europe and Britain by millions, it is seen usually in a wretched state, and yet there is something about it which prevents us seeing its bad effect in the garden, and its evil influence on the cultivation of the Rose, for we now and then see a fine and even a picturesque standard, when the Rose suits the stock it is grafted on, and the soil suits each; but this does not happen often. The term 'grafting' is used here to describe any mode of growing a Rose on any stock or kind, as the English use of the term 'budding', as distinct from grafting, is needless, budding being only one of the many forms of grafting. There is no reason why those who like the form of the Standard should not have them if they can but get them healthy and long-lived; but in that case they should train hardy and vigorous Roses to form their own stems.

While of the evil effect of the standard Rose any one may judge in the suburbs of every town, its other defects are not so clear to all, such as the exposure high in the air to winter's cold of varieties more or less delicate. On the tops of their ugly sticks they perish by thousands, even in nurseries in the south of England. If these same varieties were on their own roots, even if the severest winter killed the shoots, the root would be quite safe, and the shoots come up again as fresh as ever; so that the frost would only prune our Rose bushes instead of killing them and leaving us a few dead sticks from the Dog Rose.

Another element of uncertainty is the kind of stock used. Even if the propagator knows the right stock for the sort he may not for some reason use it, as many have found to their cost who have bought Tea Roses grafted on the Manetti stock—a stock that in any case has no merit beyond giving a few large blooms for a show the first year. And in many cases it paralyses all growth in the kind grafted on it.

There is a way to solve the question as to any kinds we are really interested in—Bouquet d'Or, Madame Hoste, or Rubens, or any other good Roses we fancy, old or new. It is easy to try a few of each kind in the same soil in the natural way on own roots, and also grafted on the wild Dog Rose or any other stock that may be recommended for a given variety, using the 'worked' kinds both as standards and half standards or dwarfs as may be preferred. The first care should be to get plants on own roots about as strong as those worked, and it is not difficult to do this with a little patience, as some gardeners and even cottagers strike Roses from cuttings very successfully. But no trial would be of any use which did not go over the first year or two, because of the dread phase of the grafting routine, that the things are grown to sell, and although they look well when they come to us, after a year or two they perish. This may look very 'good for trade,' but any practice which leads to the disappointment of the grower is not good for trade, as many people give the Rose up as hopeless when they get a poor result.

If we go into the Rose garden of the Luxembourg at Paris or any of the regular roseries in England, we shall find more than half the plants in a sickly, flowerless state. So sickly are the bushes, or what remains of them, that it is common to see a rosery without any roses worth picking after the first flush of bloom is past, and this is a great waste of time and temper. When we think of the number of beautiful things which this has to do with to their harm :—the flowers fairest of all in form, colour, and odour, from the more beautiful tea-scented Roses raised in our own days to the oldest Roses—the Moss and Provence Roses—these, too, being often seen in a miserable state in the rosery, though by nature vigorous and quite hardy, there is surely some reason for looking into ways of Rose growing that have led to this end.

Even where the Rose thrives as a standard, on deep, good loamy soils, there would be other things of interest to determine—length of bloom and endurance of the grafted plant, as compared with plants on their own roots—my own view being that own root plants generally would give the most continuous and finest bloom in the end, good cultivation and soil being understood in each case, and that in hot seasons, of which we have had severe examples of late years, the own root plants are far the best.

Why do nurserymen follow a practice to the injury of their own art and the loss to the public who support them? Unfortunately routine takes hold of every business and has taken deep hold of rose-raising to its real injury. Roses are not only propagated by the trade for the garden, but also for forcing, for sale, and for showing; and it is the quickest way to make a presentable growth that is taken. In various cases the plant is only wanted for one year, as when florists want to get strong blooms and throw the plants away afterwards. In this case the life of the plant does not matter, but to the private grower the result could not be worse.

Most of our garden Roses being grafted on the Dog Rose of our hedgerows, which does best in the heavy, cool soils of the midlands, if we want the ordinary grafted Rose to do well we must give it not less than 30 inches of like soil. This is often a rich deep soil, and it is very easy in putting in the soil to add all the manure which the Rose may want for some years, so that the surface of the bed might be planted with light-rooting rock and like plants. I have beds of Tea Roses over which the Irish mossy Rock-foil has been growing for years without the roses suffering. Beautiful groups of mossy plants of all sorts, or pretty little evergreen alpine plants associated with the earliest flowers, show that the surface of the Rose garden itself might be a charming garden of another kind, and not a manure heap. In the old way of having what was called a 'rosery' this covering the surface with manure did not matter so much, but where we put our Rose beds in the centre of the very choicest flower-garden or under the windows of the house it is a very ugly practice. The Rose can be nourished for six or eight years without adding any manure to the surface, and after six, eight, or ten years most beds will probably require some change, or we may change our view as regards them.

If we free our minds from the incubus of these usual teachings and practices, many beautiful things may be done with Roses for garden adornment.

What is wanted mainly is that the very finest Roses, and above all long-blooming ones like Monthly Roses and such Tea Roses as George Nabonnand, Marie Van Houtte, and Anna Olivier, should be brought into the flower-garden in bold masses and groups to give variety and prolonged bloom, using the choicest Tea Roses in the flower-beds, with wreaths of yellow climbing Roses swinging in the air and on the walls, especially the climbing Tea Roses.

Rose ruin. September, 1905. I have now at the end of summer the pleasure of seeing a colony of Tea Roses of the choicest kinds in fine health and flower, which were put in as cuttings not twelve months ago. Many of them are now good stout plants, though less than one year old. They are in most cases Tea Roses that perish on the Brier, or become so sickly as to be an eyesore—a common thing with the Tea Roses and others of *indica* origin.

One result is the false idea that one cannot grow Roses of this class, and the loss of beauty and that of the highest kind is great, for no other Roses are quite so fair as these. There is also incidental loss from attempts to nourish the Brier with masses of manure to keep it in health, which leads to our Roses being put away as not fit for the flower-garden. The thousands of Rose catalogues issued every year emphasize this error, and perpetuate the custom of grafting Tea and China Roses on the Brier. Very few nurserymen in Europe sell Roses on their own roots, and often when they are asked for and sent they are found to be worked on the root, or upon *Manetti* or some other poor stock, so that the question for Rose lovers is how to get over this difficulty.

After many years' experience I find it so far impossible to expect any help from the trade. The only way out of the difficulty is to take cuttings for oneself of all one's favourite Roses. Some Roses perish so quickly when grown on the Brier that it is not easy to get good cuttings before they disappear, while some, like *Marie van Houtte* and *Anna Olivier*, do better on the Brier. Weak cuttings will not do, we should always get them of medium size and of firm wood. Favourite Tea Roses that fail in the ordinary way should be put in as cuttings during September or October in warm sheltered borders inserted slantwise so as to keep most of the stem out of the weather, and with two or three leaves at the end only, three parts of the stem being in the ground. This is the way in which my Roses were put in, and in open sandy loam, and scarcely one has failed, among them being kinds slow and difficult on the Brier.

The few nurserymen in France and England who have these Roses on their natural roots deserve every encouragement, but the best of all ways is to strike the Roses for oneself, avoiding entirely the regulation soil of the catalogues.

The simplest way is to take a favourite Rose—say *Edith Gifford* or *Madame Hoste*, both of which are unsatisfactory on the Brier—and put the cuttings in where we wish them to grow, thus avoiding removal; that is to say, select the spot where the Roses will be welcome in all ways and put in enough to make groups of a kind, with a little silver sand round the cuttings, and if there are any hand-lights or *cloches* about put them over, as it makes the result a little more certain.

When the Roses begin to grow in the spring do not let them flower, but pinch all the buds off as they come, and so strengthen the plants. By persevering in this way we have graceful clean plants full of healthful vigour in the time stated. Another way is to strike the cuttings in pots, so as to ensure transplanting without a check. Inserting feeble cuttings is almost certain to end in failure. The plan advised is so rapid in its results that we see that the plea of trade growers that in grafting we gain time—the main use of the Brier—does not hold. With plants grown in this way we also at once get rid of the need for covering the soil with manure every year—assuming that the ground is well prepared and dug to begin with, and we avoid the risk of frost, which so often destroys such Roses when grafted as standards or half-standards, because the root is protected in the ground and if the frost does cut the shoots down to the roots they will still be quite safe. We also ensure a more graceful and vigorous growth, which is often absent when these things suffer on the Brier. The Tea Rose plants bought in the usual way are in some cases so weak that a good cutting cannot be got from them, and some perish wholly, as is the case with *Charles Rovelli*.

CHAPTER XII

THE FLOWER GARDEN IN AUTUMN

RECENT additions to our garden flora have made such a difference that the flower garden in autumn may be even more beautiful than in spring, rich as that is in flowering trees and shrubs.

The use of half-hardy, or bedding plants, often showy in autumn, gives a certain amount of very precious colour, and the introduction of many beautiful hardy flowers gives us the means of making the autumn garden very fine in colour effects. It would be easy to give the names of many things that are to be found in flower in gardens in autumn, but that is not nearly so important as getting an idea of many of the nobler class of plants which may be effectively used at that time, no matter almost what the season may be. Half-hardy plants for the garden depend very much on the weather of the summer, and certain seasons are so much against them that they make no show; but this cannot be said of the hardy flowers of nobler stature and beauty, which are so well fitted for our climate, like the many

Sunflowers. Certain plants may depend for success on soil and situation, or even climate, even when they are hardy as the Fuchsia, which is so much better in the coast and West-country gardens; but, when everything is left out that wants any extra culture or advantages of climate and soil, there still remain many beautiful things for the garden in the fall.

Of those that can generally be trusted for our country, I should say that, of all the gains of the past generation, the brilliant groups of plants of the Sunflower order are the finest, handsomest, and most generally useful for their disregard of any weather. The masses of fine form and colour one may have with these when grouped in picturesque ways are remarkable. With the Sunflowers are included not only the Helianthus strictly, of which there are so many good kinds now, but also other showy prairie flowers of the same natural order, which approach them in character, such as Rudbeckia, Silphium, Helenium, and other vigorous families of this numerous tribe of plants. The best character of many of these is that they thrive in any soil, and make their way in rough places and among shrubs, or in parts of gardens less precious than those we keep for our best flowers.

For delicate and fine colour, however, the first place belongs to Tea and Monthly Roses, of which the best kinds should always be grown in the open air. Of the kinds which open best in England, a delightful garden may be made in autumn, in fine seasons enduring right to the end. Until quite recently no one trusted the Tea Rose out in bold masses in the flower-garden, and hence the ordinary red Rose, not generally flowering late, was kept by itself. A greater mistake could not be, because these most precious of all Roses (the Teas) go on blooming throughout the summer and autumn, and very often they vary in bloom; that is to say, the flowers of September will not be the same as the flowers of June, the buds also varying. So we have not only lovely Roses throughout the fine season, but also variety every week, every shower seeming to influence the bloom. There is such great variety among them that every week seems to give us a new aspect of beauty. In my own garden were planted several thousands of Tea Roses in this way, not only for their beauty, but also with a view of testing the kinds best for our country. Some kinds which are fine abroad do not open well with us, but a number of beautiful kinds do, and we have never seen any picture of garden beauty equal to theirs in such a fine autumn as that of 1895. We had thousands of blooms open until the end of September, almost as showy as bedding plants, but far more refined in colour, fragrance, and everything that makes a plant precious. Almost the same thing may be said of the neglected Monthly Roses, which have this charm of late flowering, in many cases even in cold northern districts.

But the most precious, perhaps, of all flowers of autumn for all parts of the country, grouped in an artistic way, are the hardy Asters of the American woods, which lived for ages in our gardens tied in mean trusses in mixed borders. The best of these massed and grouped among shrubs or young plantations of trees, give an effect new and delightful, the colour refined and charming, and the mass of bloom impressive in autumn. Some kinds come in flower in summer, but nearly all the loveliest Asters flower in September and October, and no such good colours of the same shades have ever been seen in the flower-garden.

And not only the Asters of America, but the still more precious Asters of Europe also, which, by their extraordinary beauty, make up for their rarity. Professor Green, of California, who knows the American Aster well, on seeing a plant of Aster acris, said, 'We have none so beautiful as that.' This is the Aster with the blue purple flower so effective when massed. Under various names this plant is grown in nearly allied forms, some with specific names, enabling us to enjoy plants of unequal stature but the same high beauty, flowering at slightly different times, but always at their best in autumn. With these should be grouped the handsome large Italian Aster, which also has its half a dozen forms, not differing much, but precious for their variety, and among the prettiest plants ever seen in our gardens. It is not less valuable for being as easily cultivated as the common Balm of the kitchen garden. For the last two years I have had several thousand plants of these European Asters beneath a group of half-grown Firs, just as they might be in their wild state but rather thicker, as the spot is a cultivated one, and have never had the same beauty from anything else. Be the weather what it might, the lovely blue and purple was a picture, and landscape painters came to paint the scene.

The Sunflowers and Starworts we give the first place to because they are almost independent of soil or cool climates. Hardy as the Chrysanthemum is, the same cannot be said for it; as an outdoor flower, it must have a sandy soil and warm positions, and cool soils, even in southern England, are against it; whereas in warm and free soils, like that at Hazlemere, one may see delightful results of cottage Chrysanthemums grown against low walls or palings. Other plants which are of the highest value in endurance and freedom of bloom are the Heaths of our own islands. Their effect is good, summer and winter; but in autumn some of them flower in a pretty way, particularly the Cornish and the little Dorset Heath, and the Irish Heath in its purple and white forms.

Among the half-hardy plants of the garden perhaps the first place belongs to the Dahlia, which was always a showy autumn flower, but of late has become more precious through the beauty of what are called Cactus Dahlias, which are so much better in form and colour than the roundheaded Dahlias.

The hardy Fuchsia is in the warmer and milder districts often very pretty in autumn, especially where it is free enough to make hedges and form large bushes; but in cold and midland places the growth is often hindered by hard winters. Gladiolus is a splendid flower of the south, but coming more into a class of flowers requiring care, and if they do not get it soon disappearing; liable also to disease; on the whole is not so precious as showy. Nurserymen are raising hardier kinds, but we have more precious flowers. The last few years have brought us magnificent varieties of the Cannas through the crossing of some wild species with the old hybrid kinds. Unfortunately, although in warm valleys and under special care here and there they do well, our country is not generally warm enough to show their fine form and colour as in France and Italy. Their use in pots is another matter.

The addition of Lilies within the past generation has had a good effect on the autumn garden. Where the finer kinds are well grown, the varieties of the Japanese Lilies, with their delicate and varied colours, are splendid autumn flowers for the open air. The Anemones, usually flowers of the spring, come in some forms for the autumn garden, particularly the white and pink kinds. The handsome Bignonia, or Trumpet Creeper, is precious on all warm soils, but generally has not done so well with us as in France. Several kinds of Clematis come in well in autumn, particularly the yellow and the fragrant kinds. The Pentstemons are handsome and very valuable in warm soils and districts where they may live out of doors in winter, but in London districts they are not so good. A splendid autumn flower is the Cardinal Flower, and happy they should be who can grow it well. It fails in many gardens in loamy soil, and where there is insufficiency of water, being a native of the bogs, and thriving best in moist and peaty soil. Numerous fine varieties have been raised, and are brilliant in suitable soils; but without these they are best left alone.

The Torch Lilies are extremely effective in autumn, and in warm soils they are often among the handsomest things, but, not being northern plants, are unable to face a northern winter. Happily this is not so with the beautiful new Water Lilies raised by M. Latour Marliac, which are hardy in the open air, even with such weather as that of the early part of 1895. Though perhaps the best bloom comes in summer, they flower through the autumn, varying like the Tea Rose, according to the weather, but interesting always up to the end of September. We should also name the Hollyhock which is, however, so liable to accident from disease, and those who care for it will do well to use seedling plants. Seedsmen are now saving seed of different colours which come fairly true.

A handsome group of vigorous perennials for the autumn are the Polygonums. Some of the large kinds, such as the Japanese and Indian, are not showy, but massed picturesquely on margins of a wide lawn, and on pieces of stiff soil useless in any garden sense, are effective for many weeks in autumn, as the flower is pretty, and the foliage of one kind is often fine in colour. I have three kinds of them massed together, growing like great weeds, namely, P. cuspidatum, sachalinense, and complexum, and a very soft and good effect they give together in a rough hollow where no garden plants less vigorous than these would have grown.

Thus we have a noble array before coming to some old flowers of autumn, the Meadow Saffrons or 'autumn Crocuses', many of the common kind of which fleck the meadows in autumn. There are other kinds, too, which of recent years have been added in greater numbers to our gardens, some of them pretty, and the double kinds prettier than most double flowers. As they grow naturally in meadows, a delightful way to have them in gardens is in turf, though new and rare kinds should be grown in nursery beds until they are plentiful. They are not difficult to grow, and should often be placed in moist grassy places.

Then there are the true autumn Crocuses, which are very little seen in gardens, but are most delicate and lovely in colour. Coming for the most part from sunny lands, they do best in light soil; but some, like C. speciosus, grow in any soil, and all are worth growing. Among the best is C. nudiflorus, naturalized in Britain, in colour one of the most lovely flowers. To get little pictures from such plants we must have them happy in grass or among dwarf plants, and on sunny banks and grassy corners of the lawn.

In mid-October they have often taken away large areas of bedding plants in the London parks; while, at the same time, there are many lovely hardy flowers in perfect bloom. No doubt severe frosts may destroy any kind of flower soon, but for those who live in the country in the autumn it is something to have bright colours and beautiful plants late, and these are afforded as well by the Starworts and other hardy plants in October, as the fairest flowers that come in June. When we have a severe September about London many gardens of tender plants are shorn of their beauty, whereas the hardy flowers go on quite untouched for a month or six weeks later, and not merely bloom, as do Heliotrope and Geranium, in a fine autumn, but as the meadow flowers in summer, with vigour and perfect health. Therefore, it is clear that, whatever the charms of tender plants may be for the summer, those who live in the country in autumn are unwise to trust to anything but the finer hardy plants.

Thus, without touching on rarities or things difficult to grow, we have a handsome array of beauty for the autumn garden, even leaving out of the question the many shrubs and trees which are pretty in foliage or fruit in autumn, and there should be many of these in any well-stored garden.

CHAPTER XIII

THE FLOWER GARDEN IN WINTER

THAT winter is a doleful time for gardens is an idea which must not be taken seriously even by those who only grow hardy things out of doors; because between the colour of the stems and leaves of trees, or shrubs, there is much beauty left even in winter, and in mild winters good things venture to flower. Hitherto we have been all so busy in planting evergreens in heavy masses, that the beauty one may realize by using a far greater number of summer-leafing shrubs and fine herbaceous plants among the evergreens is not often seen. Gardens are too often bare of interest in winter, and some of the evil arises from the common error that plants are not worth seeing in winter. The old poet's wail about the dismal winter is a false one to those who have eyes for beauty. Woods are no less beautiful in winter than in summer—to some, more beautiful from the refined colour, tree form and the fine contrast of evergreen and summer-leafing trees. In any real garden in winter there is much beauty of form and colour, and there are many shrubs and trees which are beautiful in the depth of winter, like the Red and Yellow Willows and Dogwood, and even the stems of hardy flowers (Polygonum); the foliage of many alpine plants (Epimedium) are not only good in colour, but some of these plants have their freshest hues in winter, as the mossy Rockfoils of many kinds. In the country garden, where there are healthy evergreens as well as flowering shrubs and hardy plants, how much beauty we see in winter, from the foliage of the Christmas Roses (*Helleborus*) to that of the evergreen Barberries! The flower gardener should be the first to take notice of this beauty, and show that his domain, as well as the wild wood, might be interesting at this season.

For the dismal state of flower gardens in winter the extravagant practice of our public gardens is partly to blame. A walk by the flower beds in Hyde Park on Christmas Day, 1895, was not a very enlivening thing. One by the dunes of the foam-dashed northern shore, on the same stormy day, might have been more instructive—for here was a large garden carried out with the very extravagance of opulence, and not one leaf, or shoot or plant, or bush in it from end to end; giants' graves and earth puddings—these and iron rails and the lines of Planes behind. The bare beds followed each other with irritating monotony —only five feet of grass between those in line. The southern division of this garden is nearly 500 paces long and so even that those not in the habit of seeing this costly garden may imagine its ill effect in winter. Nearly 500 yards of a garden sacrificed for its kaleidoscopic effects in summer, and barer and uglier in winter than words can tell of. A more inartistic arrangement would be impossible, and there is no chance of variety, breadth, or repose, even in summer.

How are we to break up such an arid space as this in winter? One of the best ways would be to group families of the choicest flowering shrubs, which would be worth having for their own sakes, and at the same time would give relief to the wintry waste of desolation. At present any relief is only to be obtained by carrying out, in early summer, Palms and Bamboos from the hot-house, which is a very expensive and poor way in a country like ours. In forming groups of the more beautiful flowering shrubs—I do not mean anything like the present brutal treatment of shrubs in the London squares, where the surface is dug, and the shrubs are trimmed like besoms, ending in frightful ugliness—but each group of plants grown well by itself and let almost alone when once established. They would give relief in the summer; they often flower beautifully; and here and there they might form dividing masses, so as to throw the unwieldy space into parts, which would help to secure variety and contrast.

The result of planting and placing rightly well-chosen hardy shrubs would be a good background here and there; a smaller area to plant with summer things; less dependence on such feeble examples of tropical plants as one can grow in Britain; light and shade, and a variety of surface as well as more variety of plants and bushes; in short, all the life of the garden, instead of a dead waste. And not only would the winter effect be improved, but the summer also. The objection that some shrubs do not flower long enough is not serious, as we have their beauty of form and leaf, and delicate green and other fine colour of foliage. Moreover, the tropical plants put out to relieve the flowering plants do not, many of them, flower at all, and do not give such good relief as hardy shrubs and choice trees.

This is not a question of town or public gardens only, as it arises in many private places, and especially in large gardens, where much of the surface is given to half-hardy summer flowers. As to the common plan for getting rid of the winter bareness of such beds by evergreens and conifers in pots, it is impossible on a large scale, and sticking potted conifers in a flower garden to drag them away in spring is at best inartistic and a very costly business. Some permanent way of breaking up the flatness is the best way; and this way would enable us to limit the excessive area of ground to be planted with tender things, the real root of evil.

Keep the stems of hardy plants. The dead stems of all herbaceous plants, reeds, and tall grasses are very good in colour, and should always be allowed to stand through the winter and not be cut down in the way so common of sweeping away the stems in autumn and leaving the surface as bare as that round a besieged city. The same applies to the stems of all waterside and herbaceous plants, stems of plants in groups often giving beautiful brown colours in many fine shades. Those who know the plants can in this way identify them in winter as well as in summer—a great gain in changing one's plantings and in increasing or giving away plants. Moreover, the change to all these lovely browns and greys is a distinct gain as a lesson in colour to all who care for refined colour, and also in enabling us to get light and shade, and harmonies in colour. If these plants are grouped in a bold and at the same time picturesque way, the good of letting the stems remain will be far more evident than in the weak 'dotty' way generally practised, the seed-pods and dead flowers of many plants helping the picture. There is no need to remove any stem of an herbaceous plant until the spring comes and the growing shoots are ready to take the place of the brown and dead ones, which may then be cleared away.

Evergreen plants. Apart from our evergreen shrubs, so happy as these are in many parts of the British Isles, there are the oft-neglected evergreen rock and herbaceous plants, such as Christmas Roses, Barrenworts, Heuchera, Alexandrian Laurel, the bolder evergreen ferns, and the large Indian Rockfoils, (*Megasea*). In early winter these fine evergreen plants become a deeper green, some forms getting red. They have been in our gardens for years, but are seldom made a right use of; thrown into borders without thought as to their habits, and soon forgotten or overshadowed by other things, we never get any expression of their beauty or effect in masses or groups. Yet, if grouped in effective ways, they would go on for years, giving us fine evergreen foliage in winter. In addition to the wild kinds, a number of fine forms have been raised in gardens of late years. Some thought should be given to the placing of the large Rockfoils, their mountain character telling us that they ought to be on open banks, borders, or slopes exposed to the sun, and not buried among heaps of tall herbaceous and miscellaneous vegetation. They are so easily grown and increased that a little thought in placing them in visible masses is the only thing they call for; and the fact that they will endure and thrive under almost any conditions should not prevent us from showing how fine they are in effect when held together in any bold way, either as carpets, edgings, or large picturesque groups on banks or rocks.

The Alexandrian Laurel (*Ruscus racemosus*) is a most graceful plant, somewhat shrubby in character, with glossy dark-green leaves and Willow-like shoots. It is most free and happy on peaty and friable soils, growing about four feet high; in winter the effect is very good, and it is valuable for the house, to give a graceful and distinct foliage to accompany various flowers at this season. It grows very well in Ireland on the limestone. In clay soils it may want a little encouragement, and it thrives well in partial shade.

The Christmas Rose is a noble winter flower where well grown, and is lovely in its wild state in the foot-hills of the Alps, in Italy and countries near;

and, happily, it flowers in our gardens very well also, varying a little in its ways. The stout kind (*H. maximus*) flowers in the early winter in front of walls and in sheltered spots, and is hardy and free in ordinary soil. The true Christmas Rose (*H. niger*) is a little more particular; it thrives much better on chalky and warm soils, and grows best on a northern aspect or shaded place; even in its own country the finest plants are found in places where it escapes the sun. These are true winter flowers; but hardly less so are the Lenten Roses, or forms of the Oriental Hellebores. In the southern counties, five seasons out of six, no weather stops them from being fine in flower before the winter is past; they often bloom in January, and make a handsome show in February, and they are the finest of all flowers to end the winter. The Winter Heliotrope (*Tussilago fragrans*) is not to be despised, although it is a bad weed, and hard to get rid of. The way to deal with it is to put it on some rubbish heap, or gravel bank, right away from the garden, where a handful of it may be gathered when wanted.

The Algerian Iris flowers in warm sandy borders in the country around London, and in mild winters is a great treasure, not merely for its beauty in warm sheltered corners, but also for its precious qualities for the house, in which the flowers, if cut in the bud state, open gracefully when placed in moss in basins. In warm and sheltered gardens, on warm soils, others of the winter blooming Iris of the East may be grown, while in such gardens, in the south at least, the good culture of the sweet Violet will often be rewarded with many flowers in winter.

A beautiful Italian Crocus (*Imperati*) often flowers in winter, in the southern counties at least, as, where people take the trouble to get them, do C. Sieberi, Dalmaticus, Etruscus, Suaveolens and others. This habit of some of the winter flowers of the south of Italy and Mediterranean region to open in our green and open winters should be taken advantage of. The fate of these Crocuses is interfered with by the field vole, and the rat is also a great destroyer of these bulbs. Where these enemies do not prevail, and the soil favours these charming winter and early flowers, we can grow them, not only in the garden, but on the turf of sunny meadows and lawns, in which these beautiful Crocuses will come up year after year in winter and early dawn of spring.

Shrubs and Trees in the Winter Garden. The Winter Sweet (*Chimonanthus fragrans*) is in bloom often before Christmas in the country around London, and every shoot full of fragrant buds opening on the trees against south and west walls. It is invaluable both for the open garden and house. The many bright berries which adorn our country, both in the wild land and in well-stored gardens, are rather things of the autumn; and by mid-winter the birds are apt to clear them off Wild Roses, Briers, Barberry, and Thorns, American as well as British. The Pyracantha, however, stays with us late; and Hollies, Aucuba, Cotoneaster, Snowberry, and the pretty little hardy Pernettya, from the Straits of Magellan, which has broken into such variety of colour in our country, are among those that stay late. But, however the cheery berries may fail us in hard winters, the colour of the trees and bushes that bear them never does; and the Red and Yellow Willows, Dogwood, Thorns, Alders, Birch, and many Aspens and Maples, give fine colour when massed or grouped in any visible way. Still more constant are the flowering shrubs of winter, where in sheltered gardens and warm valleys any attention is given to them—Winter Jasmine, Winter Sweet, Winter Honeysuckles, Wych-Hazel, Japan Quince in many forms, Laurustinus, several Heaths, Arbutus, at least one variety of Daphne Mezereon, the pale Southern Clematis (*Calycina*) happy in our warmer gardens, Eleagnus, the Nepal Barberry, a Chinese Plum

(*P. Davidiana*), and the catkin-bearing Garrya and Hazel. The Winter Honeysuckles are a bit slow in some districts, and a better result is got from them on free soils and from walls in sheltered corners, an immense difference resulting if we can have them near the sea, with its always genial influence in favour of things from climates a little warmer than our own. In heavy soils in the inland country and around London the Laurustinus often comes to grief or fails to flower well, but has great beauty in seashore districts, and often on sandy and gravel soils is charming, even in inland places.

The hardy and beautiful Winter Jasmine, which is so free on cottage walls and wherever it gets a chance, is most precious, owing to the way it opens in the house, especially if gathered in the bud. If we have it in various aspects, such a contingency as the sun scorching the shoots after a frost and killing the flowers may be avoided, and the flowers will come later. The plant is so free that, if the shoots are allowed to hang down, they root in the ground like twitch, and therefore it can be increased very easily, and should be seen in visible groups and lines, and not only on the house or on walls, as in the milder districts it forms pretty garlands and bushes in the open. I have a little oak fence covered with it, which is usually very pretty about Christmas. In mild winters its beauty is extraordinary out of doors, and in the hardest winters the buds will open in the house.

And when the Dogwood has lost all its leaves and is a deep red by the lake, and the Cardinal Willow has nearly taken its winter colour, the dwarf autumn-blooming Furze flowers far into winter, and is in perfect bloom on the drier ground, telling us of its high value where dwarf vegetation not over a yard high is desired. It is seen in abundance on many hills and moors, but is hardly ever planted by design. A good plant for all who care for low foreground vegetation, it may be planted like common furze, but by far the best way is to sow it in spring in any bare or recently broken ground. The Common Furze, too, of which the season of bloom is spring, in mild winters often flowers at Christmas, odd plants here and there in the colonies of the plant bearing quite fresh flowers. If from the nature of these native shrubs they do not find a place in the flower garden, there are few country places where they may not be worth growing not far from the house, in covert, or by drives or rough walks, as no plants do more to adorn the late autumn and winter.

The hardy Heaths are excellent for the winter garden in their brown and grey tuftiness. The forms of the common Heather and the Cornish Heath are best for rough places outside the flower garden, but some kinds of Heath are among the best plants for the choicest winter garden of the open air, particularly the Portuguese Heath (*E. Codonodes*), which in mild winters is of great beauty; also a hybrid between the alpine forest Heath (*E. carnea*) and the Mediterranean Heath, with the port and dense flowering habit of the alpine Heath and the earlier bloom of the Mediterranean Heath. The alpine forest Heath, the most precious of all hardy Heaths, often flowers in mild winters, and in all winters is full of its buds ready to open.

So far we are speaking of districts where there are few advantages of climate; if we include others there might be more flowers in the winter garden, and many varied flowers are seen in gardens in the Isle of Wight, Isle of Man, and many other favoured places—not always confined to the southern parts of England and Ireland: the Cornish, Devon, South Wales or Cork Coasts being far more favourable. From these places Roses, Indian Daphne, and many other flowers, have often been sent to me in perfect bloom in January.

And if the snow shrouds the land, all's well, as the leaves of evergreen plants, like Carnations, are at rest in it, and some plants are all the better for the peace of the snow for a time. There is in winter no death, every root works and every bud is active with life; the wooded land is tender with colour:—Alders by the busy wintry stream and Birch on the airy hill, Reeds fine in colour round the lake or marsh, and if even our wild marsh or rough woodland be beautiful in winter, our gardens, with the flora of three continents to gather from, should not then be poor in beauty.

CHAPTER XIV

BEAUTY OF FORM IN THE GARDEN

THE use of plants of fine form has taught us the value of grace and verdure amid masses of flowers, and how far we have diverged from artistic ways. In a wild state, brilliant blossoms are often relieved by a setting of abundant green, and where mountain or meadow plants of one kind produce a sea of colour at one season, there is intermingled a spray of pointed grass and leaves which tone down the colour masses.

We may be pleased by the wide spread of colour on a heath or mountain, but when we go near we find that it is best where the long moss cushions itself beside the ling, and the fronds of the Polypody come up around masses of heather. If this be so on the hills, a like state of things is more evident still in the marsh or wood. We cannot reproduce such conditions, but the more we keep them before our eyes the nearer shall we be to success, and we may have in our gardens (without making wildernesses of them either) all the light and shade, the relief, the grace, and the beauty of natural colour and form too.

An application for £2,000 for the building of a glass house for Palms for the subtropical garden of Battersea Park throws some light on the costly system of flower gardening in this and other public gardens. It may be noted that this is only a small part of the cost of keeping the tender and half-hardy plants in a glass nursery, and not a demand of money for a Palm-house which the public might enjoy. In our flower gardens Palms can only be seen in a small state; nor can they give one any idea of the true beauty of the Palm on the banks of the Nile or the Ganges. But, worse than this, the system leads to the neglect of the many shrubs and trees of the northern world, which are quite as beautiful as any Palm. The sum mentioned as the cost of the house for young Palms would go far to plant Battersea Park with the finest hardy shrubs and trees. The number of public gardens that are being opened in all directions makes it all the more important that the false ideal they so often set out should be made clear. I do not say we should have none but hardy plants in public gardens, but the concentration of so much attention and cost on such feeble examples of tropical plants as can be grown in this country, set out for a few months in the summer, has a very bad effect. Things which can be grown to perfection in the open air in any country are always the most beautiful, and should always have the first place. It would be much better in all ways to place a like artistic value on everything that stands in the open air in a garden, and regard all parts of the garden as of equal importance without wholly doing away with tropical plants, at least those that can be grown with advantage in our country.

Looking round the London parks we see much waste in trying to get effects of form from Palms and various tender plants often dotted about without good judgement, and marring the foreground of scenes that might be pretty. Where this is done there is rarely any attempt to get effects of fine form from hardy trees, shrubs, and plants, a much simpler and easier process than building costly glasshouses to get them.

For our gardens, the first thing is to look for plants that are happy in our climate, and to accustom ourselves to the idea that form may be as beautiful from hardy as from tender things. Many tropical plants, which we see in houses cut down close and kept small, would, if freely grown in the open air in their own country, be no more striking in leaf than the hardy Plane or Ailantus. Many quite hardy plants give fine effects, such as the

Aralias, herbaceous and shrubby; Arundo, hardy and very pretty beside water; Astilbes, rough plants which can be put anywhere almost; the hardy Bamboos of Japan and India, increasing in number and very distinct and charming, and often rapid growers in genial parts of the country, especially near the sea. A considerable number will probably be found hardy everywhere. The large-leaved evergreen Barberries are beautiful in peaty or leafy soils, and, grouped in picturesque ways, effective for their leaves as well as flowers.

The Plume Poppy (*Bocconia*) is handsome for its foliage and flowers, even in ordinary soil. A great number of the larger hardy Compositae are fine in leaf, as are some of the Cotton Thistles and plants of that family. The globe Artichoke of our gardens and its allies are fine in form of leaf and flower, but apt to be cut off in hard winters in some soils. The Giant Fennels are most graceful early leafing things, thriving admirably in sandy and free soils. Plantain Lilies are important, and in groups their foliage is excellent. The Pampas Grass is precious where it grows well, but in many districts is gradually killed by hard winters. Where it has the least chance, it should be planted in bold masses.

The great-leaved Gunneras are superb near water

and in rich soil. The giant cow parsnips are effective, but apt to take possession of the country-side, and are not easily exterminated, and, therefore, should be put in with a sparing hand in islands and rough places only. The large Indian evergreen Rockfoils are fine in form, and in their glossy foliage are easily grown and grouped in picturesque ways, and they are very hardy. In sandy and free soils a handsome group of beautiful-leaved things may be formed of Acanthus. The new water lilies will help us much, especially in association with the many graceful plants that grow in and near water, as also certain hardy ferns which may be grown near water, like the Royal Fern, which in rich soil and shade makes leaves as fine as any tropical Fern. In southern districts the New Zealand Flax is effective in gardens, and the great Japan Knotworts (*Polygonum*) are handsome in rough places in the wild garden, and better kept out of the flower garden. Some of the Rhubarbs, too, are distinct and handsome, and very vigorous by the water-side, where the great water dock often comes of itself.

Better effects may be obtained from hardy plants only than from tender ones. There are the Yuccas, hardy, and unsurpassed by anything of like habit grown in hothouses; Arundos, conspicua and donax;

fine hardy plants like Crambe cordifolia, Rheum in variety, Ferula and umbelliferous plants, as graceful as tenderest exotics. Then we have a hardy Palm that through all our hard winters has preserved its health and greenness wherever its leaves could not be torn to shreds by storms.

Yuccas in groups. Wherever there is space for them, hardy Yuccas should be grown; few hardy plants are so distinct in foliage and manner of growth, but they appear best arranged in bold groups. Perhaps the best situation is a sloping ground fully exposed to the mid-day sun, and backed by evergreens. If allowed space for development, they will every year add beauty to the place. The handsome spikes of their large cream-coloured flowers are effective, especially if relieved by a good background. Yuccas like a well-drained soil; they thrive fully exposed to the sun, with shelter from rough winds.

In grouping Yuccas, a better effect is obtained if some of the specimens have the heads of their foliage from three to six feet above the soil. These tall plants should not, however, be placed in a back line, but some should be allowed here and there to advance into the foreground, some of the smaller specimens nestling at their feet. The effect of a group thus arranged charms by its irregularity and quaint beauty.

Among the more tender plants, we must choose such as grow healthily in sheltered places in the warmer parts of England. The kinds with stout evergreen foliage, such as the New Zealand Flax and the hardier Dracaenas, will be as effective here as they are around London and Paris, and to them the northern gardener should direct his attention. Even if it were possible in all parts to cultivate the softer-growing kinds to the same perfection as in the south of England, it would not be always desirable, as they cannot be used indoors in winter. The best are the many evergreen plants that stand out in summer without injury, and may be transferred to the conservatory in autumn, to produce through the cold months as fine an effect as in the flower garden in summer. One kind of arrangement in particular must be guarded against. I mean the geometric patterns seen in some parts of the London parks devoted to sub-tropical gardening. The plants are often of the finest kinds and in the most robust health, and all the materials for the best results are abundant; yet the result is not artistic, owing to the needless formality of the beds and the heaping together of many specimens of one kind in long masses straight or twisting, with high raised edges of hard-beaten soil.

Beauty of form. We should try and see beauty of form everywhere among plants that suit our climate. The willows of Britain are as beautiful as the olives of Italy, or the gum-trees of Algeria and the South of France; so that, even though the sub-tropical system of flower gardening has failed in our country generally, and can only be carried out well in the south of England and the warmer countries of Europe, we need not be deprived of the enjoyment of the finest forms in and near our gardens. The new Water Lilies take us to the water-side, and there are many good forms even among our native flowers and weeds. Of the new hardy Bamboos, also very graceful and most distinct, several of the highest value promise to be hardy in our country. What can be done with them and a few other things, we can see in the Bamboo garden at Kew, at Batsford Park, and other places. The common hardy Japan Bamboo has thriven even in London, and it is not only water-side or herbaceous plants of all kinds we have to think of, but the foliage of trees in many cases is quite as beautiful as that of the dwarfer plants. The hardy trees of North America are many of them beautiful in foliage, from the Silver Maple to the Scarlet Oak, and Acacias from the same country have broken into a number of beautiful forms, some as graceful as ferns. These trees, if obtained on their own roots, will afford us fine aid as backgrounds. The Aralias of Japan and China are quite hardy and almost tropical in foliage, while the beauty that may be got from ferns is very remarkable indeed, our native Royal Fern being of noble proportions when well grown in half-shady and sheltered places in deep soils, as at Newick Park; and the same is true of all the bold American ferns, plants too often hidden away in obscure corners, whereas the boldest of them should be brought out in our cool British climate to form groups on the lawns and turf. This applies to our larger native ferns, which, massed and grouped away from the old-fashioned fernery, often tell better. Some of the plants mentioned in this chapter are coarse, such as the great-leaved composite, many of them, on the other hand, are refined and delicate, such as the Acacias, Acanthus, Asparagus, Bamboos, and Ferns. Great Reed, Pampas and Bulrush evergreen, Barberry, and graceful Cypress, Cedar and Fir. Plantain-Lily and 'Adam's needle'—not forgetting the fine foliage of the Tea Rose.

CHAPTER XV

MARSH, BOG, AND WATER GARDENS

WHERE there is marsh or boggy ground, and the situation is a pretty one, it will often be well to preserve its natural features and to plant it with things that grow in like places and soils, instead of draining or otherwise altering it as is so often done. The soil of such places is often the best for certain plants, and indeed is better than one could make. There is hardly any such situation that cannot be planted with fine things—tree, shrub, or flower— without changing the nature of the ground; preserving the natural surface and the soil, only making a few open drains if there is any excess of water.

If we see the Royal Fern so superb throughout Europe and North Africa, in woods and boggy places never touched by man, and also the still richer Fern flora of North America in like positions, it is clear we may have like effects if we are fortunate enough to have such ground. Many places have no such advantages, and there is all the greater reason for those who have them to preserve their natural character. It is mainly a question of choice of plants, and this comes best from observation of their habits in the wild state.

I remember seeing in America the dwarf Magnolia (*M. glauca*) beautiful in bogs almost sheeted with water; and certain kinds of Azalea, Andromeda, Huckleberry, and other shrubs quite as much at home there. The Eastern States of North America and the Canadas are rich in lovely marsh-plants, including Orchids, and even in our own more limited flora we see lovely things in such ground. Over the vast range of European mountains many Primroses attain their highest health in marshy places, including our own Bird's Eye Primrose. Then, again, the dwarf and trailing mountain shrubs, often of high value, are happy in their boggy haunts. The following is an example of what can be done to turn a piece of natural bogland into a spot of beauty : It was about three acres of a natural marsh, sparsely wooded with Birch and sheltered by Spruce; some parts have been partly drained, and the whole has been turned into a garden of interesting bushes. Channels have been cut or deepened so as to allow masses of spongy peat-earth to stand clear of the water, and walks with crossings over log bridges lead one all over the enclosure. This marsh garden is not far from the house, and I shall never forget the colour and variety of vegetation that flashed upon me on a sunny afternoon in October. The colour of autumnal foliage and flowers, bright as it was, became intensified by the background, and by the ridges of black peat-earth rising here and there out of chocolate-coloured water. The rich hues and dark tones of the peat lost nothing by contrast with glistening stems and trunks of Silver Birch. To see this unique garden in April or May must be delightful, when it is a fairy-land full of Japanese and American Azaleas; even as I saw it in rainy October between the showers it was rich and full of colour. The Azaleas were dying off, and their leaves were amber and russet or purple-crimson and gold. Here and there feathery grasses and sedges contrasted with the dark peat and the water, and Sumach and Pyrus lit up the place with colour. Osmunda and other Ferns nestled at the water's edge, and in other places were carpets of Sphagnum Moss, with rainbow colouring from yellow to green, and from green to ruby red or crimson. In one place the North American Pitcher plants (*Sarracenia*) and Shortia, with its crumpled and painted foliage, seemed quite at home. It was quite a novel experience to walk up and down dry and spongy walks of peat as soft as Persian rugs, and see such a fine variety of form and colour.

An incidental gain for such ground treated in a picturesque way is the very fitting position it would afford for growing certain beautiful trees often neglected in gardens—the finer Willows, Dogwoods, Aspen and Birches, which would rise out of carpets of our native and hardy heaths of Europe, which also love such ground.

The bog garden is for the numerous children of the wild that will not live on our harsh, bare, and dry garden borders, but thrive cushioned on moss or in moist peat soil. Many beautiful plants, like the Wind Gentian and Creeping Harebell, grow on our own bogs and marshes, much as these are now encroached upon. But even those who know our own bogs have, as a rule, little notion of the multitude of charming plants, natives of northern and temperate countries, whose home is the open marsh or bog. In our own country we have been so long encroaching upon the bogs and wastes that some regard bogs and wastes as exceptional tracts all over the world, but when we travel in northern climes we see what a vast extent of the world's surface was once covered with bogs. In North America, even by the margins of the railways, one sees, day after day, the vivid blooms of the Cardinal-flower springing erect from the wet peaty hollows; and far under the shady woods stretch the black bog pools, the ground between being so shaky that you move a few steps with difficulty. And where the woody vegetation disappears the Pitcher-plant (*Sarracenia*), Golden Club (*Orontium*), Water Arum (*Calla palustris*), and a host of other handsome bog plants cover the ground for hundreds of acres, with perhaps an occasional slender bush of Laurel Magnolia (*Magnolia glauca*) among them. In some parts of Canada, where long and straight roads are often made through woody swamps, and where the few scattered and poor habitations offer little to cheer the traveller, a lover of plants will find beside the road conservatories of beauty in the ditches and pools of black water fringed with stately ferns and bog and water bushes.

Southwards and seawards, the bog flowers, like the splendid kinds of herbaceous Hibiscus, become tropical in size and brilliancy, while far north and west and south along the mountains grows the queen of the peat bog—the beautiful and showy Mocassin-flower (*Cypripedium spectabile*). Then in California, all along the Sierras, numbers of delicate little plants continue to grow in small mountain bogs long after the plains are quite parched and annual vegetation has quite disappeared from them. Many plants commonly termed 'alpine', and found on high mountains, are true bog plants. This must be clear to any one who has seen our pretty Bird's-eye Primrose in the wet mountain-side bogs of Westmoreland, or the Bavarian Gentian in the spongy soil by alpine rivulets.

Where such marsh or boggy ground is near open water, as it often is, we may then enjoy what is perhaps the finest effect of the flower gardening of our own in the bloom of the varied Water Lilies. The association together of marsh, bog, and water plants may, in the hands of those who know and care for them, lead to some of the best effects possible through merely human effort.

CHAPTER XVI

FRAGRANCE

A MAN who makes a garden should have a heart for plants that have the gift of sweetness as well as beauty of form or colour. And what a mystery as well as charm—wild Roses sweet as the breath of heaven and wild Roses of repulsive odour, all born of the earth-mother, and it may be springing from the same spot. Flowers sweet at night and scentless in the day; flowers of evil odour at one hour and fragrant at another; plants sweet in breath of blossom, but deadly in leaf and sap; Lilies sweet as they are fair, and Lilies that must not be let into the house; with bushes in which all that is delightful in odour permeates to every March-daring bud. The Grant Allens of the day, who tell us how the Dandelion sprang from the Primrose some millions of years ago, would no doubt explain all these things to us, or put long names to them—what Sir Richard Owen used to call 'conjectural biology',—but we need not care where they leave the question, for to us is given this precious fragrance, happily almost without effort, and as free as the clouds from man's power to spoil.

Every fertile country has its fragrant flowers and trees; alpine meadows with Orchids and mountain Violets; the Primrose-scented woods, Honeysuckle-wreathed and May-frosted hedgerows of Britain; the Cedars of India and of the mountains of Asia Minor, with Lebanon; trees of the same stately order, perhaps still more fragrant in the warmer Pacific breezes of the Rocky Mountains and Oregon, where the many great Pines often spring from a carpet of fragrant Evergreens, and a thousand flowers which fade away after their early bloom and stand withered in the heat, while the tall Pines overhead distil for ever their grateful odour in the sunny air. Myrtle, Rosemary, and Lavender, and all the aromatic bushes and herbs clothing the little capes that jut into the great sea which washes the shores of Greece, Italy, Sicily, and Corsica; garden islands scattered through vast Pacific seas, as stars are scattered in the heavens; enormous tropical forests, little entered by man, but from which he gathers on the outskirts treasures for stove and greenhouse; great island gardens like Java and Ceylon and Borneo, rich in spices and lovely plant life; Australian bush, with plants strange as if from another world, but often most delicate in odour even in the distorted fragments of them we see in our gardens.

It is not only from the fragile flower-vases these sweet odours flow; they breathe through leaf and stem and the whole being of many trees and bushes, from the stately Gum trees of Australia to the sweet Verbena of Chili. Many must have felt the charm of the strange scent of the Box bush before Oliver Wendell Holmes told us of its 'breathing the fragrance of eternity'. The scent of flowers is often cloying, as of the Tuberose, while that of leaves is often delicate and refreshing, as in the budding Larch, and in the leaves of Balm and Rosemary, while fragrance is often stored in the wood, as in the Cedar of Lebanon and many other trees, and even down through the roots.

It is given to few to see many of these sweet plants in their native lands, but we who love our gardens may enjoy many of them about us, not merely in drawings or descriptions, but the living, breathing things themselves. The Geraniums in the cottage window bring us the spicy fragrance of the South African hills; the Lavender bush of the sunny hills of Provence, where it is at home; the Roses in the garden bring near us the breath of the wild Roses on a thousand hills; the sweet or pot herbs of our gardens are a gift of the shore-lands of France and Italy and Greece. The Sweet Bay bush in the farmer's or cottage garden comes with its story from the streams of Greece, where it seeks moisture in a thirsty land along with the wild Olive and the Arbutus. And this Sweet Bay is the Laurel of the poets, of the first and greatest of all poet and artist nations of the earth—the Laurel sacred to Apollo, and used in many ways in his worship, as we may see on coins, and in many other things that remain to us of the great peoples of the past. The Myrtle, of less fame, but also a sacred plant beloved for its leaves and blossoms, was, like the Laurel, seen near the temples of the race who built their temples as the Lily is built, whose song is deathless, and the fragments of whose art are Despair to the artists of our time. And thus the fragrant bushes of our gardens may entwine for us, apart from their gift of beauty, living associations and beautiful thoughts for ever famous in human story.

It is not only odours of trees and flowers known to all we have to think of, but also many delicate ones, less known, perhaps, by reason of the blossoms that give them being without showy colour, as the wild Vine, the Sweet Vernal, Lemon, and other

Grasses. And among these modest flowers there are none more delicate in odour than the blossoms of the common white Willow, the yellow-twigged and the other Willows of Britain and Northern Europe, which are all the more grateful in air coming to us

> O'er the northern moorland, o'er the northern loam.

What is the lesson these sweet flowers have for us? They tell us—if there were no other flowers to tell us—that a garden should be a living thing; its life not only fair in form and lovely in colour, but in its breath and essence coming from the Divine. They tell us that the very common attempt to conform their fair lives to tile or other patterns, to clip or set them out as so much mere colour of the paper-stainer or carpet-maker, is to degrade them and make our gardens ugly and ridiculous, from the point of view of Nature and of true art. Yet many of these treasures for the open garden have been shut out of our thoughts owing to the exclusion of almost everything that did not make showy colour and lend itself to crude ways of setting out flowers.

Of the many things that should be thought of in the making of a garden to live in, this of fragrance is one of the first. And, happily, among every class of flowers which may adorn our open-air gardens there are fragrant things to be found. Apart from the groups of plants in which all, or nearly all, are fragrant, as in Roses, the annual and biennial flowers of our gardens are rich in fragrance—Stocks, Mignonette, Sweet Peas, Sweet Sultan, Wallflowers, double Rockets, Sweet Scabious, and many others. These, among the most easily raised of plants, may be enjoyed by the poorest cottage gardeners. The garden borders of hardy flowers bear for us odours as precious as any breath of tropical Orchid, from the Lily-of-the-Valley to the Carnation, this last yielding, perhaps, the most grateful fragrance of all the flowering host in our garden-land. In these borders are things sweeter than words may tell of—Woodruff, Balm, Pinks, Violets, garden Primroses, Polyanthuses, Day and other Lilies, early Iris, Narcissus, Evening Primroses, Mezereon, and Pansies delicate in their sweetness.

No one may be richer in fragrance than the wise man who plants hardy shrubs and flowering trees—Magnolia, May, Daphne, Lilac, Wild Rose, Azalea, Honeysuckle—names each telling of whole families of fragrant things. From the same regions whence come the Laurel and the Myrtle we have the Laurustinus, beautiful in our sea-coast and warmer districts, and many other lovely bushes happy in our climate; one, the Winter Sweet, pouring out delicious fragrance in mid-winter; Sweet Gale, Allspice, and the delightful little Mayflower that creeps about in the woodland shade in North America. So, though we cannot boast of Lemon or Orange groves, our climate is kind to many lovely and fragrant shrubs.

Even our ugly walls may be sweet gardens with Magnolia, Honeysuckle, Clematis, Sweet Verbena, and the delightful old Jasmine, still clothing many a house in London. Most precious of all, however, are the noble climbing Tea Roses raised in our own time. Among the abortions of this century these are a real gain—the loveliest flowers ever raised by man. Noble in form and colour, and scented as delicately as a June morn in alpine pastures, with these most precious of garden Roses we could cover all the ugly walls in England and Ireland, and Heaven knows many of them are in want of a veil!

CHAPTER XVII

THE FLOWER GARDEN IN THE HOUSE

ONE of the real gains in any flower garden worthy of the name is that we have in it lovely forms and delicate colours for the house, from the dawn of spring, with its noble Lenten Roses on sheltered borders, until autumn goes into winter in a mantle of Starworts. Many English and all German and French flower gardens in parterres offer us only Lobelias, and various plant rubbish of purple or variegated hues, very few of them worth cutting, whereas our real flower garden is a store of Narcissus, Azalea, Rose, Lily, Tulip, and Carnation, and all the fairest things of earth. All we have to care about is placing them in simple ways to show their form as well as colour. Apart from the good plan of having a plot for the culture of any flowers we wish to cut for the house, a true flower garden will yield many flowers worthy of a place on an artist's or any other table, and worthy of it for their forms, colour, or fragrance. Many of these, from the Narcissus to the Tea Rose, give flowers so freely that we need not be afraid to cut; indeed, in many cases, careful cutting prolongs the bloom (as of Roses). Many shrubs we may improve as we cut their branches for the house, for example, Winter Sweet, Forsythia, and Lilac.

It is not merely the first impression of flowers, good as it may be, that we have to think of, but the charms which intimacy gives to many of the nobler flowers—some opening and closing before our eyes, and showing beauties of form that we never suspected when passing them in the open air. In the changing and varied lights of a house we have many opportunities of showing flowers in a more interesting way, particularly to those who do not see them much out of doors, and now we have in gardens many new flowers of great beauty of form—Californian, Central Asiatic, Japanese, even the mountains of China and India giving precious things, as well as the rich flora of North America, as yet not as much seen in our gardens as it deserves to be. So that it will be seen how good is the reason why care should be given to show the flowers in the house when we have them to spare out of doors.

At first sight there may not seem much against our doing justice to flowers in the house, but our flower vases have shared the fate of most manufactured things within the past generation, and suffer from being overdone with designs called 'decorative', which at the South Kensington schools is supposed to have some connexion with 'art'. Every article in many houses being overcharged with these wearisome patterns, it was not to be expected that the opportunity of 'adorning' our flower pots would be lost, and so we may have ugly forms and glaring patterns where all should be simple in form and modest and good in colour. The coalscuttle, with its 'decoration', does not stand in our way so much as the flower vase in which we have to put living things in their delicate natural colours and shapes, and to look at these stuck in vases with hard colours and designs is impossible to the artistic mind.

And when we have seen the ugliness of much of this work, what is to be done in the way of remedy, as the shops are so much against us? The first need is a great variety of pots, basins, and jars or vases, so that no flower that garden, wood, or hedgerow can give us shall be without a fitting vessel the moment it is brought into the house. What are known as the Munstead glasses are a great help, because their shapes are carefully made to suit various flowers, and they are very useful and good in form and made of plain glass. But, however good this series is, it is well to use a variety of other things in any simple ware that comes in our way, very often on the way to the rubbish heap, such as Devonshire cream jars in brown ware. Nassau seltzer bottles in the brown ware may well take a single flower or branch, while old ginger pots and quite simple shallow basins in yellow ware and other articles made for use in trade come in very well.

There is no need to exclude finer or more costly things than these if good in shape and colour, but for various reasons we prefer the simpler wares, in which the flowers look often quite as well as in any others. A mass of Edith Gifford Rose looks very well in a good old silver bowl, and good china, silver, or bronze vases or basins may be used for choice positions or occasions, though it is generally best not to submit fine or fragile vessels of this kind to the risks of constant use. Among the finest things ever made in the shape of vases for cut flowers is the old Japanese work, which is often as lovely in form and as beautiful with true ornament as anything made by the old Greeks; but the Japanese, like others, have taken to 'potboiling' in bronze, and many of the things now seen at sales in London are coarse in workmanship. It might be worth while to have good and avowed reproductions of some of the more useful old forms —the slender, uprising ones are so good for many tall flowers; Italian bronze bowls are often useful too; and the darkness within the bronze vessels tends to keep the flowers longer than the glass vessels exposed to the light.

Japanese ways of arranging flowers are extremely interesting, and may sometimes be imitated with advantage; but the Japanese way is not so necessary as a system, for given a variety of vessels of good shapes and materials, we can place any single flower, branch, or bunch in a way that it will look well, with very slight effort and in very little time. Any way involving much labour over the arrangement of flowers is not the best for us or for the result—far from it.

Having got a good and constant supply of flowers and a variety of vessels, the question of arrangement only remains to be thought of, and it is not nearly so difficult a question if we seek unity, harmony, and simplicity of effect, rather than the complexities which we have all seen at flower shows and in 'table decorations', many of them involving much wearisome labour, when a shoot of a wild rose growing out of a hedge or a wreath of honeysuckle would put the whole thing to shame from the point of view of beauty. In all such matters laying down rules leads to monotony, and yet there is much to be said for ways distinct from the old nosegay mass and the modern jumble, and generally it is best to show one flower at a time, especially if, like the Carnation, it varies finely in colour. The baskets and basins of Carnations arranged by the late Lady Henry Grosvenor, at Bulwick, were lovely to see, and the best were of one Carnation of good colour. These were from her fine collection of outdoor Carnations, so useful for cutting in summer and autumn, when people are enjoying their gardens. But the improved culture of the Carnation as a plant for winter and spring bloom under glass gives us quantities of this precious flower for six months more after the outdoor supply is over. These are among the best flowers for the dinner table as well as the house generally, and on the dinner table the effect by artificial or natural light of one or two flowers of the season is often better than that given by a variety of flowers. What is said of the Carnation applies to various noble groups of hardy flowers, such as the Tulip, Narcissus and Lily.

It is not only in vases we see the good of showing one flower or group at a time; a good result will often come with a single spray or branch of a shrub. The Japanese have taught us to see the beauty of form and line in a single twig or branch, with its natural habit shown, apart from any beauty and form or colour of its flowers. This is important, in view of the many shrubs that flower in our climate in spring, and of which, if flowering shoots are cut when in bud, the flowers open slowly and well in the house. They are best placed in Japanese bronze or other opaque jars. The taller Japanese bronze jars with narrow necks are very useful for this, and it is an excellent practice to cut the bud-laden shoots of Sloe, Plum, Apple, Crab, and like plants, and put them in jars to bloom in the house. By this means we advance their blooming time; and in the case of severe weather, the beauty of early shrubs may be lost to us unless we adopt this plan. We see how the French practice of growing Lilac in the dwelling-house prolongs the beauty of this shrub, and it is not difficult to do something of the kind for the hardy shrubs and early trees that come with the Daffodils, but are not so well able to brave the climate. These shoots of early shrubs are usually best arranged each by itself, though some go well together, and graceful leaves of evergreens may be used with them. One advantage of dealing with one flower at a time is that we show and do not conceal the variety of beauty we have. For, all thrown together, that variety will be much less evident than if we make clear the colour and form of each kind.

Some proof of this may be seen in the work of the best flower painters. In the work of M. Fantin-Latour, for example, his nosegays of many flowers, evidently bought at some country market stand, are painted as well as his simple subjects, but these last are by far the best pictures. However, there is such a wide range of plants, shrubs, and woodland and hedgerow flowers, that we must not hesitate to depart from any general idea if it tends to keep us from making the best of things in simple and ready ways.

Water Lilies and water-side plants for the house. Often the water and the water-side will give us fine things for house decoration, and the new Water Lilies of rare distinction help very much, as cut in the freshly expanded state they keep very well for some days and give us quite a new order of beauty. For this purpose we want bold and simple basins, as if we can put some of their handsome leaves in with them the effect will be all the better. Although very fine in the open water, where they do admirably, the effect of the flower near at hand in the house is quite different and very beautiful, and as these plants increase their value as cut flowers for the house will be found to be great. There are also plants of the water-side which may help with foliage or flower, one of the best being the Forget-me-not, which flowers so well in the house, and the great Buttercup.

Leaves. Many as are the flowers of the open air excellent for house, the leaves of the open-air tree or shrub or plant are hardly less useful for the same end: notably the foliage of evergreen shrubs in warm and sea-coast districts, from evergreen Magnolia, Poet's Laurel, Cypress, Juniper and Thuja, Cherry Laurel, and Bamboo. Even in the coldest districts we have the evergreen Barberry, and more than fifty forms of the best of all evergreen climbers, the Ivy, and the Holly with its scarlet, yellow or orange berries. The trees in autumn give us leaves rich in colour—Maple, Medlar, Mespilus, Parrotia, Tulip-tree and many others. The shrubs and climbers, too, help—Bramble, Wild Roses, Water Elder (Viburnum), Common Barberry, with its graceful rain of red berries; Vines in many forms; hardy flowers, too, help with Acanthus, Alexandrian Laurel, Solomon's Seal, Iris, Plantain Lily; Rock plants are rich in good leaves: Cyclamen, Heuchera, Christmas and Lenten Roses, the large Indian Rockfoils and the Barrenworts; and then there are the hardy ferns of our own country and Europe, and also those of North America as hardy as our own.

A great help in a house is ready access to water

supply in a little room near the flower garden or usual entrance for flowers, where vessels may be stored and flowers quickly arranged, used-up water and flowers got rid of, and so planned that the mistress of the house, or whoever arranges the flowers, may use it at all times without other aid. This greatly helps in every way, and makes the arrangement of flowers for the house more than ever a pleasure.

CHAPTER XVIII

EVERGREEN TREES AND SHRUBS

INTO our brown and frozen northern woods come a few adventurers from southern lands that do not lose their green in winter, but take a deeper verdure—Ivy, Holly, and Yew, enduring all but the very hardest frosts that visit our isles, some bright with berries as well as verdure; giving welcome shelter to northern and wind-swept gardens, and in our own time each varying into many noble varieties. These native evergreens and their varieties are, and for ever must be, the most precious of all for the British Isles.

When after a very hard winter we see the evergreen trees of the garden in mourning and many of them dead, as happens to Laurels, Laurustinuses, and often even the Bay, it is a good time to consider the hardiness and other good qualities of our British evergreens and the many forms raised from them. If we are fortunate enough to have old Yew trees near us, we do not find that a hard winter makes much difference to them; even winters that brown the evergreen Oak. We have collected within the past 200 years evergreen trees from all parts of the northern world, but it is doubtful if any of them are better than the common Yew, which when old is often picturesque, and which lives for over a thousand years. Of this great tree we have many varieties, but none of them quite so good as the wild kind when old. In the garden little thought is given to it, and it is crowded among shrubs, or in graveyards, where the roots are cut by digging, so that one seldom sees it in its true character when old, which is very beautiful. The Golden Yew is a variety of it, and there are other forms, one of which, the Irish form, is well known, and too much used.

After the Yew, the best of our evergreen shrubs is the Holly, which in no country attains the beauty it does in our own; certainly no evergreen brought over the sea is so valuable not only in its native form, often attaining forty feet high on the hills, but also in the varieties raised from it, many of them being the best of all variegated shrubs in their silver and gold variegation; in fruit, too, it is the most beautiful of evergreens. Not merely as a garden tree is it precious, but as a most delightful shelter around fields for stock in paddocks and places which want shelter. A big wreath of old Holly unclipped on the cold sides of fields is the best protection, and a grove of Holly north of any garden ground we want to shelter is the best evergreen we can plant; the only thing we have to fear being rabbits, which when numerous make Holly difficult to establish by barking the newly-planted trees, and in hard winters even barking and killing many old trees. As to the garden, we may make beautiful evergreen gardens of the forms of Holly alone.

Notwithstanding the many conifers brought from other countries within the past few generations, as regards beauty it is very doubtful if more than one or two equal our native Fir. In any case few things in our country are more picturesque than old groups and groves of the Scotch Fir; few indeed of the conifers we treasure from other countries will ever give us anything so good as its ruddy stems and frost-defying crests.

Again, the best of evergreen climbers is our native Ivy, and the many beautiful forms that have arisen from it. This in our woods arranges its own beautiful effects, but in gardens it might be made more use of, and no other evergreen climber comes near it in value. The form most commonly planted in gardens—the Irish Ivy—is not so graceful as some others, and there are many forms varying even in colour. These for edgings, banks, screens, covering old trees, and summer-houses, might be made far more use of. In many northern countries our Ivy will not live in the open air, and we rarely take enough advantage in such a possession by making both shelters, wreaths, and screens of it. It requires care to keep it close on our houses and on cottage roofs or it will damage them; but apart from buildings there are many pretty things to make of it, and among them Ivy-clad and Ivy-covered wigwams, summer-houses, and covered ways, the Ivy supported on a strong open frame-work.

Box, which is a true native on certain dry hills in the south of England, is so crowded in gardens that one seldom sees its beauty as one may on the hills full in the sun, where the branches take a charming plumy toss. To wander among natural groves of Box is pleasant, and we should plant it in colonies by itself full in the sun, so that it might show the same grace of form that it shows wild on the chalk hills. It is, I think, the best of our native evergreens for garden use, making pretty low hedges, as at Panshanger—for that purpose for dividing lines near the flower-garden it is better than Yew or Holly.

Also among our native evergreens is the common

Juniper, a scrubby thing in some places, but on heaths in Surrey, and favoured heaths elsewhere, often growing over twenty feet high and very picturesque, especially where mingled with Holly. The upright form, called the Irish Juniper, is not nearly so good in gardens as the wild Juniper, though more often grown.

The Arbutus, which borders nearly all the streams in Greece, ventures into Ireland, and is abundant there in certain parts in the south. This beautiful shrub, though tender in midland counties, is very precious for the seashore and mild districts, not only as an evergreen but also for the beauty of its flowers and fruit. Still, it is the one British evergreen which must not be planted where the winters are severe in inland districts, and it usually perishes on the London clay. It is the best of our native evergreens, and deserves to be preferred to the heavy Laurels and various evergreens which are not even hardy, so that after a hard frost we often see the suburbs of country towns black with their dead.

Ugly Evergreen Trees and Shrubs. One of the most baneful things in our gardens has been the introduction of distorted and ugly conifers which often disfigure the foregrounds of beautiful houses. These are often sports and variations raised in modern days, as is the case with the too common Irish Yew. It is not only that we have to deplore the tender trees of California, which in their own country are beautiful, though unhappily not so in ours, but it is the mass of distorted, unnatural, and ugly forms—the names of which disfigure even the best catalogues—that is most confusing and dangerous. In one foreign catalogue there are no less than twenty-eight varieties of the Norway Spruce, in all sorts of dwarf and monstrous shapes—some of them, indeed, dignified with the name monstrosa—not one of which should ever be seen in a garden. The true beauty of the pine comes from its form and dignity, as we see it in old Firs that clothe the hills of Scotland, California, or Switzerland. It is not in distortion or in little green pincushions we must look for the charm of the Pine, but rather in storm-tossed head and often naked stems; and hence all these ridiculous forms should be excluded from gardens of any pretence to beauty.

Another most unfortunate tree, as helping to fill out gardens with graceless things, is the western Arbor vitae (Thuja occidentalis). This, which is a very hardy tree but never a dignified one, even where it grows in the north about Lake Superior and through the Canadas, is, unhappily, also hardy in our gardens, and we may see in one catalogue no less than twenty-three forms of this tree all dignified with Latin names. There are plenty of beautiful things, new and old, without filling our gardens with such monstrosities, many of which are variegated. Of all ugly things, nothing is worse than the variegated Conifer, which usually perishes as soon as its variegated parts die, the half-dead tree often seeming a bush full of wisps of hay.

Evergreen Weeds. In many once well-planted pleasure grounds the Pontic Rhododendron almost runs over and destroys every other shrub, and hides out the most beautiful tree effects, growing often a little above the line of sight. Even where people have taken the greatest trouble to plant a good collection of trees, the monotony of it is depressing; always the same, winter or summer, except when dashed by its ill-coloured flowers. The walk from the ruins at Cowdray to the new house is an example amongst a thousand others of a noble bank of trees, varied and full of beauty, but, in consequence of this shrub spreading beneath them all along the walk, showing nothing but a dark wall. This ugliness and monotony came about through the use of the Pontic kind as a covert plant, and also, owing to its facility of growth, for grafting the beautiful sorts of Rhododendron on. In a garden where there are men to look after plants so grafted and pull away the suckers, this plan may do, but when planting is done in a bold way about woods, or even pleasure grounds, this is not and indeed cannot be done, so that the suckers come up and in time destroy the valuable sorts. The final result is never half so pretty as in the most ill-kept natural wood, with Bracken and Brier in fine colour and some little variety of form below the trees. Therefore everybody who cares for the beauty of undergrowth should cease this covering of the ground with this poor shrub, which is not so hardy as the splendid kinds of American origin often grafted on it to die. With the Cherry Laurel and the Portugal Laurel it is the main cause of the monotony and cheerless air of so many pleasure grounds.

The nurseryman who grows rare trees or shrubs very often finds them left on his hands, so that many nurseries only grow a few things, mainly those that grow freely or weed-evergreens like Privet, without beauty, and offensive in odour when in flower. The presence of such things is one cause of the miserable aspect of the shrubberies in many gardens, which might be very beautiful and interesting with a varied life. Many shrubs of little or no beauty very often destroy by their vigour the rare and beautiful garden vegetation, so that we have not only the ugliness of a brake of Laurel, or half-evergreen Privet, or Pontic Rhododendron to survey, but often the fact that these shrubs have overrun and killed far more precious things. And this nursery rubbish having killed every good thing begins to eat up itself, and hence we see so many shrubberies worn out.

The Nobler Evergreen Flowering Shrub. It is not only the ill-effect of these all-devouring evergreens we have to consider, but also what they shut out. Evergreen flowering shrubs and trees of the highest beauty of colour as well as of foliage, and the many hardy Rhododendrons of finest colour, if we would only cease to graft them, and get them instead from layers on their own roots, we should not be overcrowded with the R. ponticum of the present system. They are not only hardy in the sense that many of our popular evergreens are hardy in favoured districts or by the sea, so kind as it is to evergreens, but also everywhere in England. I mean the many broad-leaved Rhododendrons which have mostly come to us from the wild American species, and are hardy in North and Eastern America. Apart from the use of such things, by carefully selecting their colours we may have not merely an evergreen background of fine and varied green, but also the most precious flowering shrubs ever raised by man and in their natural forms, often varying in fine colour and form too, if we will only cease to compel them to live on one mean and too vigorous shrub.

The kinds of Rhododendron raised from the Pontic kind or even from the Indian Rhododendrons, are not in any way so good as the varieties raised from the North American kinds, which have the fine constitution of R. Catawbiense in them, and many of which are hardy not merely in Old England but in the much more severe winters of New England. Apart from plants of these kinds from layers we may also have them as seedlings, though the named kinds from layers give us the means of grouping a finely coloured kind which may often be desirable. It is also probable that, as various regions of the northern world are opened up, we shall introduce to cultivation other fine wild species, and get precious races from them; so, for many reasons, the sooner the better we get out of the common routine of the nurseries of grafting every fine kind we already have on R. ponticum. And if this plan be wrong with the varieties, what are we to say to grafting any of the fine wild species that come to us on the same Pontic kind kept in every nursery for the purpose?

For however vigorous the growth at first, the stock is sure to get its head in the end, and then good-bye to the precious natural species.

The Nobler Evergreen Trees. Apart from trees of poor forms, there are others which are stately in their own country but a doubtful gain to ours, like the Wellingtonia and other Californian trees, and the Chili Pine. Sometimes the foregrounds of even fine old houses are marred by such trees, and unfortunately people use them in the idea that they are doing something old-fashioned and 'Elizabethan', whereas they are marring the beauty of the landscape and of our native trees, beyond the bounds of the garden. We ought not to spoil the beauty of our home landscapes by using such things, which are so abundant in many places that the nobler exotic evergreen trees like the Evergreen Oak are forgotten. This European tree, from Holkham in Norfolk to the west of England and in many gardens round the coasts of our islands, is a noble evergreen tree and a fine background and shelter.

Then there is the Cedar of Lebanon, which is perhaps the finest evergreen tree ever brought to our country, and as hardy as our own trees. If we use evergreen trees they ought to be the noblest and hardiest. The loss of this tree by storms could not happen to anything like the same extent if people went on planting young trees. The many catalogues issued help towards the neglect of the really precious trees by 'bringing out' novelties from all parts of the world—absolutely unproved trees, whilst such grand trees as the Cedar of Lebanon and the Ilex of Europe are often forgotten. A mistake in Cedar planting is that of planting isolated trees with great branches on all sides—an enormous surface exposed to strong wind. In their own country Cedars are naturally massed together, and although the gales are severe, the trees are not destroyed by wind in anything like the same degree. The Cedar of Lebanon is beautiful as a 'specimen', but it is at least equally beautiful massed in groups. In their own countries, in addition to being massed and grouped together, the soil is often stony and rocky, the growth is slower, and the trees take a firmer hold, whereas in our river valleys, where the Lebanon Cedar is often planted in an isolated way, the growth is softer and the resistance to wind less; a more artistic and natural way of planting would lessen the accidents to which this noblest of evergreen trees is exposed.

Shelter and Wind Screens in and near the Flower Garden. Few countries are so rich in the means of shelter as our own, owing to the evergreens that grow freely with us and thrive in seashore and wind-swept districts. Shelter may be near flower beds, or wind-breaks across the line of prevailing winds and the north and east winds, and may be of Yew, Holly, Cedar of Lebanon (never of Deodar), native Fir, and a few other hardy Firs, and the Ilex. In old times shelter was often obtained from clipped hedges of Yews and Limes, but the fine evergreen shrubs we now possess make it more easy and effective, as naturally grown shrubs soften the wind better than clipped lines, while often themselves beautiful in leaf and bloom. There is, indeed, the danger of planting too densely at first, so that after some years the garden becomes dank and the house itself is made cheerless. The pretty young conifers planted are not thought of as forest trees, and parts which should be in the sun are gradually overshadowed—a great mistake in a climate like ours.

Walls, thickly clad with climbers, evergreens and others, are often the best kind of shelter for close garden work, because they do not rob the ground, as almost any evergreen tree will, and themselves may bear many of our most beautiful flowers. Half-hardy evergreens, like the common Cherry-Laurel and Portugal Laurel, should never be planted to shelter the garden, because they may get cut down in hard winters. But even in the most exposed places a good many hardy flowers may be grown with success, such as Carnations, Pinks, and many rock plants which lie close to the ground, and are therefore little exposed to the wind, and which thrive in exposed places where soil and cultivation are not against them. English gardens are often well sheltered by the house itself and by old walls and enclosures, so that in old gardens it is easy to secure shelter for plants.

Planting near the Sea. Some doubt the wisdom of planting near the sea, considering the bleak look of things and the cutting winds. Yet even in places where the few trees that are planted are cut sharp off by the sea wind above the walls, as in Anglesey, we may see how soon good planting will get over difficulties that seem insurmountable. By the use near the sea of small-leaved trees like the Tamarisks, Sea Buckthorn, and small Willows, we very soon get shelter, and by backing these with the close-growing conifers like our common Juniper and some of the sea-loving Pines like Pinaster and, in mild southern and western districts, the Californian Cypress and the Monterey Pine, we soon get shelter and companionship for our trees, and fifty yards away we may soon walk in woods as stately as in any part of the country. Having got our shelter in this way, the growth of the hardy Pines of the northern world seems as easy by the sea as anywhere; indeed, more so, because if there is any one place where the rather tender Pines are grown well it is in places around our coast, where, if the soil is good, one has not to be so careful about the hardiness of trees we select as we have to be in inland places.

The Ilex. The Evergreen Oak takes a lead among the trees near the sea, and it ought to be largely used; but as it is not very easily transplanted from nursery-bought plants, it is just as well to raise it on the place and plant it young. Seed may be scattered with some advantage in places we wish it to grow in, as it grows freely from seed. This Evergreen Oak withstood the great gales of 1897 in the south and west of England better than any other. At Killerton and Knightshayes, and many other places where the destruction was greatest, I was glad to see that the Evergreen Oak was not among the many victims. It is a precious tree for the south and west, and all seashore districts, and should never be forgotten for any of the crowd of novelties among trees, not one out of fifty of which is worth naming beside it. Like many other trees, it suffers from indiscriminate planting with other and sometimes coarser things, and is rarely grouped effectively, although here and there, as at Ham House, Killerton, and St. Anns we may see the effect of holding it together in groups or masses.

In addition to the common evergreen trees of Europe, the Scotch, Spruce and Silver Firs, we have the noble Corsican Pine, which, from its habitat in Calabria and in Corsica, can have no objection to the sea. The Pines of the Pacific coast, too, are well used to its influences, and hence we see in our country good results from planting them near the sea, as, for example, Menzies' Spruce at Hunstanton, the Monterey Pine at Bicton and the Redwood in many places. One good result of planting in such places is that we may use so many evergreen trees, from the Holly to the Cedar, and so get a certain amount of warmth as well as shelter.

Though our country generally is not perhaps fitted for the growth of the Cork Oak, a fine evergreen tree, it is here and there seen in southern and sheltered parts on warm soils, as in certain parts of Devonshire, and on the warm side of the Sussex Downs even, in good condition. We have an example in the Cork Oaks at Goodwood of all that could be desired in health and beauty. This Oak naturally inhabits the southern parts of Europe and the northern parts of Africa, and it is interesting to see that it can attain the size of a stately tree in some favoured places in our country, but the Evergreen Oak for our islands is the Ilex and its various forms.

CHAPTER XIX

THE ORCHARD BEAUTIFUL

THE spirit of beauty was at the birth of the trees that give us the hardy fruits of the northern world—Crab, wild Plum, Pear and Cherry—yielding back for us in their bloom the delicate colours of the clouds, and lovelier far in their flowers than Fig or Vine of the south. The old way of having an orchard near the house was a good one. Planted for use, it was precious for its beauty, and not only so when the spring winds bore the breath of the blossoms of Cherry, Plum, Apple, and Pear, as there were the fruit odours too, and the early Daffodils and Snowdrops, and overhead the lovely trees that bear our orchard fruits — Apples, Pears, Cherries, Plums, Medlars, Damsons, Bullaces, and Quinces. To make pictures to last round the year, I should only ask for many of these orchard trees on a few acres of ground, none the worse if too hilly for the plough; a belt of Hollies, Yew, and Fir on the cold sides to comfort trees and men; with careless garlands of Honeysuckle, Rose, and fragrant Clematis among them here and there; and in the fence bank plenty of Sweet Brier and Hawthorn. If we see fine effects where orchards are poorly planted with one kind of tree, as the Apple (in many country places in our islands there are no orchards worthy the name), what might not be looked for of an orchard in which the beauty of all our hardy fruit trees would be visible? If we consider the number of distinct kinds of fruit trees and the many varieties of each, we may get some idea of the pictures one might have in an orchard, beginning with the bloom of the Bullaces in the fence. The various Plums and Damsons are beautiful in bloom, as in the Thames valley and about Evesham. The Apple varies much in bloom, as may be seen in Kent and Normandy orchards, where the flowers of some are of extraordinary beauty. The Pear, less showy in colour, the Medlar, so beautiful in flower and in foliage, and the Quince, so pretty in bloom in Tulip time, must not be forgotten. The Cherry is often a beautiful tree in its cultivated as well as wild forms, and the Cherry orchards in parts of Kent, as near Sittingbourne, are pictures when in bloom. There is no better work in a country place than choosing a piece of good ground to form an orchard, and a dozen acres are not too much where there is land to spare.

Poor Soil should not hinder. Some may be deterred by the fear that their soil is too poor and planting is more successful on the fruit-tree soils of Devon, Hereford, and Kent than in some other districts; but the difference in soils is no reason why some counties and districts should be bare of orchards, and in many the soil is as good as it need be. Indeed, south of London, where much of the land is taken up with orchards, we may see the trees suffering more from drought in dry years than orchard trees do on the sandstone soils of Cheshire or in Ireland and Scotland, where there is a heavier rainfall. Few of our orchard trees require a special soil, and where chalky or warm soil occurs, the best way is to keep to the kinds of fruit it favours most. But though the orchard beautiful must be of trees in all their natural vigour, and of forms lovely in winter as in spring and summer, the trees must not be neglected or allowed to perish from drought, or to become decayed from bug, scale or other pests, and it should be the care of those who enjoy their beauty to protect them from all such dangers. The idea that certain counties only are suited for fruit growing is erroneous, and need not deter us from planting the hardier trees and good local kinds. Much of Ireland is as bare of orchards as the back of a stranded whale, but who could say this is the fault of the country?

The Trees to take their Natural Forms. Where we plant for beauty we must have the natural form of the tree. Owing to the use of dwarfing stocks, fruit gardens and orchards are now beginning to show shapes of trees that are poor compared with the tall orchard tree. However much these dwarf and pinched shapes may appeal to the gardener in his own domain, in the orchard beautiful they have no place. For the natural form of all our fruit trees is good indeed, winter or summer. We know what the effect in flower-time is in the orchard pictures of such painters as Mark Fisher and Alfred Parsons, if we have not taken the trouble to see the finer pictures of the orchards themselves, seen best, perhaps, on dark and wet days in flower-time. Lastly, the effect of finely-coloured fruit on high trees is one of the best in our gardens. Therefore, in every case, whatever thinning of the branches we do, let the tree take its natural form, not only for its own sake or the greater beauty of natural form generally, but also for the interesting variety of form we get even among varieties sprung from the same species.

Clearly, if we prune to any one ideal type of tree we can never see the interesting variety of form shown by the varieties of one species, as the Apple and Pear. Keeping to the natural form of each tree, moreover, does not in the least prevent thinning of the branches where overcrowded, which is the best way of pruning.

Root Pruning in the Orchard. We have not only to avoid ugly forms of training and pruning, but never in the orchard, where the true way is to let the tree take its natural and mature form, should the practice of root pruning be allowed. Our orchard trees—especially the trees native of Britain like the Apple and the Pear—are almost forest trees in nature, and take some years first of all to make their growth and then mature it. In gardens, for various reasons, men try to get by artificial ways the fruit that nature gives best at maturity, so root pruning was invented, and it may have some use in certain soils and in limited gardens, but one would hardly think it would enter into people's heads to practise root pruning in the orchard; though the word is a catching one and leads people astray. I have several times had the question seriously put to me as to how to root-prune forest trees— where all pruning is absurd save in the way effected by the forest itself. The trees in the orchard should be allowed to come freely to maturity, and in the way the years fly this is not a long wait. By planting well-chosen young trees every year the whole gradually come into noble bearing, and the difference between the naturally grown and laden tree and one of the pinched root-pruned ones is great.

Cider Orchards. Cider orchards are picturesque in the west of England and in Normandy, and so long as men think any kind of fermented stuff good enough for their blood, the cider apple has on northern men the first claim for the beauty of the trees in flower and fruit, and indeed throughout the year. The cider orchard also will allow us to grow naturally-grown trees and those raised from seed. Cider orchards are extremely beautiful, and the trees in them take fine natural forms. They have a charm, too, in the brightness of the fruit, and also in the lateness of the blooms of some, many of the cider Apples flowering later than the orchard Apples. In some cider orchards I saw near Rouen (Lyons-la-Forêt) the finest, tallest, and cleanest trees were raised from seed. The owner, a far-famed cider grower, told me they were his best trees, and raised from seed of good cider Apples; if he found on their fruiting that they were what he wanted as cider Apples he was glad to keep them; if not, he cut their heads off and regrafted them with good cider sorts. These were free and handsome trees with good grass below them, just like the Cherry orchards in the best parts of Kent, where the lambs pick the early grass. But however beautiful such an orchard, clearly it will not give us the variety of form and beauty found in the mixed orchard, in which Cherry, Apple, Plum, Pear, Medlar, Quince, Walnut, and Mulberry take a place; where also the various interesting trees allied to our fruit trees might come in, such as the true and common Service tree, Almond, Cornelian Cherry, and Crab.

Grafting. Where we make use of grafted trees—and generally there is no choice in the matter—we should always in the orchard *use the most natural stock*. It is much better to graft Pear trees on the wild Pear than on the Quince, a union harmful to the Pear on many soils. If we could get the trees on their own roots without any grafting it would often be much better, but we are slaves to the routine of the trade. The history of grafting is as old as the oldest civilizations—its best reason is the rapid increase of a given variety. In every country one or two fruit trees predominate, and are usually natives of the country, like the Apple in Northern Europe and the Olive in the South. When men found a good variety of a native fruit they sought to increase it in the quickest way, and so, having learned the art of grafting, they put the best varieties on wild stems in hedgerows, or dug up young trees and grafted them in their gardens.

This eventually became stereotyped into the nursery practice of grafting many varieties of fruit trees on the same stock, often without the least regard to the health and duration of the trees so grafted. In some cases when we use the wild form of the tree as a stock for the orchard tree we succeed; but grafting is the cause of a great deal of the disease and barrenness of our orchards. Where we graft, it is well to graft low; in the case of Cider Apples, for example, it is much safer and better to take a tree grafted close to the ground than grafted standard high, as the high graft is more liable to accident and does not make so fine a tree. In the orchard the good old practice of sowing the stone or pip of a fine fruit now and then may also be followed with interest.

Starved Orchards. Even in the good fruit counties like Kent one may see in dry years orchards starved for want of water, and the turf beneath almost brown as the desert. Where manure is plentiful it is well to use it as a mulch for such trees, but where it is not, we may employ various other materials for keeping the roots safe from the effects of drought. Not only do the tree roots want water, but the roots of the competing grass suck the moisture out of the soil. The competition of the grass could be put an end to at once, and the trees very much nourished, by the use of any easily found mulching from materials which are often abundant in a country place. Among the best of these, where plentiful, is the common Furze; if cut down in spring and placed over the ground round the base of young or poor orchard trees it prevents the grass from robbing the trees and lets the water fall through to the ground, helping to keep it there, too, by preventing direct evaporation; moreover, the small leaves falling off nourish the ground. So again the sweepings of drives and of farm or garden yards are useful, and also any small faggots which are often allowed to rot in the woods after the underwood is cleared. Then also there are the weeds and refuse of gardens of all kinds which form detestable rubbish heaps that would be much better abolished, and all cleanings from the garden placed directly over the roots of young orchard trees. Even rank weeds, which swarm about yards and shrubberies, would help, and one of the best ways to weaken them and help towards their destruction is by mowing them down in the pride of their growth in the middle of summer—nettles and docks, as the case may be—and instead of burning them or taking them to the rubbish heap use them over the tree roots. Even the weeds and long grass growing round the base of the trees, if mown and left on the ground, will make a difference in the growth and health of fruit trees. Such care is all the more needed if our orchard is upon poor or shaly soils in the drier counties: in naturally rich and deep soil we need it less.

Fencing the Orchard. All fences should be of living things, as at once the most enduring, effective, and in the end the best. We see the hideous result of the ironmonger's fence in marring the foregrounds of many landscape pictures. Holly, Quick, or Cockspur Thorn, with a sprinkling of Sloe or Bullace here and there, give us the best orchard fence, and once well made, far easier to keep up than the iron fence. Yew is a danger, and a hedge of it should never be planted where animals come near, as they usually do, the orchard, and if the Yew comes by itself, as it often will, it should be cut clean out and burnt as soon as cut down. Holly is the best evergreen orchard fence for our country, and we should be careful about getting the plants direct from a good nursery—clean seedling plants not much over a yard high. The best time to plant Hollies is in May if growing in the place, but on light soil plant in autumn, and all the more need to do this if we bring the plants by rail. Unless the soil is very light I should make the fence on a bank, because a turf bank is itself such a good fence to begin with, and a free Holly hedge on a good bank, with, perhaps, a Sloe here and there through it, is one of the prettiest sights of the land, and forms the best of shelters for an orchard in our country. Where shelter is much sought the hedge should not be clipped, and is much handsomer if free grown. The orchard fence should not be cut in every year to a hard line, but Sloe, and May, and Sweet Brier, and wild Rose left to bloom and berry, the hedge to be a shelter as well as a fence, and not trimmed oftener than every ten years or so. Then it should be cut down and woven together in the strong way seen in parts of Kent on the hills.

Kinds to Plant. The English fruit garden is often a museum of varieties, many of them worthless and not even known to the owner. This is wrong in the garden, and doubly so in the orchard, where the fruit trees should be trees in stature and none of poor quality. Too many varieties is partly the result of the seeking after new kinds in the nurseries. In orchard culture we should be chary of planting any new kind, and with the immense number of Apples grown in our country already, we may choose kinds of enduring fame. It is the more necessary to do this now when good Apples are coming from countries where men do not plant a collection when they want a crop of a few first-rate kinds. So we should in our orchards never plant single trees, but always, if possible, choose a good kind and plant enough of it to make it worth gathering. Local kinds and local circumstances often deserve the first attention, and some local kinds of fruit are among the best. When in doubt always choose kinds of proved quality rather than any novelties that may be offered. Any fruit requiring the protection of walls or in the least tender should never be put in the orchard. It is probable that some of the fruit trees of Northern and Central Europe and Russia would be well suited for our climate, but as yet little is known of these except that they are interesting and many of them distinct. The vigour of the tree should be considered and its fertility. Kinds rarely fertile are not worth having, always bearing in mind, however, that a good kind is often spoiled by a bad stock or by conditions unsuited to it.

The Flowers of fruit trees. The beauty of flower of certain varieties may well influence in their choice. Once when talking with Mr. Ruskin of the beauty of the fruit as compared with that of the flower in our northern fruit trees, he said : 'Give me the flower and spare me the stomach-ache!'

In view of the confusion brought about by fat catalogues, new varieties of doubtful value, the number of early kinds worthless for winter and spring use, and the planting of untried kinds, a good rule would be to put any kind we propose to plant under separate study as to its merits in all ways, and only plant one kind a year. The kind chosen for orchard culture should be of undoubted merit and distinction, and of high quality when cooked, without which apples to keep are worthless. In fixing but one kind a year, the first consideration should be its quality, and the second its constancy in bearing, as to which there is a great difference in apples. Hardiness and vigour are essential, and our judgement as regards orchard planting should never be influenced by the produce of trees grafted on the paradise or other stocks which limit the natural growth of the tree.

Apples known for many years, like the *Blenheim, Kentish Fillbasket, Wellington, French Crab, Sussex Forge, Warner's King, Yorkshire Greening, Tom Putt, Reinette Grise, Bramley's* and *Alfriston*, should never be left out of our consideration, as, however they may be affected by situation or soil, their value has been proved. And that is a great point, as in the case of new varieties chosen for some one minor quality, such as colour, it is only after they have been grown for years that we begin to find out their bad qualities.

Pear Orchards for beauty. Some of the most beautiful things in our garden or home landscapes are the orchards of the west of England, more often planted with the Apple than with the Pear. The Pear tree in this country should be much more grown as an orchard tree, for its beauty even if not for its fruit, which yearly grows in value. Some Pears of our own time, like Doyenné du Comice, are worth a score of the old kinds. The Pear tree is finer in form and stature than the Apple, and it is not rare to see trees in Worcestershire the size of forest trees. Such trees, with their varied and picturesque form, are worth thinking of when planting for beauty.

The use of the Quince as a dwarfing stock for many years past in England has been against the Pear as an orchard tree. No Pear grafted on this stock ever succeeds as a standard tree. In our fertile valleys and the rich soil of gardens the Quince is for some kinds often a good stock, but over a large area of poor sandy and chalky land it is worthless; and its use has done much harm to Pear cultivation. In using the Pear, or natural stock, we may hope that it will do well on any land, be it heavy wealden clay or on upland soils. It is true we must wait for results; the standard Pear is a forest tree in its way, and must be allowed time to mature, but it is surely better to let the years run by than to plant trees which may never succeed as standards. For trees so planted to endure we should choose good kinds that ripen in our country, and see, in every case, that they are grafted on the wild Pear—their natural stock—since we cannot easily get them on their own roots, though it would interest me much to see them on their natural roots, and I have two Pears so grown which look far healthier than any others. The most important point is that of varieties. We should never plant any but good Pears, which, as standards, will ripen in our country under any fair conditions, such Pears as *Beurré Giffard, Jargonelle, Beurré Goubault, Beurré Dumont, Beurré d'Amanlis, Beurré Hardy, Fondante des Bois, Louise Bonne, Rousselet de Reims, Doyenné du Comice, Marie Louise, Urbaniste, Soldat Laboureur, Triomphe de Jodoigne, Comtesse de Paris, Nouvelle Fulvie, Bergamotte Saumier, Charles Cognée, Doyenné d'Alençon, Josephine de Malines, Suzette de Bavay.*

Much has been said of late about the advantages and disadvantages of planting in grass; but most growers of Kent and other orchard counties have long known that in hop, arable, and any other land, the trees show quicker growth and greater vigour at first. It is not every one, however, that cares to break up grass to plant an orchard, and we can do very well without grass by mulching the ground round each tree for a few years, until it has gained a good hold.

Wild Pears. And here we may also say a word for some of the Wild Pears of Europe, particularly the little-known species of the region of the Danube and Southern Russia. Some of these eastern kinds are distinct and beautiful in growth and appearance, and their leaves take on the richest autumn colouring, in shades of purple, crimson, orange, and gold, which would give fine effect in the wild garden even if valueless in other ways. The autumn colour of some of our orchard Pears is also beautiful, particularly in some soils; an orchard of Pears is finer in this way than one of any of our other fruits.

And apart from these are the Pears grown for Perry, an interesting group of which we have little knowledge in the home counties, though in some parts of the west they are grown.

Staking Orchard Trees. Fruit trees grown in any way are fair to see in the time of flower and fruit, but our orchard must be in turf if we are to have the best of its beauty. In fruit gardens where the whole surface is cultivated with small fruits below and taller trees overhead, we may get as good, or it may be better fruit, but we miss the finer light and shade and verdure of the orchard in turf, the pretty incidents of the ground, and the animal life among the trees in spring, as sheep in Kent, and the interest of wild gardening in the grass. Also the orchard turf, by its shade or shelter, or in some way, becomes most welcome nibbling for lambs and calves in the spring. A gain of the orchard in turf is that we can plant it on any ground, however broken or steep, and in many parts of the country there is much ground of this sort to be planted. Now, while we may in the garden or the fruit garden plant trees without stakes, we cannot do so in the grass orchard, because of the incursions of animals; therefore staking is needed, not only to support the tall and strong young trees which we ought to plant, but also to guard against various injuries. The best way is to use very strong stakes and make them protect and support the trees, and also carry the wire netting which is essential wherever rabbits, hares, goats, or other browsing animals exist. The best way to do this is to have a very stout stake of Larch or old Oak. Sometimes in the repairing of old sheds a number of old Oak rafters are rejected which are excellent for staking young trees in orchards, first digging the hole and putting the stake firmly in to a depth of 3 feet below the surface. Cradles of Oak and iron are much in use; the first is very well in an Oak country where labour is plentiful; iron is costly and ugly, and not so good as the single stout stake, which is easy to get of Larch or stub Oak in many country places. The common way of tying a faggot of Quicks or any thorny shrub is often good when done by a good fencer. The trees should be tied carefully with soft ropes of straw or jute, and when planted be loosely but carefully wired with netting well out of the reach of browsing animals. This wiring is well supported by the strong stake, and it keeps rabbits and hares, as well as cattle, at bay, and, worse than all for trees, young horses. A usual way in Kent is to drive in three stout stakes, 6 feet or more in height, round the tree, and fasten crossbars to them. This can be done at a total cost of about 10*d.* a tree, and should last twelve to fifteen years.

The Orchard Wild Garden. One of the reasons for a good orchard, from the point of view of all who care for beauty, is its value for wild gardening. It is so well fitted for this that many times Narcissus and other bulbs from the garden have even established themselves in its turf, so that long years after the culture of the flowers has been given up in the garden, owing to changes of fashion, people have been able in old orchards to find naturalized some

T

of the most beautiful kinds of Narcissus. Where the soil is cool and deep, these flowers are easily grown, and in warm soils many of our hardiest and most beautiful spring flowers might easily be naturalized. On the cool side of the orchard bank, Primrose and Oxlip would bloom long and well, and on all sides Daffodils, Snowflakes, Snowdrops, wild Tulips, or any like bulbs spared from the garden; and from the garden trimmings, tufts of Balm and Myrrh to live for ever among the grass of the bank. The robin would build in the moss of the bank, the goldfinch in the silvery lichen of the trees, and the thrush, near the winter's end, would herald the buds with noble song.

Climbers on Orchard Trees. Bold planters need not hesitate to adorn some of their orchard trees with graceful climbing plants. A few of these climbers would be too vigorous eventually for the fruit tree, but a good many are never so on vigorous orchard trees. The most picturesque planting I ever did was to put a number of white Indian Clematises (*C. Montana*) with some orchard trees. They grew in a most picturesque way, and took a different habit on almost every tree. The autumn-flowering Clematis (*flammula*) is such a light grower that it would not make much difference to the tree, and there are numbers of wild Clematis with the same light character that would not hurt an orchard tree. Some of the fine-leaved Vines, too, would give a dash of rich colour in the autumn, and do little harm, and some of the more fragile Honeysuckles might also be tried. In the south of France the common blue Passion-flower and various kinds of climbing Roses will often reach out from the garden hedge and take possession of the nearest trees, and Olive and Orchard trees may be seen beautifully robed in this way. Even the hardy winter Jasmine, when crowded by other things upon a bank, I have known to clamber up into the branches of a little Cherry tree, with very pretty effect. One of the prettiest effects I have every year is a cross, due to a plant of the white Traveller's Joy (*Clematis viticella alba*) growing on a double Cherry tree. We first have the bloom of the Cherry, and then weeks after comes the fair white Clematis, flowering for weeks all over the Cherry and doing no harm.

CHAPTER XX

LAWNS AND PLAYGROUNDS

THE lawn is the heart of the true British garden, and of all forms of garden the freest; and it may be the most varied and charming, adapted as it is to all sorts of areas from that around the smallest house. It is above all things the English form of garden made best in the rich level valley land, and, with the least amount of trouble and labour to make or keep it, certainly gives the best result in effect. The terrace garden, we have seen, in its origin and best meaning arises from wholly different sort of ground from that on which we make a lawn. If the Italians and others who built on hills to avoid malaria had had healthy and level ground they would have been very glad of it and have thought it beautiful. With the lawn there is little or no trouble in securing fine background effects, variety, pretty dividing lines, recesses for favourite flowers, freedom, relief, air and breadth. There is room on the lawn for every flower and tree, from the cedar, or the group of fruit trees planted for the beauty of their flowers and fruit, down to rich beds of lilies or smaller flowers. In a recent book by an architect we are told that there is no such thing as a garden to be made except within four walls. Many of the most beautiful gardens in the British Isles are made without any trace of walls, which are absolutely needless in many situations to get the most artistic results in a garden. Lovely gardens may be made around lawns without marring the breadth and airiness which is the charm of a lawn, or interfering with the use of its open parts as a playground.

Climber-covered Alleys around Play Lawns. Where there is space enough there are reasons in country places for cutting off by a hedge a playground from the garden or pleasure ground, as at Madresfield and Campsey Ash and in many of the older gardens; and what is used generally is the yew or holly hedge, but clipped hedges give little shade and no flowers. Now, if in the like position we adopt the pergola, we get shade, and many graceful flowers. Clematis, tall Roses, Wistaria, and almost every beautiful climber could be grown thereon, some even better than on walls, because we can allow them more freedom, and it is not so easy to crucify vine or climber on a pergola. We can have evergreens too if we wish, with garlands of handsome Ivies among them, and players might rest in the shade and lookers-on sit there to see the play. Various bold openings should be made on the playground side, and the whole so arranged as to form a sort of living cloister. Apart from its shade and coolness and use as a dividing line it might be a garden of a very graceful kind. Pergolas have various uses in covering paths which are too much exposed to the sun, and there is no better way of growing beautiful climbing plants than a green covered way, whether supported by oak posts, or brick or stone pillars as in Italy.

The ordinary covered ways made in England are often too narrow. In forming all such things a certain amount of freedom is essential, and we cannot enjoy the air in the usual narrow covered way, which is also soon made narrower by the growth of the things upon it. It should always be at least wide enough for two people to be able to walk abreast. Where oak is not distinctly preferred, 14-inch brick pillars are best, and the plants take to them very soon. Common brown or rough stock bricks are far better for this use than showy red bricks, which are often too the most costly. In stone districts stone would do as well or better and need no fine dressing or designing after any pattern. It is better, in fact, done in the free way the Italians do it; but then in

Italy every man is a mason, or knows what to do with stone, and also the stone there comes out in long posts or flakes, which serve as posts. This is also the case in the north of England, where beautiful posts of the green stone may be seen in use on the farms. In Cornwall, too, it would be easy to have stone pillars. We are in the iron age, and many resort to iron, ugliest of all materials; but simply done and not disfigured with galvanized wire, even iron may help our purpose if painted carnation green or some other quiet colour. We may take from its hardness by tying wooden trellis work over it, which is better for tying the climbers to than iron or wire, using the most enduring wood we have for this purpose. For this an excellent aid will be found in the bamboo stakes which now come in quantities to our ports as underpacking for sugar cargoes. These are sold at a reasonable rate, and are an excellent aid in making the iron pergola, wired across and along the iron supports. Thus we get an enduring material, good in colour and excellent to tie the shoots of rose, clematis, or vine to.

Beautiful climbing shrubs and other plants would find a congenial home on such a pergola. Various graceful forms of our grape vine, as well as the Japanese and American wild vines, a group which now includes the Virginian creepers of our gardens, would be also useful, but not so good as the true vines. The lovely Wistaria, and not only the old Chinese kind, the best of all, but also the beautiful Japanese long-racemed kind (*W. multijuga*), and various others too, though we think none come near to these in beauty; the brilliant flame Nasturtium in cool districts, and where light shade is desired; the green Brier (Smilax) of America, and also the South of Europe, for warm soils; handsome double and white-stemmed Brambles; wild and single Roses; Box Thorn, with its brilliant showers of berries; European, American and Japanese Honeysuckles; Jasmines; over fifty kinds of Ivy, the noblest of northern and evergreen climbers; Evergreen Thorn, with its bright berries; Cotoneasters of graceful habit; Clematises, especially the graceful wild kinds of America, Europe, and North Africa; in mild districts particularly, the winter blooming clematis of North Africa and the Mediterranean Islands, which flowers in winter or early spring—all these would be very pretty and give light shade. The showy Trumpet flowers (*Bignonia*), quite hardy in southern and midland counties; and the Dutchman's pipe (*Aristolochia*), with its large leaves, would also be useful. The fine-leaved Lardizabala of Chili, the brilliant coral barberry of the same country (*Berberidopsis*); the graceful, if not showy Silk vine (*Periploca*) of Southern Europe; the Chinese Akebia; the use of the rarer climbers depending much on the climate, elevation, soil, and nearness to the sea.

Fine Turf in and near the Flower Garden. Fine turf is essential in and near the house and garden wholly apart from the open park or playground. Flower beds are often set in turf, or small grassy spaces near the house or the garden, on the good effect of which depends very much the beauty of the home landscape, as coming so much into the foreground of what should be pictures. One reason why we should take care to get the best turf which the conditions of soil or climate allow is that no other country can have such good turf. In many countries, even in Europe, they cannot have it at all, but grass seed has to be sown every year to get some semblance of turf. With natural advantages so great, our care should be to get the full benefit of them, and though in many places the turf, through the goodness of the soil, is all that could be desired, in other places a very poor turf is often seen, and much effort is often given in vain attempts to get it worthy of a flower garden. Many people think that any rough preparation will secure them a good sward, and merely trench and turf the ground; even experienced ground workmen fail to get a fine turf for the flower garden, though they may lay turf well enough for a cricket ground. Others think that turf will come of itself, and are often rudely disappointed.

CHAPTER XXI

HOME WOODS

At the beautiful gate of the woods one happiness awaits us, in being free from vain considerations about 'styles'. Our home wood should be only a nobler kind of garden, and may be so treated without spoiling its value as a wood. We may see on a spring day in one place more beauty in a wood than in any garden, from the bushes and plants wild in the place: Furze, Crab, Cowslip, Wood Hyacinth, Primrose on northern slopes, Marsh Marigold in wet copses, and Sloe. But this great beauty often has to be sought through briery paths and dense underwood, and the best of it is not easily brought into relation to the home grounds. In many country places, where people labour for years with a wretched stereotyped kind of garden, they take no trouble to see the beauty of the wild bushes and plants that grow near naturally and without cost or care. The supreme beauty of our native trees is often a sealed book to them, while they perhaps spend time and money on trees that are tender, ugly, and useless in our land either for wood or garden.

The wood is a mighty worker for man, a precious gift of beauty as well as profit. For the wood, unlike the farm, wants few costly labourers, no weeding or ploughing, finds its own manure, its own watering, its own shade and shelter, all this and much more and without the aid of the colleges now thought necessary to make the good gardener or farmer. If all the wit of man, backed by all the learning of the colleges, were on one side and a wood of our best native trees on the other, the wood would certainly give a better return than could be got from any labour or capital applied to the same class of land in other ways.

Evergreen Woods for Beauty. Even in the most frequented lines of country we are often dismayed by the ugliness which results from neglecting to plant that most precious gift of the hills, the Mountain Pines. With few exceptions the best of these are the trees of northern Europe and America, massed in serried armies on the mountains, and grown on the hilly ground to a vast extent in central Europe. The first good reason for planting evergreen woods is their beauty. This we do not get in the kind of pleasure-ground planting of which the object is to grow each tree as a specimen dressed down to the ground in a green 'crinoline'. It is only by grouping and massing hardy evergreen trees that we can see their highest beauty, which in most kinds is in the mast-like stem. Nothing in the form of trees may so much influence the look of country as these evergreen trees.

Shelter. In continental countries, where the winds are powerful enough to destroy the crops, shelter-belts of evergreen trees are a great defence; much more so in our wind-shorn coast land we have reason to seek shelter. If, owing to the vast length of exposed coast, we neglect to give shelter, the trees and shrubs are cut off as by giant shears above the walls. But where we have the evergreen wood (beginning with wind-resisting shrubs working up to the higher trees) we have perfect shelter, as at Bodorgan in Anglesey, on one of the most wind-shorn coasts.

Planting poor Land. In dealing with poor land the question of profit cannot be excluded, and to what better use could one put bad land, poor rocky slopes, starved sandy flats, boggy hills (as in Ireland), and wet districts, and land too cold and poor to be ploughed with any profit, as in some southern wealds? There is no way we can use such land so well as by planting it with the true evergreen forest trees. There is no

Saturday night in the woodland; it puts on its profit without other care, adorning and sheltering the land, helping the living creatures that haunt the woods, and adding in many ways to the charms of the country. Few know the power of evergreen trees to grow on the poorest land. We cannot grow Oaks on nothing, but I have seen young Pines sow themselves on land from which the top soil had been entirely removed by gold hunters. Many poor, cold, ill-starred hill-sides of the north of England, Wales, and Ireland could grow the Mountain Pines as well as they grow in their native lands. The Corsican Pine makes a growth of from 20 inches to 3 feet a year in a quarry I know from which every bit of soil has been removed.

Quickness of Growth. Another reason for choosing evergreen trees for planting poor land is that woods can be so quickly raised. If we make a right choice of young plants and wire against rabbits and hares before planting, we may raise sheltering woods in ten years. Little plants, after a few years' struggle with the turf, settle with it and are soon tall enough to give us the shelter and effects which only evergreen woods can give. Our climate helps us if we only know how to take advantage of it, because of its affinity to the sub-alpine conditions in which the great Pines of the world so often grow in lands below the snow-line.

All the Pines of Europe are easily grown as forest trees in our country, because the conditions are something like those of their natural climate. If we go to North Africa we find the Cedars growing far above the wide sea of arid hills where the snow lies late, our wild flowers and our Thorn and Yew growing with them. A man after middle age could easily raise noble woods of these trees in his lifetime, while a young man, owner of a poor, treeless estate, might clothe the hills with a stately forest.

Fuel. In the country house, all the cooking and heating might be much better done with wood fuel; the British kitchen range is a costly deception, and, if all our coal mines failed, every country parish might grow its own fuel and light. Yet it is a common thing to see people bringing coals from Newcastle and carting it miles from a railway station, whilst abundance of fuel lies rotting in their woodlands. The wealth of Britain in coal has been our loss, in leading us to forget the old ways of cooking and warming. The architect and the housemaid, and the modern grate and chimney, are all against us, and it is not uncommon in a country house to see people shivering round an ugly grate with a coal fire. Our evergreen wood is not such good fuel for the open fire as the native hard woods—Oak, Beech, Ash, or Maple—but for closed ranges and furnaces it makes a good fuel. I have lately been staying in a country house in Hungary, where all the cooking was done with wood, there being thirty-five people to provide for. Even the electricity for lighting the house and offices was generated from the grubbed stubs of Fir trees which in this country would be left to rot. Every cottage on the estate was warmed with wood only, and with perfect comfort.

The objection to the greasy coal of northern England, apart from its cost, is that it pollutes the air of the country as well as that of the town, and many good gardens and country houses are defiled by it. I have placed in cottages a wood-burning kitchener which answers well, and people are grateful for the cleanliness and the good cookery and baking done with it. The fuel we use is such as may often be had in old shrubberies and underwoods—batwood it is called—of slight value in the district. Some simple means of cutting it up is all that is needed for economy.

As some of the Pines grow three feet a year in soil too poor for any agricultural use, few words are needed to give an idea of the enormous amount of firing that might be grown in this way, even from the mere thinning of the woods. And here it should be said that we must in all cases follow the true forest way of close planting, only thinning when the thinning will pay for the labour, and when the trees to remain are close enough to keep the shade canopy overhead.

Tree Colour. Another reason for giving more thought to the woodland as a nobler kind of garden is the lovely colour of trees throughout the year in good planting. Mr. J. Meehan, writing to an American paper, describes the trees of England as 'keeping up their dark green-hued foliage to the last!' He must have left us too soon, as our woods are often full of colour right through the autumn, and some of the American trees, where people have the art of grouping them in an effective way, have as fine a colour in our country as in their own. It is a mistake to suppose that our native trees have not fine colour, for scarcely one of them is not remarkable for it. The autumn Oak woods around London are superb in colour, and the Beech woods fire every year from Scotland downwards. To the eye, open to delicate gradation and variety of good colour, that of British woodlands is as good as any, and the winter effects often most beautiful, from Alders by the busy stream to Oaks massed with silvered stems. Almost every native tree and shrub is beautiful in colour of flower, leaf, or fruit. Scarlet Dogwood, red and yellow Willows, Gorse, Broom, Holly in berry, Mountain Ash brilliant in fruit, our native Barberry (a lovely thing in fruit in groups), the Spindle Tree, and Viburnum, are among our trees that give the most showy effect; but for refined colour that of our common woodland trees in picturesque planting is best of all. The colour lacking in many districts is that of the nobler Pines, with their fine variety of perennial verdure, from the Hemlock, Spruce, and Yew that toss their branches so finely in storms, to the silvery Californian trees and the trees noble in colour of stem, the Yew and the Scotch Fir, and indeed nearly all matured Pines.

The planting of evergreen woods is then an important question, and from the number of merely new trees in lists not always a very simple one. We have a few hardy evergreen trees which everybody plants, but so many trees have been introduced which possess good qualities in their own country that people are apt to plant things which can never become in Britain timber trees of any value, however well they may look in nursery rows, or singly on the lawn with perhaps a dozen loads of good loam under each tree. The mountains of Europe give us the best trees for our islands, as they need no special soil or care, and with them thrive the trees of Northern Asia and Asia Minor with its noble Cedars of Lebanon. There is always gain in having a tree from a like climate. If we go to California and warm regions for our evergreens we may make mistakes, and costly ones. There are fine trees in the North Pacific region, but for British evergreen woods we ought to take the hardiest only.

We shall have to steer clear of many pitfalls made for us by catalogues in giving pompous Latin names to mere 'states' or slight varieties of each tree; of fine trees not hardy save in favoured spots, as the Deodar and Sequoia; of false names like Retinospora; of failures like Cryptomeria; of trees starting too early in the spring, owing to our open weather; of weedy, poor trees like the western Arbor-vitæ, and to whole lists of poor varieties of such trees, rubbish from a woodland standpoint, and little better for the pleasure ground.

Shelter. The next thing to consider in our evergreen wood is where to plant, and this will differ a good deal according to the ground and district. The shelter line is all-important, not only for the garden and the house but also for crops. For the country house it is often desirable to have a sheltered retreat in all weathers, and nothing will give this so well as the evergreen wood, free from labours of all kinds after planting, unlike most underwoods, which are the scene of much labour and delay. A house on high ground, with open land to the north or the east, offers one of the most tempting situations to plant a hardy Pine wood in, not merely for the sake of effect, but also for shelter from the north and east. I have planted such a wood, and raised it in ten years to dignity and beauty. A simple Pine wood with rides cut through is far better for effect, shelter, and the growth of trees than the labelled and sticky 'Pinetum', which gives neither timber, shelter, nor beauty. In many districts we see iron-bound clumps dotted over beautiful ground, and worse than useless for effect; also skinny belts not deep enough to keep out the wind. As the common ways of planting are so hopeless, what others have we? Well, this is a question of district, of whether the land is valuable or not, and whether it is rich plain or rough upland. Large areas of land have been broken up in all parts of Britain when prices were good, which ought never to have been broken up at all and are not fit for anything but timber. Think of ploughing with four horses in clay land and expecting to get anything back. The same field which breaks a man growing corn at the present prices would give a steady profit if well planted. It is well, therefore, to plant cold and poor fields, no matter what their shape, and from the first year that we plant them we shall have some useful covert. It is not only fields poor from coldness of soil on the clay that are not worth cultivating, because some light lands would be much better planted.

Very often, in diversified country where the land is not valuable, the old way of very small fields for the stock has become almost useless for the present needs of farming. If there are rabbits about, anything grown in the field is eaten up, trees begin to spread in, and there is often hardly room to swing a plough. Then it is often a good plan to plant the whole of the field, suiting the tree to the soil and taking care to bring in now and then a change of tree. For example, in the woodlands south of London we often see hundreds of acres without an evergreen tree anywhere. This cannot be good from the points of view of shelter, game, or beauty, and, therefore, it is often well to plant some of these small fields with hardy evergreen trees. Never look in the direction of Californian trees, which are not everywhere successful, but keep to the evergreen trees of Europe—Scotch, Silver Fir, Spruce, Corsican, Austrian, White Pine of

Canada, and the Cedar of Lebanon, which people use as a pleasure-ground tree only, although it is as easily raised from seed, and as free and vigorous, as any Pine.

Tail ends of fields running into woods, which often necessitate much fencing within a very small area, are also good places to plant, especially with an evergreen tree which we wish to encourage, as such corners and tail ends are often sheltered by the woods about them. By planting these, and making a line of fence round the field, we improve both the field and the wood and also simplify fencing, which is always worth doing.

Apart from taking advantage of the incidents and nature of the ground, there may be a reason to plant for covert in certain positions, and then we must take what ground we can, always keeping to the principle of massing and grouping rather than the narrow straggling clumps which are so common and, generally, fenced with ugly iron. The larger the mass we plant the easier the fencing becomes and the simpler for everybody, both in making and keeping. For cold and wind-swept districts it is often good to plant on the north and east sides of favourite fields or gardens, and it is pleasant to see how much one can do in the way of shelters with evergreen trees, even in ten years, if we exclude rabbits and choose the right kind of tree. The common idea that good planting means big planting is a great hindrance to getting artistic results or even good timber, and it is well to learn to enjoy the beauty of little trees and woods, which we may raise in ten years, even by the use of small plants, which, after all, is the true way. It is an error to think that because we put in 'large stuff' we shall get a better result. In many cases trees not a foot high will beat those bought in nurseries a yard high. My Corsicans came in a basket, in little bundles not bigger than bunches of groundsel, and in ten years they formed a handsome sheltering wood. Certainly the Pine babies make a far from dignified appearance the first year; but I am quite content to plant small, knowing how vigorously they will grow in a very few years, and how much better an effect I shall get than by planting tall plants to wobble in the wind. Now, to plant in this way and get a good result for all the future life of the grove, we have not only to know the greater trees of the Northern World as distinct in kind, in beauty of form or leaf and in height, but also in relation to time; and hence arises one of the questions concerning good planting for the future, for which all good planting should be.

We have much evidence how quickly woods may be formed by planting in well-considered masses and by the association of things of like nature, as Firs and Pines; and how a man even beginning after middle age may in his own lifetime hope to see noble woods of his own planting. If anything in the world would be enviable by a tree lover it would be the lot of one still young, with much poor land to plant, as he certainly could in his own lifetime raise stately forests. Such good and rapid results, however, can only be got by the absolute exclusion of hares and rabbits and the still worse attacks of young horses or grazing creatures of any sort.

The stock of the ordinary nursery, being in most cases grown for planting gardens and pleasure grounds, should be avoided in forest planting. For that we must go to the true forest nursery, which will give us young and healthy seedlings, by far the best for all purposes of planting. One or two instances of this may convince the planter of the gain of getting very young trees. In planting a field of Larch, some of the plants received were so very small that the men put them thickly in lines at one side of the field (in stock as it were) to allow them to get bigger. Left there and forgotten, they grew much better than the regularly set-out plants, although much more thickly planted. In another case of planting a field of Corsican Pines and Scotch, mainly small plants, some parts of the field were planted with larger ones, about a yard high, which happened to be in the place, where they stood too close. While the little trees never failed, about two-thirds of those of the larger size perished the first season. Thus will be seen at once the advantage of always getting very small and young trees in all planting of woodland and forest. As distinct from pleasure-garden planting I am sure we in the end gain instead of lose time by beginning with baby trees.

Time in planting. Where we plant good trees in a liberal way, for which there is so often room to spare in poor ground, a plan seldom followed, but a very good one, is that of dating the wood on a stone-block, as in the Oak wood at Althorp; or on stout iron posts, as in the woods near Virginia Water. It is very interesting when examining a well-grown wood to know its age, which may also be duly recorded in an estate book of planting—a useful book to have on every estate where the woods are of any extent.

A source of failure. A common source of failure with the nobler evergreen trees is the mixed, muddle way which is common everywhere with us, and fatal as regards the evergreen wood. Planters think merely of the effect of the pudding-like masses they form at first, and follow no principle, the planting being too often a mixture of evergreen shrubs of the south of Europe, forest trees of the north, and conifers of California, or any other country, in one mass, usually uniform back and front, and planted for size only. In nature trees have distinct habits of growth, and some notice should be taken of this in planting for the sake of effect or for timber. We rarely or never see a mixture of conifers, evergreens, and summer-leafing trees growing naturally in one place; the Oak and the Pine run together sometimes and, as we go up high mountains, the Beech and the Birch, but the association ceases eventually, and we have the Pine on the higher hills, as we have the Oak on the plain and the Willow in the marsh. Nothing like the incoherent mixture which we see in Britain is ever seen in nature, nor should be seen in any good planting. These remarks as regards stupid mixed-plantings are not addressed to the true forester, but to the many people who, often with good opportunities of planting, never think of the matter from that point of view; so that we see under their forest-evergreens the remains of flowering shrubs and rare evergreens which are quite unfit for such association, but which grouped by themselves in right positions would have given a beautiful result. I do not say that some association with summer-leafing trees is not right in the Pine wood; in fact, such trees often come by themselves. Oak, Beech, and Ash in a forest country are blown in, or in some way come uninvited and often with good effect. Birch and Beech might even be planted among Pines; but that way has nothing in common with the mixing, which is so wrong, of hard-wooded trees with Californian conifers and every conceivable tree that happens to fit in at first, to make a show of size. And this is but one of the many important things we have to think of, if our planting is to be true and beautiful and lasting.

The beauty of the Pine-stem. A mistake running through the whole of our planting, doing infinite harm from an artistic and even a cultural point of view, and as difficult to eradicate as Twitch or Bishopsweed, is the common one of planting every precious tree we have as an isolated specimen on the grass. I have seen in an interesting garden a Monterey Pine (*P. insignis*), a tree about seventy years old and in fine health, but instead of the stem, such as a Pine should show, its huge branches were massed close to the ground and one could scarcely get under it, thus offering an immense target for rain, or wind, or (worse than all) wind-carried sleet. It grew in grass as usual, and that it throve in the climate of the district was clear from its healthy foliage; but the timber was very much less than it would have been if the tree had been planted rightly, for, instead of being (as in a forest Pine) massed in the stem, it was wasted in twenty great arms. In this way of planting, trees like the Scotch Fir, the Cedar of Lebanon, and the Monterey Pine grow too much to branches, not losing their lower limbs but pushing them out until they become the enemies of the main stem, whence it is we have so many trees thrown down by storms, as well as other evil results from the practice. Other Pines, like the Columbian Fir (*Abies nobilis*), never assume this bushy habit but go up like arrows, their lower branches getting weaker as the tree grows higher; massed together, as in nature, the trees lose their lower branches quicker. When the bare stem is seen, many who have not seen the trees in their native home attribute it to loss of health, whereas they are merely throwing off tired branches for which they have no further need. In nearly all forest trees, and Pines more than any, it is a distinct gain in beauty to show the stem. The trees escape the wind, and do not suffer from exposure or from being set on grass, which during summer or light rainfall takes all the moisture. They shelter each other, and the mast-like stems are sufficient to uphold them in any storm. What is the remedy for the mistake so often made in planting pines? Certainly grouping the trees closer together, and so gaining those stately columns, good effect, and timber. If there is not room enough to group each kind separately, that is no reason why different Pines should not be grouped together. Much of the time and energy of writers and students is wasted in the attempt to draw distinctions where none exist, ranging from the abysmal profundities of Kant to the last issue of some publication dealing with the simple facts of country life. Attempts are made to set up distinctions in kind where it is only a question of degree. We have the table hen and the exhibition hen, which proved so distressing a bird to Sir Henry Thompson; we have men endeavouring to separate garden from exhibition Roses; critics who write of all sorts of 'schools' in art instead of showing the harmony with nature of all true work in art; and now books of woodcraft show the same tendency and, instead of being simple and clear, use a jargon of German and bad English in order to be as obscure and pedantic as possible. The tree growing by itself, as our English trees often do, is discussed on 'arboricultural principles'; trees growing in a wood are discussed under another set of principles called 'sylvicultural'. This and much like talk is very apt to confuse. Some of the noblest trees for beauty as well as size are in the forests, and I would much rather have Oaks from the forest of Marly or Bercy in the pleasure-garden than any merely bushy tree usually grown therein. The greater Pines of the northern forest should be grown as they are found in natural forests generally, that is to say, close enough together to get the true form and stature of the central stem.

CHAPTER XXII

THE WOODLAND GARDEN

IN several country places I have lately seen woods of singular tree beauty—woods with all the natural advantages of soil, air, and country, and well placed near the house—a charm which does not always occur. There was all the dignity and grace of trees planted with loving care by past owners; but such woodland is very often neglected until ugly plants such as Nettles, Dog's Mercury and, most hateful of all, the common Elder and Privet take possession.

In such woods covert is sought for game, shelter and other ends, and there is no reason why it should not take a beautiful form. No situations about a country house offer such opportunity for beauty as these woodlands, where we can mass and enjoy many of the most beautiful of native and other shrubs for which there is not always room in the garden. They would be far better in the woodland garden than in the usual mixed shrubbery; and while good wholesome undergrowth does not interfere with the trees but rather helps them, the growth of weeds and grass rankling over the ground is hurtful in many ways. Some of the finest natural woods have a natural undergrowth of evergreen shrubs, as for instance in the Californian forests with their beautiful undergrowth of evergreens, the trees rising with clean stems far above them.

The first aim should be to get rid of the enemies by light grubbing, and plant in bold free masses things that will fight the weeds. I know of nothing that clears the ground below it more thoroughly than the Red Dogwood; its foliage is so close. An inexpensive shrub, it gives bright winter-effect in marshy or wet places beside streams and ponds, and will also grow apart from water.

Our native Holly, Box, and Yew make much more beautiful and effective groups than the weedy trees which usually have possession. The common evergreen Barberry from North America is a beautiful covert shrub, with its foliage all through the winter and its fragrant and effective blooms in spring, but it should be held together in natural masses, and close enough to keep the ground clear. The too common way of having a lot of coarse Laurels clipped down to one level is stupid and ugly, because there are so many things that give a very fine undergrowth without clipping. The large Partridge-berry (*Gaultheria*

Shallon) of North America, as it may be seen at Coolhurst—what an excellent undergrowth it makes, and yet how little grown.

Evergreen Barberries might alternate with our common native Barberry so brilliant in fruit, and wide masses of Aucuba and Yellow Azaleas, now so easily raised. Such excellent evergreen covert plants as Cunningham's White Rhododendrons can be bought on their own roots. Rhododendron are a host in themselves, but there is too much of the dull *ponticum*. We should encourage the bright-coloured kinds such as *Jacksonii*, and never put in a grafted plant. There are splendid kinds in the country if people will only layer them, or even allow them to layer themselves, as they often will when let alone. Kinds good in colour can be picked out in flowering time at the lowest rate the nursery trade offers. Only hardy things will be used, and in southern places we may have a little more variety of evergreen undergrowth. Some of the new Bamboos would help very much for effect, such as *palmata*, which keeps the ground clean and is very fine in habit. In open and poor soils the Heaths would tell well, such as the Cornish Heath, and the Common Heather in its stoutest varieties. Sweet Briers, Wild Roses, and Brambles, would naturally be welcomed, and it would be well to encourage native bushes like Viburnum, Sloe, and the beautiful Spindle Tree (*Euonymus europaeus*), and plants such as Solomon's Seal and the Ferns, which often form a pretty undergrowth in woods. Wherever natural covert exists, as it often does in large woods in the shape of tall evergreen Sedges like *Carex paniculata*, or handsome masses of Bracken or Brambles—it should be kept, as there is no better covert.

The planting of covert had better be done from early autumn until March or April, but much may be done throughout the year in clearing the ground and getting rid of objectionable plants. That is even better done in summer, as we are then more certain to make an end of them than if done in winter or autumn. When planting Holly in places overrun by rabbits it will be necessary to wire, and if we plant in large, bold masses, as we always ought, the wiring is easier. Happily rabbits do not attack Box, which is a great gain when seeking covert for hungry soils or poor dry bluffs.

Woodland Rides. Besides, it is important in such woods to have the rides airy, clear, and green, and not less than 18 feet wide. In dry places there is little to do besides clearing them, but in wet soils it may be necessary to form a dick on each side outside the 18 feet line, the soil from which should be thrown up to make the rides drier. We lose nothing by having such rides, because the trees enjoy the light and air, and the best timber often grows alongside them. Much can be done by direct sowing on the ground; I raise acres of Broom and Furze by simply throwing the seed out of hand. In freshly cleared spaces these seedling plants would come more freely still. The seed should be sown not too early in the spring—I mean it is better to sow in the first week of May than in March, as it gives the rabbits a little less time in which to gnaw the small plants before they get well started. At least two kinds of Broom and two kinds of Furze are excellent to sow in this way, and not a few other things might be raised from seed in case of scarcity of plants. But most covert plants are to be had in quantity in forest nurseries, and only young healthy plants should be bought for this purpose.

CHAPTER XXIII

THE GREATER TREES OF THE NORTHERN FOREST

I HAVE shown reasons for the planting of evergreen woods: for shelter, profit, use of poor lands, rapid growth, varied uses, and for their beauty in the landscape. The man who does not love the woodland and the tree will never make a beautiful country place; for the questions which cluster round the house itself are as nothing compared with what we have to face if we wish to get the best the ground may give us. We have now to think of the chief question in planting, the choice of stately and first-rate trees; kings of the northern evergreen forest they should be. From many points of view, the planting of evergreen woods is an important one, and, from the number of merely new trees in lists, the question is not always simple. We have a few hardy evergreen trees which everybody plants, but so many trees have been introduced, possessing good qualities in their own country, that people are apt to plant things which can never become in Britain timber trees of any value, however well they may look in nursery rows, or isolated in the pleasure ground with perhaps a dozen loads of good loam under each tree. The mountains of Europe give us the best trees for our islands, needing no special soil or care, and with them thrive the trees of Northern Asia and even Southern Europe and Asia Minor with its noble Cedars of Lebanon. There is always a gain in having a tree from a like climate. If we go to California and warm regions for our evergreens we may make mistakes, and costly ones. There are certainly fine trees in the North Pacific region; but for the evergreen woodland we ought to take the hardiest trees only.

But we have to steer clear of many pitfalls made for us by catalogues in giving pompous Latin names to mere 'states' or slight varieties of each tree; of fine trees not hardy save in favoured spots, as the Indian Deodar; of false names like Retinospora; of failures like Cryptomeria; of trees starting too early in our spring; of weedy, poor trees like the western Arbor-vitae, and to whole lists of poor varieties of such trees, rubbish for woodland, and little better for the pleasure ground.

Useless Evergreen Trees. Much has been spent and wasted in planting these, owing to the excitement over the Wellingtonia and other Pacific coast trees.

For these, people almost ceased to plant the best native trees and the really good Pines for our land, the main result in many cases, except in the most favoured places, being ugly sticks often half dead. The effect, also, is so ugly in what is called the 'Pinetum' that people might well be tired of planting conifers. But the true 'Pinetum' is the Pine wood, where no tree should ever enter which is not as hardy as the Scotch Fir or the Yew.

The Deodar Cedar is unfit for the woodlands of our country, being tender. The Redwood of California, which is a fine tree in its own country and grows pretty well with us, is injured almost every year even in southern parts of England, though it may thrive as a close wood. The Wellingtonia is worthless from a forest or other point of view in this country. Araucarias should never be planted in any woodland work, nor should any merely curious conifer, and many absurdities are described in catalogues serving to obscure the value of the really noble Pines.

Design. It is important to get out of our heads skimpy ideas of planting, wrong in effect for shelter, timber, and simplicity of working. North or south, east or west, we often see that, if any planting of evergreen trees is done at all, it is done in narrow skirtings to roads, so that the winds cut through the line in an instant, whereas when trees are massed rightly the edge of the wood impedes the prevailing wind, and within fifty yards the trees are in shelter and warmth. The best way to plant is to take a piece of ground which is not valuable for arable or any other use, and plant it as wood. If, as often occurs, there are few or no evergreen trees among the hardwood trees of the place, it is all the better if we can place an evergreen wood in the midst of Oak and like woods; birds can get more protection in such woods, as in estates with hard woods only it is too easy for the poacher to see the pheasants clear against the sky on the leafless trees. All planting of these trees should be in masses, bold groups or 'clouds' on the hills. It is not a question of space; an acre or two rightly planted would be better than miles of the mean skirtings to roads called 'plantations', and the round clumps with which so many country places are spotted and disfigured.

The following are the greater trees for the evergreen wood :—

The Corsican Pine. The tallest Pine of Europe, reaching 160 feet high and over in Calabria and its own country, Corsica, and of very rapid growth in our country, as I have raised woods of it in ten years.

The tree shows much variety of habit and even foliage, and, if one liked to do anything so foolish, one could give Latin names to several forms found in one wood. The Calabrian variety has been reckoned as a species by some, as it is a more vigorous tree, especially in poor soils. A lovely tree for all the southern parts of Britain at least, and good in every way. Plant small; two-year-old plants do best.

The White Pine (*P. strobus*). One of the noblest forest trees of the northern world, sometimes reaching a height of over 170 feet, with a girth of trunk of 30 feet. Owing to the cutting of the woods in Canada and Northern America, it is seldom seen in its native dignity in the settled parts. It forms dense forests in Newfoundland and Canada, and westwards and southwards along the mountains, and in our country thriving best in gritty and free soils. I find it perishes when growing on wet clays, and this is not owing to any want of hardiness, as it is as hardy as any northern tree.

The Cluster Pine (*P. pinaster*). A rapid-growing Pine of pleasant colour, 70 feet or more high, native of the Mediterranean region, often by the seashore, and useful in our country near the sea, but often thriving in inland places, best in free and sandy soils. It is used much in France to aid in fixing sand dunes.

The Scotch Pine. Our native Pine, and, when old, one of the most beautiful. It is of very wide distribution in Northern, Arctic, and mountain regions, and also on the mountains of Italy and Greece. The Riga variety is a more erect and stronger grower. A number of varieties are mentioned in books and catalogues, and some hybrids, compact and dwarf varieties, including variegated ones, none of any consequence compared to the wild tree. This Pine sows itself in rough heaths, and is rapidly spreading in that way in some districts.

The Monterey Pine (P. insignis). A grass-green Pine of California, often thriving in the southern and western parts of our country, but in inland places occasionally suffering in hard winters, and therefore not good for general planting, except on high ground. The tree is so distinct and beautiful that it should not be forgotten in the southern and milder counties.

The Swiss Pine (P. cembra). A noble alpine Pine of distinct, close-growing form, a slow grower in our country, as well as in its native land on the mountains of Central Europe or in Siberia, where it attains a maximum height of 100 feet. This is a tree of rare beauty and fine quality; its slow growth at first does not lessen its great value.

The Austrian Pine. One of the hardiest trees;

distinct in form and colour, attaining a maximum height of nearly 100 feet; of close, dense growth when young, thriving on calcareous, poor, stony or rocky ground and on clay soils (but not on poor sands). Owing to its close 'covert' and habit it nourishes the ground beneath it so well with its fallen leaves that it is self-supporting and gives precious shelter. It is often planted in Britain, but generally set out in the usual 'specimen way', so that it is slower in taking its true form than when grouped as Pines should be. The final form of the tree is very picturesque, with a free open head; giving valuable wood, however massed it should be freely thinned so as to allow of its full development. In books this Pine is sometimes classed as a variety of the Corsican Pine, but, from a planter's point of view, the trees are as distinct as any other Pines in colour and form.

The Cedars of Lebanon and Atlas. Noble trees of the mountains of Asia Minor and India; some hardy. Planters should not forget that it is to the Cedars of the northern mountains they must look—the Lebanon and Atlas Cedars, which have been proved so hardy and so well fitted for our country. In books a form called *Cedrus atlantica* is considered distinct enough to merit a separate name, but, having seen the trees on their native mountains, I think the Atlas Cedar is the same species as the Lebanon Cedar (*C. Lebani*). The seed of the tree is plentiful in Asia Minor and North Africa, and it ought to be grown in forest nurseries and offered among the other forest trees. The seed being as easy to raise as that of any other conifer, we should not buy the tree in the 'specimen' state, but in the smaller state, a much safer way. These Cedars should be grown as woodland and forest trees, and they will take a very high place in the ranks of such.

The Common Yew (*Taxus*). Our best native evergreen, though neglected by gardeners as a tree, must not be left out in planting evergreen trees, as it is such a welcome shelter for game, and when old very beautiful with its finely-coloured stem and everlasting verdure. In woods, too, we have the best chance of growing it out of harm's way, as no asp of tropic jungle is more deadly, and thousands of precious living creatures have been killed by Yew. Plant as far in the centre of woods as may be. Keep all old trees with reverent care. The lower branches of Yews should be cut off where there is any danger of stock reaching them.

Lawson's Cypress (*Cupressus Lawsoniana*). A tall and beautiful tree of the Pacific coast of North

America, 100 feet high, and very free in our climate. Unfortunately, owing to propagation from cuttings instead of in the natural way from seed, the tree often breaks into a number of stems, which interferes with its natural habit and beauty. It varies very much into what is called 'sports'. There are a number of fastigiate forms, but they are malformations, and only the natural wild form raised from seed should be planted.

The Canoe Cedar (C. nootkatensis). A distinctly beautiful tree, hardy, a native of the northern Pacific coast, and with even more than the grace of the Italian Cypress. It thrives in cold, ordinary soils, and it is a pleasure to see it at all seasons. In its native land there is a copious rainfall, and it thrives in wet districts in our country. Syn. *Thuiopsis borealis.*

The Great Japanese Cypress (C. obtusa). A beautiful evergreen tree of the mountains of Japan, better known in our gardens under the wrong name of Retinospora. It grows nearly 100 feet high, and in its own country it is much used to form avenues. It has many varieties within Latin names, but few of them of real value as they grow old, and these varieties and their Latin names and propagation by cuttings will no doubt do their sorry work in blinding us to the value of the wild tree. Only plants from seed are worth planting for woods.

The Douglas Fir. One of the most valuable trees introduced, and now a common tree in Scotland, grown for timber. It should be planted in sheltered valleys or woods, but will live in all soils ranging from light sands and gravels to moderately stiff clay. There are several varieties of the tree, that known as the Colorado variety being considered the hardiest but not the best grower. Its growth in Ireland is very fine.

The Sitka Spruce (Abies sitchensis). In places where this Spruce thrives it is a beautiful tree with bluish silvery-grey leaves. In a damp climate, where the soil is deep and moist, it grows into a noble tree, but in dry soils it is poor. It comes from a very cold part of the northern world, and is a precious tree for Britain, and among the best evergreen forest trees.

The Rocky Mountain Spruce (Picea pungens). A valuable tree for this country, as it is very hardy, quick in growth, and withstands exposure in high-lying places. It is most generally known in gardens by its variety *glauca*, which is perhaps the most silvery of all conifers, the whole tree being like a cone of frosted silver. This Spruce is largely raised from seed in order to select from the seedlings these silvery varieties, and it is the green kind which is of less value for gardens that is so useful for exposed plantations and shelter groups. I find this tree very good in poor stony and dry ground.

The Norway Spruce. One of the most planted of trees, and yet often failing in the southern and dry counties, except near water or in wet bottoms. It is a mistake to plant it on high exposed places or in very dry soil, but over a large area of the western country it is valuable, and in Ireland and Scotland. Its failure in the southern counties is owing to their low rainfall.

The Silver Fir. A noble tree of the mountains of Central Europe, often planted in Britain, and growing well over 100 feet high in many places. It was the first of the Silver Firs planted in Britain, and one of the best. When young it grows well in the shade of other trees, and it is an excellent tree to plant for shelter, as it will grow in the most exposed situations, and in peaty as well as most soils, but it is slow to start growth in some clays and adhesive soils.

The Giant Arbor-vitae (Thuja gigantea). A tall and noble tree, fine in stature and form, hardy in our country, thriving in ordinary soils, and a free and rapid grower, even without the special attention in the way of soils such conifers often receive. It attains in its own country a maximum height of 150 feet, and its wood is fine-grained and good. N.W. America, finest on the Columbia river (syn. *T. Lobbii*).

The Puget Sound Fir (A. grandis). A beautiful and stately tree of over 200 feet high, with dark-green cones 2 to 3 inches long, and dark shining leaves, white below. Hardy and free in various parts of Britain; best in moist soils. N.W. America.

The Columbia Fir (Abies nobilis). A mountain tree 200 to 300 feet high, with rich silvery foliage, tipped with bright green as the young growths start in spring, and set with handsome brown cones 5 to 7 inches long. It is hardy in this country save in cold low lands towards the north, and when sheltered and well suited as to soil it thrives remarkably. Shelter is of importance, for the tops of vigorous young trees are not infrequently blown away in a gale, if too much exposed. Old trees develop a broad rounded head with short rigid branches. They seed freely in this country, and soon make timber, but coarse and straight-grained, only second-rate in quality, and not very durable. The finest trees in this country are upwards of 80 feet high, with a girth measure of 8 feet. Oregon.

The Crimean Fir (Abies Nordmanniana). A beautiful tree of 100 to 150 feet, and closely allied to the Common Silver Fir, with rigid branches, dense dark-green foliage, and large cones. It is hardy and of rapid growth when well placed and fairly established, the new shoots making and ripening their growth within a few weeks. It will grow in almost any soil, and even in dry sandy places where many Firs refuse to thrive; but in such soil it is particularly liable to a blight like the woolly aphis so common on fruit trees, which spoils the appearance of the trees and finally destroys them. This pest follows the tree so persistently in some places that many planters have abandoned its use, spite of the merit of the mature wood. Mountains of the Caucasus and Crimea.

The Red Cedar (Juniperus virginiana). A graceful, hardy tree on the hills and mountains of N.E. America, giving somewhat of the effect of the Eastern Cypress in Italy, and in our islands a good sheltering tree thriving in the poorest of soils and rocky places.

The Hemlock Spruce (Tsuga canadensis). A tree sometimes over 100 feet high with a diameter of 4 feet in the trunk, inhabiting cold northern regions from Nova Scotia to Minnesota. This tree has been much planted in England, but it has not attained the stature and form that it shows in Canada. It is of too high a character among the nobler northern trees to be left out in any varied planting of evergreen forest trees, choosing for it cool soils or river banks.

The Western Hemlock Spruce (*T. Mertensiana*). A nobler tree of graceful habit, a larger tree than the Canadian Hemlock Spruce—sometimes 200 feet high, with a trunk diameter of ten to twelve feet. A native of Puget Sound, British Columbia to Alaska, and coming from such fog-moistened regions hardy in our island climate. The foliage, as graceful as a fern, is of a lustrous green, and silvery white beneath. It is a tree beyond price for our country.

The Yellow Pine (*Pinus ponderosa*). A noble American tree covering a vast area in its own land, where it thrives under a variety of conditions and in many soils. Fully grown trees attain a height of nearly 250 feet, with stems upwards of 6 feet in diameter. In this country it has not been much planted except as a pleasure-ground object, though it grows well in most parts of Britain, is hardy, and of rapid growth. It thrives in free and gritty soils, and is at home in poor Surrey sands where few of our native trees would thrive. Its appearance is very distinct, with a sturdy trunk and few branches, coming in regular whorls, and drooping with age. Tried on poor limestone soil at Grignon in France, it has outstripped the Corsican Pine, and promises to be one of the best timber trees. Its wood is heavy, tough, and durable, yellow-brown or light red in colour, and heavily charged with resin.

Jeffreys Pine (Pinus Jeffreyii)—better known in this country—is a mountain form of the same tree, not quite so rapid in growth, but more resistant to the Pine Beetles and certain diseases which attack the Yellow Pine.

The White Fir (Abies concolor). Perhaps the most valuable of the American Firs, it is remarkable for vigorous growth and resistance to heat and drought. It reaches a height of 200 feet and upwards, with a trunk diameter of 6 feet, a narrow pointed crown, and spreading frond-like masses of foliage. The wood is light, soft, and not very durable, but easily worked and valuable for temporary uses. Brought to this country only forty years ago, there are trees already upwards of 60 feet high with a girth of 7 to 9 feet. It is a variable tree, with several forms—*Abies lasiocarpa* with an erect habit and slender stem, and *A. Lowiana* with a stouter trunk and more spreading in its outline. All, however, grow freely on well-drained land, in places not too liable to spring frosts. Along the coast of New England it has been freely planted in seashore gardens, and some of the finest trees are to be found fully exposed to the fierce winds sweeping in from the Atlantic—winds which frequently drench the trees with salt spray without any ill effects. It should be tried under similar conditions on our coast, and deserves far more consideration as a forest tree. Syn. *Abies Parsonsiana.* N. W. America.

Caucasian Spruce (*P. orientalis*). An elegant tree with somewhat the appearance of the Norway Spruce, but it is a smaller-growing tree with much shorter leaves and branches, of denser growth, and retains its lower branches. It is of a deep green, and on this account is especially suitable for grouping with the larger conifers. It is very hardy, and thrives best in moist soils. Massed it forms a fine shelter.

Tiger-tail Spruce (*P. polita*). A Japanese tree of comparatively recent introduction, but, judging by the largest trees in various parts of the country, it is one that will have a future in these islands. It is a handsome tree of very rigid pyramidal outline, and with leaves the stiffest and sharpest-pointed of all. It stands exposure well, and is a tree for high windy places.

P. Morinda. No other Spruce has such gracefully drooping branches as this Himalayan tree, and it is worthy of a place among the finest trees, but it must have a deep, moist soil, more heavy than light, and the position not too sheltered. Under these conditions it flourishes in the bleakest parts of the eastern counties, where are some of the finest trees of it. Syn. *P. Smithiana.*

Himalayan Pine (P. excelsa). A handsome tree, much planted in Britain, with long, slender, drooping leaves and pendent cones. It is a native of the Himalayas, and of very wide distribution in Asia, and also in another form inhabits the mountains of Greece and South-Eastern Europe on high elevations. In our country it thrives best in warm and well-drained soils.

Cascade Mountains Fir (Abies amabilis). A tall massive tree with deep blue-green foliage and dark purple cones. It grows rather slowly with us, the tallest tree being not much above 40 feet, whereas in the mountains of the Western American States it attains a maximum height of 250 feet with a trunk 4 to 6 feet in diameter. It is a noble tree, the branches sweeping down in graceful curves, clothed with dense foliage more silvery on the under-sides of the leaves than *A. Nordmanniana*, and during May conspicuous for the fine red catkins of the male flowers. It is still a scarce tree in this country, and difficult to get true to name and on its own roots. It is too often increased from side-shoots, which seldom develop a good leader. The wood is light, hard, finely grained, and of a pale brown. British Columbia and southward to Oregon.

The White Spruce (*Picea alba*). A graceful tree of pyramidal habit in its early state, broadening and rounding off with age, while the slender branchlets are finely pendulous. It grows best in cool and moist places, upon the banks of lakes and streams, decreasing in size and vigour southward where exposed to heat and drought, which it cannot endure. It is abundant in Canada, reaching a height of 150 feet, and is much used in the manufacture of paper-pulp and for fitting interiors. The mature wood is light and hard, finely grained, and readily stained or polished. Syn. *P. canadensis*.

The Big Tree (*Sequoia gigantea*). At first I intended to omit this tree from the greater trees of the Northern Forest, because of its failure in many pleasure grounds. Is this not largely our own fault in placing the tree? The best thing to do would be to give it a fair trial as a forest tree in sheltered woodland valleys, or where there are none of these to plant in a sheltered wood, and always among trees and cover of some kind which would help to keep the sun out and the ground cool. Coming from one of the finest climates, with a constant sun and gentle Pacific breezes, the least we can do with it is to take care to place it in the best woodland conditions. We should in such ways give it all the chance of growth our climate affords, and get rid of the toy-tray look of our garden lawns which arises from sticking such trees about in them. The fact that over much of the northern and midland country we may not hope for success with it should be another reason for growing the tree where the woodland conditions are most favourable.

The idea that these trees should be planted far apart is wrong. They should, like other forest trees, be planted young and close, say 4 to 5 feet, and thinned in after life without losing the canopy overhead. The popular idea is expressed in Veitch's *Manual of Conifers* :—' For whatever purpose it is planted, a space having a radius of not less than 20 feet should be allowed for it, and a free circulation of air on all sides thus secured.' The Big Tree, or any tree, should never be planted in this way. Many trees might go in that space and be all the better for it. It is this popular and erroneous way of planting which is so much against the growth and natural beauty of character of the greater forest trees in this country.

CHAPTER XXIV

EVERGREEN COVERT

THERE is nothing about which more loose talk is indulged than the matter of covert plants. One famous sportsman tells people to put Privet where they want covert near water—a most weedy and evil-smelling shrub, besides bad covert, its rapid growth being its only recommendation. It is a mistake to use a weedy bush merely because it grows quickly. Most hardy shrubs grow quickly enough, and some of the most rampant growths are the soonest to go back. On the whole, the best covert plants, especially for woods near the house, are the native and other hardy evergreens. In the choice of such plants their beauty should not be overlooked, and things of offensive odour and other bad qualities like the Privet should be rejected.

Rhododendrons. There is a shrub which is hardy and beautiful as an evergreen covert plant, fine in colour, and of vigorous constitution. It is 'Cunningham's White', an old kind which, although called white, is a rosy-lilac colour in bud. It is one of the best plants for growing in any cold, or rough, or even clay soil, forming far better covert than the pontic Rhododendron, and having also the advantage that it can be bought on its natural root in some nurseries. It is easily increased, and grows in any soil. I have had a healthy group of it in clay (part of the dug-out foundation of a building) for over a dozen years; it never turns a leaf in any frost, and is a close and excellent covert.

Rhododendrons are often planted, but it is the common pontic kind, which, used as a stock, ends by killing the good kinds grafted on it. If, however, we take to layering our brilliant kinds of hardy Rhododendrons, then we shall have such underwood effect as no garden can rival. It is not necessary to put the finer and hardier Rhododendrons, raised mostly from the hardy North America kinds, on the somewhat tender *ponticum*, and, if nurserymen will not layer them, everyone who has a good kind should layer it for himself wherever the plant grows. Some of the best nurseries now have already good stocks of the finer kinds on their own roots, and are preparing more. These in cool woods would almost layer themselves, and give a splendour of colour in summer that no man's planting could surpass.

Box. There is no more useful evergreen covert than this for chalky, light and warm soils, and for growing where it would be hard to establish covert from foreign shrubs. Few who only see Box weary and drawn in the shrubbery have any idea of its beauty massed on an open down. As an evergreen group on a hot and poor bluff in a wood it is fine in effect, and an excellent and warm covert. Happily, this native evergreen loves our poorest and driest soils, of which there is such a vast area in the southern counties. Box will thrive on chalky wastes where no other shrub appears, and, fortunately, it is so distasteful to rabbits that it is let alone in places infested by them.

The Evergreen Barberry (Berberis Aquifolium). This is a pretty evergreen, and a free grower in many peaty, open soils, but not so free in certain heavy soils. As, however, these occur in certain parts of the country only, it may be included among the very best shrubs for evergreen covert.

The 'Sweet Bay', or True Laurel (Laurus nobilis). I had never seen this used as covert, but having many bushes of it to spare I tried it in old woodland, and was pleased to see how well it looked. It is very cheery in colour in the winter season, and it grows very freely in southern and seashore districts. Even if not generally used as covert it can be made to form very pretty groups in woods, but rabbits soon destroy young plants of it if not 'wired'.

Holly. Though often a tree, Holly is an excellent covert, and in some free or gritty soil even runs at the root, as in certain parts of Epping. It loves poor, stony ground, and, mixed with Juniper, forms beautiful covert; but only seedlings of the wild form should be planted, and in establishing colonies of Hollies in rabbit-infested ground it is necessary to wire well.

Juniper. Our native kind is meant here; it makes very good covert for the poor, dry and chalky soils too frequent in the southern half of the country. Junipers can be had from various parts of the world, but our own native Juniper is as worthy of cultivation for this purpose as any, and we have so few really hardy evergreens. In the valleys in Surrey it grows to a height of 18 to 24 feet, though usually only a bush.

Savin (Juniperus sabina). This is one of the most graceful and hardy of all dwarf evergreens, and admirable for cold hills or stony ground no matter how wet or poor. It is a dwarf Juniper that clothes those parts of the mountains of Central Europe too bare to support anything larger. If not easily bought in quantity it can be readily increased by pulling up the branches, which often throw out many rootlets.

These should be planted firmly and a stone put over the part left out of the ground, or it can be pegged down to stop wind-waving.

Ivy. This is undervalued for its use and beauty in woods, and is too often cut away. It would be well in many places where the large-leaved Ivies are grown to put them here and there in copses. They are of all things the most easy to increase, the young shoots pulled off wall or tree rapidly rooting in moist earth. The Ivy is among our best native evergreens, as, after carpeting the wood and clothing the tree-stems, it takes the tree form, and is as good an evergreen as any.

The Great Partridge Berry (Gaultheria Shallon). A valuable covert bush, difficult to obtain in many nurseries. It has been neglected by nurserymen, owing to the small demand for it for gardens. It will thrive in ordinary soils and runs about apace in wet peaty places. In Scotland it seems to be better known than in the south, for it has been largely planted there for covert, as at Balmoral. It is one of the shrubs that will thrive in the shade of Pine plantations.

The Cherry and Portugal Laurels. The Cherry Laurel (usually, but wrongly, called the Laurel) is, perhaps, more used than any other bush, but has certain defects, being not hardy in severe winters even in Ireland, and also, it is too vigorous for underwood covert, and when chopped back, as it very frequently has to be, it is ugly. Some of the newer forms, however, are hardy, especially that from the Shipka Pass; and its beauty is best seen in a wood allowed to grow in its own natural way. In some southern and mild districts the Portugal Laurel and some of its handsome forms are very free-growing, but in cold and inland districts they are apt to be cut down in hard winters. They are so free and handsome in the south and west, however, that they may be used with good effect.

Yew grows well in the shade, and gives warm covert, but should only be put in the interior of woods owing to its poisonous nature, and the woods should be fenced or much trouble may arise from stock eating it. It is naturally common in some districts, and cannot be excluded from our plantings, and the safest way with it, perhaps, is to put it in a dense group towards the centre of a wood, where its shelter will be very welcome to birds in winter.

The Palmate Bamboo (*Bambusa palmata*). I first had this in a moist wood in rather black soil, and then took a fancy to moving it to the water-side, and although we took the plant out carefully from the wood, a number of roots remained, and from these arose the most graceful colony of plants I ever saw, so fresh and fine a green in the middle of winter as almost to make one forget the season; the shoots are handsome enough to cut for the house in winter, the growth close, and the form good. It was also quite free by the water-side, where its fine reed-like habit goes well with Reeds and Willows.

The Japanese Bamboo (B. Metake). This is very free and hardy in varied conditions, and a fine covert plant. It has long been cultivated in Surrey nurseries, and is easy to secure; it increases quite freely either in woodland or near water. Some of the older Bamboos, such as used to be grown first of all, as *B. falcata* so well in the south of Ireland at Fota, give tall covert of a graceful sort, but not so good as these.

A Beautiful Evergreen Covert Plant. We often see lists given in catalogues of covert plants like Privets, which are only of slight beauty and value, and inferior to our native Briers, Bracken, and Furze as covert plants. There is one bush, however, not always known as a native be it said, which makes the most beautiful of all evergreen covert, especially in sandy, chalky, stony, or dry gravelly soils, where few other things will thrive. The Box is common in shrubberies, but is rarely seen in its natural form of a spreading plumy bush on an open sunny hillside. I know nothing more beautiful among evergreens than Box trees fully exposed, as there they have a charm never seen in 'shrubberies'. A great quality, and one which raises it entirely in value above Laurels and the other evergreens commonly used for this purpose, is that rabbits do not touch it owing to some poisonous property. In the last two years, in the hope of getting some evergreen covert, I tried the hardiest form of the Cherry Laurel, and also (a great favourite of mine) the true Laurel or Sweet Bay; though accustomed to the depredations of the rabbit, I never saw anything so sad as the disappearance of both, many plants being absolutely bitten to the ground, whilst in the same woods Box of all sizes remains untouched. For this reason above all, as well as for reasons of shelter, pleasant colour, and hardiness, it should take the first place among evergreen covert plants. There is a vast range of our country in which it grows well: and even where compact soils abound—which it dislikes—it is often possible to find patches of gravel or sand in which it will thrive. It is at home on arid soils and on hillsides and mountain slopes; large tracts of forest are covered by it in Southern and Western France and other parts of Southern Europe, Northern Africa, and Northern and Western Asia; it is also found in some of our southern and western counties—Kent, Surrey, Sussex, and Gloucester. Long-living and slow-growing as it is, it will, in the best conditions, rise to a height of 20 feet or over, and sometimes be as much as 6 feet round the stem. But grand specimens like these are the exception, and most often it is seen as a compact shrub. It is easy to establish or move at any age, but for covert use is best small, when it can be bought very cheaply. It seeds freely in our country, and on arid slopes might be increased by scattering the seed on the surface. To many the odour of Box is agreeable, and its colour also is very beautiful.

Hedges and Shelters of Holly. Our country is fortunate in having as a wild tree the most beautiful evergreen of Western Europe, and one denied to much of the country in Central and Northern Europe and a vast region in North America, where it will not withstand the winters. In beauty other evergreen Hollies are inferior to it, hence its berried branches are sent in quantities to North America at Christmas. Of all possible living evergreen fences the best is Holly in close but not stiffly clipped lines. Better still is the free unclipped Holly hedge, as it makes a fine shelter as well as a good background. In Warwickshire and other counties it often makes as good a shelter round fields as any shed. Of the clipped Holly hedges fine examples are at Woolverstone in Suffolk. Where land is not valuable—either from its poverty or elevation or other reasons—it matters little whether the hedge is clipped or not, especially round woodland and for cutting off woods from pasture fields. For such a case the finest hedge is that of unclipped Holly, because then we get its fruit and protection and fine-form. Such hedges might be either of Holly alone or mixed with Sloe or Quick. Where from the nature of the soil it is not easy to raise Hollies from seed—as they should have friable open ground in the young state—it is best to buy small plants from the forest nurseries. The worst enemy of the Holly hedge is the rabbit. I have lost thousands of plants in that way, and although many places are not so much infested, still great care must be taken, or in hard winters the Hollies are sure to be destroyed. Where Holly comes naturally, as it does in many parts of the country, the destruction is not noticeable except after hard winters, when even old woods of it are destroyed. Being a close-growing shrub it forms a shelter for cattle, and as it grows much better than the

Hawthorn under hedgerow trees it ought to be more often used for enclosing meadows and pastures. It keeps itself almost free from weeds, owing to the closeness of its branches at the bottom, and it is free from insects. Holly is found flourishing on dry gravelly land as well as on strong clay, but sandy loams are the soils it delights in most.

Covert from seed. If in any bold or varied planting in poor soil we succeed in one-half what we attempt we are fortunate; and the best thing I ever did in planting was sowing a bare field with Gorse. It was about to be planted with little forest trees, when I scattered the seed broadcast over the field; the field was wired to keep out rabbits, and after five or six years the effect of the Gorse, with the young Pines and Larch growing up and standing a little above it, was splendid. An artist friend came, and amid the Oaks in a shaw near drew a picture of the field looking towards the distant hills.

The warm colour of Gorse as a covert in winter is pleasant. No other shrub does so much for us, and I have sown without covering it several hundredweight of seed. In old woods it has less chance owing to the rabbits and partly to shade. On railway banks, or bleak, dry, 'brashy' places, it thrives and looks at home. Where in clearing fences or old fields a difference of level often occurs as the result of ages of ploughing, it is a good plan to sow Furze on the little rough terraces. There would be no particular advantage in seeking this Furze treasure where the bush abounds, as in many parts of Ireland, Cornwall, and Devon; but in districts where, owing to heaviness of soil or other causes, it is absent, it is one of the handsomest bushes one could raise.

In sowing among young forest trees I take advantage of the spaces between them, and, instead of the Furze being a hindrance to the young trees, it is a gain, inasmuch as Furze thickly planted is a soil-maker, its leaves falling thickly, and the rapid-growing Pines, closely planted, as they ought always to be, will, after some years, get clean above it and finally get the field to themselves. In making the best of fences, the live fence, Furze seed scattered along the banks comes up very soon; it looks beautiful in such places, and helps to make the fence a more sheltering dividing line. There is nothing to be gained by sowing such seeds early. A very good time is in April, when the nightingale comes, May, or early in June; and, as there is no covering or transplanting, it does not much matter if the seeds are sown at night. It must not, however, be thought an altogether haphazard business, because the man with the bag is supposed to know his plants and the places that are likely to suit them. The common Furze seed is sold at a low price by all the great seed houses of Europe if bought in any quantity; other kinds of Furze I have tried in like ways, and find that the tall one known as the Foxbrush (*Ulex strictus*) does equally well. It is a very rapid grower, and a fine, useful aid for the farm, as it faggots more compactly than any other Furze; but the seed is not so easily procured. Much less vigorous than this is the dwarf Furze (*U. nanus*), which abounds in rough heaths in many parts of the country, but the seed is not common. Sown in places where a compacter growth is wanted, it is as free and easy as any, and may be sown just in the same way. In all these sowings there was no covering given, the seed was simply thrown over ground likely to suit the plants. The dwarf Furze is beautiful in autumn when all the other bushes are losing their charms, and best for low foregrounds and rather bare, stony places.

The Brooms. Though very beautiful I never fancied these so much as the Furzes, owing to their scraggy habit when old not forming good covert. The best, the Spanish Broom (*Spartium junceum*), flowers much later than the others, and is a showy, handsome plant, growing on any gravelly or sandy place, no matter how dry. Standing on the top of a railway bank I scattered the seed and let it fall on a steep slope formed of débris without soil. The natural soil of the place is about as poor as any on the habitable earth—simply shaly rock; and the bank was overrun by rabbits. After some time the Spanish Broom began to sow itself. I was encouraged to sow more in spite of the rabbits, and there are now thousands of bushes on this waterless, soil-less bank, and a beautiful bloom comes in midsummer after most of the flowering shrubs are past, the effect being good as far as it can be seen. Our native Broom is a beautiful plant, though it does not make such good covert as the Furze. I have sown large quantities of it with success where rabbits are kept out, but it is more apt to perish from their attacks than the Furze. I have had, on a sandy bluff, bushes 12 feet high, and it is very graceful where it grows here and there in quarries or rough, stony places. The seed is usually very cheap; and it must not be forgotten in any sowings of this sort. The Portuguese (or white) Broom (*C. albus*) is a graceful bush, and comes freely from seed, which should be sown in sandy, warm places early in June. One of my reasons for sowing the seeds of these bushes is the difficulty of transplanting them if not bought very young, and even then they often fail. Besides, there is the expense of transplanting and no end of labour entirely got rid of by bold sowing, and my friends and myself see better effects from this work, simple as it is, than has been got in other ways with many times the expense and labour.

CHAPTER XXV

UNDERWOODS AND WHAT TO DO WITH THEM

In our woodlands nothing was so firmly established as the underwood so often seen in the southern and other parts of the country, an old system, and for many years a profitable one. Underwood so planted and cut every ten years or so gave a good rent, while the 'top' wood which arose among it was cut to profit now and then, the matured trees taken and the growing trees left. But this system is a good one no longer; underwood which once paid from £15 to £25 an acre now only fetches a few pounds, and is often not saleable at any price. In hop-growing districts better prices for useful growths are paid, but, generally, underwood has ceased to pay much more than enough to mend the fences, and its cutting and clearing is often a never-ending labour in woodland work. I often wished, looking at the masses of growth removed in one cutting of underwood, that the strength of it all had gone into tall Ash, Beech, or Oak, sound native timber, instead of stuff so little in demand that the men who buy it often leave much of it on the ground to rot. The question is important for owners with many acres of underwood, poor, thin, worn-out growths not even pretty to look at. Generally we should convert as much as we can of the underwood into trees—slow work, and yet work that must be faced if our woods are ever to be worthy of our land either for profit or beauty.

An example. Some account of what has been done on an estate with much underwood may be of interest. The woods being often on rough ground—slopes and gullies—with Oak, Beech, or Ash standing amidst the underwood, it was difficult to fence against rabbits, as we could have done new plantations of little trees; and so, to avoid the expense of wiring, the plan was adopted of selecting healthy young saplings as tall as could be transplanted with safety (10 to 12 feet high) and planting them at about 12 feet apart among the underwood stools in the more open spaces. As they came from the nursery each bundle of trees was plunged roots and stems up to about one-third of their height in a mixture of adhesive earth and fresh farmyard manure. The dip is good for the roots, and keeps off the rabbits for the first year; some mixture of quassia-juice or other offensive bitter will help in bad cases.

Wind-waving. Wind-waving, almost as great an enemy as rabbits in the case of tall saplings, was stopped in a simple way by *cutting off all the side shoots.* Strong young forest trees 10 feet high so treated showed no sign of 'wind-waving', and grew well the first year. The leading shoot was not cut back, but simply the side shoots which catch the wind; this done before the trees are planted need not be repeated, as the vigorous young saplings soon come to anchor in the earth and are then less liable to wind-waving. *Instead of the heavy labour of staking we made each young tree a stake.*

Native Trees best for Replanting Old Woodland. In selecting trees for this end it is best to choose native trees, and for the most part Oak, Ash, Beech, Chestnut, Poplar, Sycamore, and White Willow. If we go beyond these it should only be for European and North American trees of proved vigour as forest trees. By planting these we have a chance of varying our ordinary woods, and we shall vary the wood best by planting each kind in colonies or masses, the trees intermixing with others on the outside of the masses. The planter should take advantage of every incident of the ground and variety of soil, and plant in accord with them as far as he can—Tree Willows by the streams, Beech on the dry hills, Oak in cool soils. The market value of timber should rarely influence the choice, as a few years often make a marked difference in the value of timber, and the best way is to plant the trees that make best growth in each class of soil. It would be wise in all cases to study the soil, climate, and other conditions that may affect the growth of trees, as some of these conditions are often not found out until we have made costly plantings. Even in our islands there are vital contrasts as regards tree-life— chalk hills and poor, hot sands, stiff wealden clays, wide peat bogs, uplands with a light rainfall and hills and plains with a heavy one. There are hills bare of trees always, and within sight of them hills of the same altitudes thick set with our finest native trees. The best time to plant is as soon as we can after the cutting of the underwood, but as the preparing and clearing of this usually takes the whole of the winter, spring, and summer, we cannot plant until the following autumn, and we do well if we get the trees in before Christmas.

Replanting Woods without Grubbing. This is a good way if we would baffle our animal enemies, as the underwood itself gives a canopy of leaves until the young trees provide their own. But costly as grubbing is, it is worth doing now and then, and in certain places, especially if we plant evergreen trees. These are usually much better for being planted small, and, therefore, not so well fitted to fight their way in underwood. In one case a slip of underwood came quite near the house on the stormy side, and, as its frequent cutting was disfiguring, the piece of rough ground was grubbed and planted with Holly, Cedars of Lebanon, Corsican Pine, Giant Arbor vitae, and the Nootka Cypress, all in free groups. These took well, and in a few years gave shelter and a fine evergreen-grove effect from every point of view, long before those resulting from the ups and downs of the underwood crop. But treating woodland in this way is a costly labour, and only worth facing where there is a real gain in effect from the change from ordinary woodland to the forest evergreen growths.

Renewing Woods from Underwood Growths. If underwood has been well planted, and it is not too old, it is often easy to get a great many young trees from it. In some districts the underwood is mixed, and we find clean saplings of good native trees which will thrive if freed from their neighbours. All underwood should be carefully marked before sale, and every 'teller' worth saving singled out and the number in each piece written down. If this is not done serious loss to the wood often occurs; and even if it is done, in many estates where the woodland is neglected and there is no resident agent or owner to care, the trees may be destroyed, not only the marked 'tellers' being taken by the buyers, but even young Ash and other trees of value. Ash, which planted small is so quickly destroyed by rabbits, may often be saved in carefully cut underwood, young trees soon arising from healthy stubs. Nor should we fear to leave them pretty thick on the ground (6 to 8 feet is not too near), as Ash wood is useful in many states, and thinning should not be done until the trees close together overhead. Even Alder may be left for the sake of its leaf-canopy. If patches of Hazel or Withy are here and there, then replant with stout Oak or Sycamore saplings about 12 feet apart. These trees resist rabbits the best of all that I have tried. Underwood buyers should be carefully watched, and where pieces of underwood are old, of little value, and not great in extent, it is often better not to sell, but to keep every 'teller' that is worth keeping, even as close as 8 to 10 feet apart, as useful thinnings will come in the following years. Small pieces come in as faggots for home use, and there is then no motive for destroying the most valuable part of the wood for that purpose; but excepting what is needed for home use any large cutting of underwoods is a sure loss to the owner. Such tall saplings as are spoken of above must be sought for in nurseries for forest trees, or raised at home; I have planted thousands of them every winter, and have not lost five per cent. from any cause. Any smaller trees will not fight the underwood growth; but these keep up with it and, after some years, begin to meet overhead and soon settle it. In any after cutting of underwood the young trees should be marked by washing them 3 or 4 feet from the base with a mixture of clay and earth and a little lime, so that no mistake need arise as to their cutting, and also it will help to keep off rabbits.

CHAPTER XXVI

NATIVE AND EUROPEAN TREES BEST

If we have eyes for the highest beauty in tree-life, we may find that after looking for it round the world and having gone through all the books and pictures of Californian and other giant trees, we may have to seek for it at home among the trees of Europe and Britain. But we live in a time when the pursuit of things exotic is so active that the value of native trees is often forgotten. We see in books of much show of learning, like Brown's *Forester*, trees named as being fit for forest work in Britain which are not only of no proved value, but even require a greenhouse to live in, like the Norfolk Island Pine. Catalogues, too, nourish the delusion that we must look to other lands for all our good things, and we see men planting many costly and useless trees who never plant native trees. Wretched plantations these costly exotic trees often make, as all may see who watch them for a few years. While with the native tree on a suitable soil there is no going back, with the foreigner all is risk. It is not a matter of hardiness only; a tree may be as hardy as the Spruce on the mountains of Central Europe, and yet do poorly in Southern England. The native tree is ready to respond to every impulse of the season, is happy with our rainfall—often a slight one in some districts—and, given the soil right for it, soon makes in growth an end of all the pretensions of exotic rivals. Soil and right situation every tree must have; the rock from which springs the column of the Pine will do nothing for the Oak, and any tree, native or exotic, is profitless and often ugly on ground it does not thrive on.

Wood value. For quality and value of wood the native tree is by far the best. Nothing else that can be done with the land that suits our native Oak will pay so well with so little labour. The natural Beech woods of Normandy and Britain are among those that more than repay the owners. No foreign tree we grow, except the Larch (now stricken in many districts by a disease which threatens to make it useless for us), equals in value the wood of our Oak, Ash, and Tree Willows. The facility of increase of our native trees should also be thought of; and it is clear from what we may see in a neglected field that the wealden land in Kent or Sussex would soon be a forest of Oak if let alone. If we plant Pines in an arable field that has been under the plough for years, we shall probably find Ash, Oak, and Birch, sown by squirrels, mice, or winds, starting up here and there and keeping pace with the quickest growing Pines. But it is not only the value as timber of our native trees I wish to show, it is their beauty; no trees introduced from other countries equal in that our native ones, with the exception of the Cedar of Lebanon. In many districts there are no natural old woods where our native trees can be seen in their forest forms; but the beauty exists for all who care to see it, and in many ways. What various forms the Oak assumes in chase, or park, or wood, and, perhaps most impressively in old Oak woods, where the trees stand tall and close. The tree varies in different countries; such stately Oaks as we may see by the roadside in Warwickshire we never see south of London, where there are many Oaks in many forms. So, too, the Beech, a true northern tree in its vigour; how fine it is in many conditions—on chalky hills and also in the level land, whether in Surrey or on the Lothians. It is more precious than the Oak in one way, that we get it in a fine state over such vast areas, trees in Denmark being as fine as those in Northern Greece. The Ash—

one of our best timber trees—is often fine in form in old states. There is a whole string of Elms and their varieties in catalogues, but by far the best is our native Wych, or Mountain, Elm; a noble tree in beauty and dignity, attaining sometimes a girth of trunk nearly, or quite, 50 feet and a height of 120 feet. Our native Poplars are often neglected, the Abele and Grey Poplars being stately trees, and the wood more valuable than it used to be. Among Pines, we have none which surpasses our native Fir in form and colour; when old, valuable, too, for timber. The field Maple is a neglected tree, but beautiful trees of it can be seen here and there in woods, as at Mereworth and Brede. The Sycamore Maple is fine in form, as we may see at Knole and other places. It is supposed to be a naturalized rather than a native tree, but over a large area of the coldest parts of Europe no tree surpasses it in vigour and rapidity of increase. It is storm resisting, thrives near the sea, as in Anglesey, and is altogether one of the best trees for planting.

Tree Willows. The Tree Willows of Britain have value as timber, but are neglected by planters even of gardens, though none of the variegated rubbish of the nursery gives anything like so good an effect as the white, red, and yellow Willows in winter or summer. The common Lime is not a native of Britain, but two other kinds (*Tilia cordata* and *T. platyphyllos*) belong to our native flora. The Hornbeam is a true native, neglected by planters, though common in some old woods. The Yew should never be forgotten in woodland, where its shelter for game is welcome. It is too much planted near houses, to the danger of animals and to the loss of all good flower-gardening, owing to its roots. The Holly, usually in gardens a shrub, is on the hills and in land that it likes a tree 40 feet high, and therefore never to be omitted in seeking evergreen effects.

Trees for beauty. Trees of secondary value as timber are often of great value for their beauty, and should never be forgotten by planters. Thus Crab, Hawthorn, Aspen, White Beam, Wild Cherry, Bird Cherry (often a fine tree, as at Longleat), Mountain Ash, Wild Pear (the Pear in good deep soil, as in Worcestershire, is a forest tree, and a very fine one), and the Wild Service Tree with its finely coloured foliage in autumn, though rarely planted and only here and there seen so well as at Blackdown. The Crab is as handsome as any flowering tree; the Alder gives us good colour by the streams in spring. The Mountain Ash, or Rowan, is really deserving the epithet splendid when it is grouped on the hills, or almost anywhere else; but it is beloved by the rabbit, and many I have planted in the hope of adding its fine colour in autumn to old woodland have been all gnawed round and destroyed. On rocky ground it is lovely, where it takes various dwarf forms. The White Beam is an effective tree at various seasons and well deserves to be made more of, as also its varieties or hybrids (like *P. latifolia*). Some of the trees which we admire individually are not so often seen grouped, though there is nothing more beautiful than a free group of Aspens on a limestone soil in autumn. Birch, too, which we often see in the north of Germany, with the white stems rising like silver columns all round, might be more often effectively grouped. Nor is any introduced tree so fine in form when grouped as the Ash, as one often sees it round a farmhouse on the hills or in the North.

In all the changes of fashion as to trees there never was one in which people were so carried away as by planting the giant conifers of Mexico and California, nor one in which failure has been so complete. And we have not only to suffer the loss of these trees, but there is the penalty of our neglecting the trees of the forest plain, from Oaks to Maples, which are far more suited for a lowland country than the conifers of those lovely mountains fanned by Pacific Ocean breezes. Similarity of climate is what we should always remember, and the more like the climate of our own country, the more certain success will be. The region of the Corsican Pine, and that of the Cedars of North Africa, is so high in altitude that it has somewhat the same conditions of climate as our own country, the proof being that we see our own hardy wild flowers and shrubs growing there. Our aim should be not the increase of species, but making good and artistic use of those that not only endure but thrive in our climate. Hardiness is only one of the conditions, as the hardiest trees may fail.

CHAPTER XXVII

OF MIXED WOODS

IN countries where forestry is best practised there is much evidence of the utility of having woods formed of trees of different kinds, ages, and times of cutting. The reasons are many, but perhaps the most serious are the following: When we plant a tree like the Larch, putting them in solid masses of the same age, any disease that comes to the tree is much more likely to sweep through the wood than it would be if trees of various kinds were intermixed. Wind, often a destroyer of trees, is far less severe in the mixed wood, not only because some of the kinds are wind-resisting, but also because the different ages and heights of the trees help to break its force. Mixed planting is more likely to lead to a better annual output, as the roots of mixed trees get more out of the ground than a wood of one kind of tree only. It also allows us to associate light-seeking trees, like the Pines, with others, like the Beech, that do well below them. It commits us to no monotonous or regular mixture, for it allows of varying the wood in a way that is good for it, either for effect or growth, and of adapting the tree to the soil. A boggy spot we may plant with Willows; a rocky knoll, with wind-resisting Beech; a wet stretch near a stream, with Spruce.

We may see in the forest-clad mountains of the Tyrol how often trees grow naturally together— Larch, Scotch Fir, and Norway Spruce. Where the conditions suit a given kind completely we see it prevail, but there are many other conditions in which several kinds of trees grow equally well— groups of Larch among colonies of Scotch or Norway Spruce—also single trees of each kind scattered here and there with a sprinkling of Birch and Beech, until the ground rises so high that the trees of the Pine tribe clothe the rocks. Why should we not more often follow this way, by which vast and steep mountain ranges are clothed in some of the most picturesque forest regions of the world?

Mixed planting. Mixed planting is, in many conditions, the most profitable. It is the way, too, that best aids us to adapt the soil to the tree; all the more so in broken ground, or the many places where we find striking differences of soil in a small area. To take an example from a few acres of ground I have lately dealt with, we have a wet piece of ground near a stream, where there is a good chance for the Norway Spruce, which so often starves in dry soil, and above this wet ground there is a nearly level bed of stiff soil, which grows Oak of the best quality with a few Ash among it. Above the level Oak bed there are some acres of a shaly soil, on which the Oak starves; so the stunted Oaks are cleared, to plant with Larch and Scotch and Silver Fir; and these conditions occur in a wood of about twelve acres. It is not intended that any hard lines should be drawn between any of the trees, but that the kinds shall 'run into each other', as they so often do in natural forests where the soil or altitude changes.

In forming mixed woods the fine vigour of our native trees may often aid us by their persistent way of coming from seed where we least expect them. If, in a woodland district, we plant an arable field with Pines of various kinds, we shall often find vigorous Oak, Ash, and Birch seedlings keeping company with the young Pines which had the start of them by a few years. Mice, birds, and other natural agents carry the seed, and instead of cutting out the young and often healthy saplings, it is better to leave them to vary the wood.

Mixed planting by no means confines us to a fixed rule, but, on the contrary, enables us to take best advantage of the natural variations of soil and aspect. We might, in varied soils, enjoy the effect of one tree, passing gradually into mixed masses of evergreen and hardwood trees. The trees being of different ages and cut at different times, the wood would never at any time be shorn of its vigorous and constant forest growth. And this plan would be in no way against beautiful planting, as where it is in use there are not only many instances of good tree growth from surfaces absolutely valueless for any other purpose, but examples without end of tree grouping as an effective aid to landscape beauty.

CHAPTER XXVIII

UNDERPLANTING

In the present state of our woodlands, when through the decay of the trade in underwood and the neglect of the trees many woods are thin and worn out, 'underplanting' is a subject to be thought about. Pines, that in youth might have covered the earth with their branches, have grown and shed most of their boughs, and grass has begun to invade the ground, bringing in its train starvation or death to the trees, the sun and drying winds completing the ruin of the unsheltered woodland. Now this cannot happen if a wood is managed in the best forest way, which never allows the overhead canopy to be broken. The thin, scraggy plantations, so common by British roadsides and fields, are more open to the attacks of sun and drying winds than the broad, natural woodlands in the best planted counties and estates. The remedy for the stale woodland is 'underplanting'. That means, when woods get thin or scraggy from any cause, the introducing of young trees, usually of other kinds and what are called 'shade bearers'. In replanting old woodlands we must choose trees which will thrive in partial shade; and as in old woodland it is difficult to protect young trees from rabbits, we must, if we can, choose those that are not so loved of that pest. Where the nakedness of the wood occurs in large patches we can plant and wire, but in large woodland areas we must plant the young trees singly among the older trees, and hence the necessity for choosing kinds that will thrive in partial shade. Among the summer-leafing trees the best for underplanting is the Beech, of which in certain forests of the north of Europe trees of 50 to 60 feet may be seen thriving under Pines nearly 100 feet high, and both close set. Inter-action of the roots of trees of different kinds is rather beneficial than otherwise. After the Beech may be named the Hornbeam, Oak, Ash, and, on sandy or rocky soils, the Chestnut—(not the Horse Chestnut, which is not a Chestnut at all). Most of the trees named—except the Ash—are not very subject to the attacks of rabbits, and they also bear planting as saplings of 6 to 8 feet or even more, though beyond that size it is risky. In all cases we must avoid trees too old for transplanting. We cannot with success plant Pines of large size, but with a little care in buying from forest nurseries we can get tall saplings of the summer-leafing trees that will grow well.

Among Firs the best for underplanting is the Silver Fir, which may often be seen in the German forests growing well under the other trees, all closely set. Spruce, in wet land, is also good; and in our southern and western country the Douglas Fir is excellent and soon gets its head up among the other trees, the shelter of which is a help to it at first.

The effect of underplanting in the best cases is good, and woods treated in this way can be very beautiful, varied, and full of life; but in order to enjoy such woods well-considered rides should be made through them, so that they may be airy and accessible in all weathers.

CHAPTER XXIX

FORMING WOODLAND RIDES

GOOD rides through woods are necessary for shooting, for the clearing of the woods, driving, hunting, and the pleasure of riding or walking in them, and they are often best dealt with in replanting worn-out underwoods. The older and more picturesque the woodland, the easier the task of making rides pleasant to the eye as well as right for use, though it is not unusual to see many woods without rides of any value. It is easy to improve them by making them a little more open, and cutting away here and there to bring good groups of trees into view, or any helpful incident, such as a gully of Ferns. Native plants are often beautiful in masses near rides, and their effect seen in any clear way in shade is as good as could be given by any exotic plants. These are among the right places to have beautiful native plants, such as Solomon's Seal, Lily of the Valley, and Willow Herb, and also many of our hardy Ferns, in moist spots, such as the Royal Fern. Groups of neglected native shrubs might also be planted here and there, and native trees such as the Aspen and Field Maple, not often planted in the usual mixtures. In warm and sea-shore districts not subject to severe frosts we may have groups of Pampas Grass, New Zealand Flax, and hardy Bamboo here and there, though generally it is better to trust to good native things even in such districts. If we go beyond these, let us take care that the shrubs are as hardy as any of our own; it is easy to find such among the hardy Azaleas and Rhododendrons and the beautiful Mountain Laurel (*Kalmia*), where the soil is not against us.

Woodland rides should be not less than 18 feet wide, and it would be no loss from a shooting or other point of view to make them a few feet wider, and if a ditch be made on either side it ought to be in addition to the 18 feet. The surface should be Grass, Moss, dwarf Heather, Thymy turf, brown leaves, according to soil and elevation and other conditions. A reason for this is that such surfaces drink up and keep for their own use the rainfall, which if it fell on bare surfaces might turn our rides and paths into watercourses. In very hilly ground we may have to cut rides out of the hill-side, of shale or rough gravel, sand, or peat. In these conditions or on any surface where we cannot find a protecting carpet of vegetation of any kind we shall have to form little ducts aslant the walk to carry off the storm-water. Woodland drives should want no care beyond the annual 'fagging' which the gamekeepers do to remove Briers and all interloping rank growth before shooting begins. But in woods near the house, it may be worth while to rough mow the rides now and then.

Sunny Spots in Woods. Shade is one of the charms of the woods in summer; but where the shade is too great for any of our plants or bushes, we have our chance for sun-loving things in glades or open spaces, so often seen in natural forests. These are to be sought for the sake of various things—game, sun, light and shade, and the variety of tree form which is often seen around such openings. The floor of these glades may be of turf, Fern, Ivy, or any mixed plants of the woods, and they are also good places for evergreen or other covert, e.g. Savin, dwarf Mountain Pine, Partridge Berry, Heaths, either Cornish Heath or the more vigorous forms of Heather and, if we can spare them, brilliant bushes like Azaleas. Bushes needing sun and warmth might be grouped in such spots, and in districts where the cold does not strike hard, as in a great length of the shore-lands of our islands, other exotics might be tried. But they should be chosen with care, and only for some distinct quality. The incidents of the wood itself will often offer the best places for our sunny spots, and there might be small openings, too, in shade, suggested often by wood-plants like Gerard's well-named Stubwort (*Oxalis*) and Primroses. As trees take the place of underwood there is more need for woodland sun-spots, and also for more open and airy rides, avoiding always the too common way of thinning so that each tree stands singly, a harmful though well-established British practice, and against all profit or other good from woodland.

Without planting choice shrubs, we may by studying carefully the lines of easiest access and grading in hilly districts, and the convenience of the varied labours or pleasures of the woodland, often gain a very beautiful result. I have made several miles of rides during the past winter, and no labour has ever given me greater pleasure in the result. Where the ground is level the work consists of merely taking out old and often worn-out stubs. Where it is sloping it is a little more laborious, but even then not difficult. Where the woods have been a little neglected and are rather worn-out, it is often easy to get a good line where the ground is bare of trees and thus avoid felling timber. Sometimes I crept under a great group of Oaks or Beech trees for the beauty of their fine stems, and got a better effect than if I had avoided them, besides using ground where nothing else would grow. In some cases the result was so striking that parts of the woods, before unnoticed, became picturesque even in the eyes of artists; the airy foreground and the fine view along the clearances giving good pictures when the trees happen to come in the right way. Where there is much disturbance of the ground I sow mixed grass seeds as soon as possible afterwards, mainly in April, but also in the summer and autumn. As to game, the airy rides are a distinct improvement in every way, creatures of all sorts getting a chance to air and sun themselves in the clearances. The gamekeepers like it much better, and the timber surveyor tells me that he always finds the best trees near the open rides.

Woodland Shade. It is said by many who have lived under warmer skies than ours, that hot weather in Britain is more oppressive than in countries where the temperature is often much higher; and this is one reason why we should pay more attention to shaded rides and airy shade under trees. In a large area of country in the home counties many woodlands are wholly without airy and picturesque access, except for narrow rides closed up every year with briers and underwood.

Airy Rides. In olden times, when underwood was valuable, people begrudged the space to form airy rides, but this reason no longer holds. Making such rides in no way lessens the value of the wood, because every inch of the ground is occupied by the roots of the adjacent trees, and timber surveyors know that the best timber trees often grow near rides. If we can make rides beneath good old trees or groves all the better, as beneath such trees the undergrowth lessens, and the clearance is easier. By all such rides the lower boughs of the trees should be removed for the sake of showing the wood and stems; such branches are usually without value to the tree in its forest state. Nearer the house there is a way to get pleasant shade and air by removing the lower branches of trees, which are often a nuisance in preventing air and movement. In the case of fine old trees, the tree itself is very often trying to get rid of its lower boughs, and yet we often see them impeding all progress about the lawns. Where there are good rides through old mixed or evergreen woods it is important not to let the undergrowth close in on each side, as it is very apt to do.

No clipping back. It is difficult to give an idea of the difference in the effect of such a ride when light and shade are let into it, and when, as is commonly the case, Yew, Box, and other things are clipped back to hard walls, good views, fine trees, and groups being all shut out. It is better not to clip in such cases, but always to work back to a good tree or group, and so get room for the air to move, the shade of the trees above being sufficient in each case. The pleasure of driving or walking is much greater when the air is moving, and when one can see into the wood on each side and perhaps beautiful views into the country beyond.

CHAPTER XXX

WASTE IN PLANTING

EVERYTHING which tends to simplify planting is a gain in all ways, and much of the work given to it is needless and wasteful, particularly trenching and draining, two costly labours. I live in a cool country with a wet soil, and never drain for any kind of planting in woods, but adapt the trees to the soil, which is the true way. There are trees, American and European, that will almost stand in water and be none the worse for it.

Another costly and, I think, needless labour is trenching. I have young woods of Pine planted in arable fields not of specially good soil, which people say they have never seen surpassed in vigour and beauty for their age, yet the ground for them was neither trenched nor dug. The poor hill-lands that are now recognized as worth planting seldom need draining, as they are often uplands and naturally drained. One of the pleas for planting such lands is that it arrests denudation and conserves the moisture and fertility of the soil. And even where the soil is too wet much can be done to drain it by a good choice of kinds. The Poplar, Willow, and Spruce, if planted thickly enough, prove very good drainers.

Draining. In certain cases, owing to a low uniformity of surface, draining may be needed, but in forest work generally it is needless. Even in heavy soils I avoid draining. Light sandy soils, and hill soils generally, seldom or never need draining, except when they lie upon a hard pan, such as is here and there found in peaty districts, and where the water stands, however light the rainfall may be. Where the surface soil in such cases is not deep, and an outfall can be found—not an easy matter on level tracts—the surface water can be led off by open drains, but when the peat is deep the water will not subside below the drain levels. Some of the best German foresters hold that in many soils the best system is that of planting trees of different ages, different kinds, and different times of cutting, and grouping the trees according to soil and situation, and that this way helps one to avoid the heavy costs of draining and trenching. It is certainly a better way than the level mixture of trees we so often see, and which has to adapt itself to all conditions. The grouping and massing way also leads to beauty, as by its means we keep and accentuate any varied incidents of the surface. Planting Austrian Larch, Scotch Fir, and Beech on the drier ground, Spruce, Sitka Spruce, and Douglas Fir in the sheltered and moist hollows, Oak, Ash, Sycamore, and Elm on the cool ground, and Poplar, Willow, and Alder wherever the soil is deep and moist, is a better plan than the mixing of kinds together on the same spot, no two of which are alike in their wants.

Trenching. Trenching does not add to the staple of poor soils such as are generally planted with forest trees, useful though it may be in rich garden ground, where a rank, quick growth is sought. Even if we can face the great cost of trenching, the labour is not always to be had. I have seen a countryside denuded of labourers in order to trench ground for planting, and the result no better than could have been got by a plough run through the land, or even if the trees had been planted in the sod. One of the best things about a wood is that it finds its own soil, and if we plant closely and well, and choose the right trees, it very soon begins to do this as many of the finest natural woods have done it for ages. Woods planted a dozen years will be found to have a good deposit of leaf-soil—this is in cases where the tree suits the ground and where the young trees are thick enough. In the open, loose way of planting we may look in vain for any such deposit, as the grass absorbs it all. The effect of a heavy fall of leaf-soil from the lower branches of Pine and other trees is that, in hot and dry seasons, when farmers and gardeners are at their wits' end to get water, the wood is cool and safe.

Trees as Soil-makers. To the pleasure-ground planter these ideas will seem folly; he considers all such costly work as drainage and trenching essential to the success of his shrubbery. From his point of view, which is to get a rapid growth in the rampant growers that he usually plants, this may be desirable; but where is the shrubbery that can show as good a growth as many a woodland or forest? It does not exist. Pursuing the same ideas, we wish now to show how well trees will often grow in abandoned scoriae, mine-rubbish, and other hopeless and ugly earth surfaces. My first lesson in this way was in the foot-hills of California, where goldseekers had washed away the whole surface for over 20 feet in depth, and I saw vigorous young Pines growing out of the bare surface. But the planter of such surfaces must look a little to kinds and their habits as well as to soil. In the planting of lands of no 'quality' or poor situation the kind of tree is important, as each has its preferences, and though many hardy trees will grow in almost any situation, it by no means follows that we get good timber from them. Oak, Ash, and nearly every hardwood tree will grow almost anywhere, but not always be worth cutting. Oak is much affected by the quality of the land, and, even where it grows rapidly, is often not as good timber as that grown less vigorously. Spruce on a wet western hillside will make growth such as we never see in Southern Britain, and our quick-grown Scotch Fir is never so valuable for timber as the same tree from the poor mountains of Western Europe. Rainfall also has much effect on trees, and also elevated situations; in such we might venture to plant trees which would be started too early by the milder climate of the south. In the wood we need no manure cart, and in the hottest years the trees maintain their freshness. Vast areas of European mountains are covered with Pines, although there is scarcely a trace of soil over the ribs of the mountain. Those who are now seeking to plant with a garland of trees the hideous refuse heaps of the Black Country are right in their efforts; however poor the land may be when the trees are first planted, the annual layer of fallen leaves soon forms a deposit of mould, between which and the natural soil the roots of the trees are always found in great numbers. The older the wood the deeper the leaf-soil: in old Beech and other forests it is extraordinary to what an extent this leaf-mould has accumulated. If it were not for it, generation after generation of the same tree could not have succeeded each other on the same ground. Mountains which unplanted would have been almost bared to the rock by constant denudation, have a deep covering of leaf-mould; the same may be said of Fir and Spruce woods, in which the fallen Pine-needles have formed a bed of black mould. Tree crops manure themselves and enrich the ground on which they grow, a fact that should never be lost sight of in considering the planting of poor lands.

CHAPTER XXXI

FENCING FOR WOODLAND

An immense amount of energy in our country is devoted to fencing, which is wholly avoided in some other lands. Our way of keeping stock in the open air instead of in sheds, and the abundance of game destructive to young trees, makes fencing a necessity, and to simplify it as far as may be and to make it enduring is worth thinking about. Many act as if the iron and wire fences were the best—a serious error, as the wood should fence itself, and there are no fencing plants so good as those which grow naturally in woodland, such as Quick. The worst of all are iron and wire fences, which give no shelter, and moreover are ugly and dangerous.

To reduce the extent of fencing. This is one of the motives which should lead us to plant in more visible and natural masses. In the common ring, specimen, and spinney planting there is often more fence visible than plants. No artificial fence that man can invent is half as simple, enduring, easy to keep up, or effective as a Quick hedge set on a turf bank. The cost of this should be less than that of an iron fence. Even in badly-infested places, when we are obliged to use an iron fence to support barbed wire, we should always plant a Quick fence inside it to provide for the future fencing of the wood. The weak point about the Quick fence is that the plants are usually so small that it is expensive to protect them. In many places it would be an excellent way to lay down an acre of Quick and let the plants get into a bushy state, and then we should only have to send the cart for stout bushes, which would at once form a fence. I know nothing in woodland work that would be more useful than such a store of Quick. We can buy small Quick everywhere, but it is difficult to get it really strong, and impossible to get the bushes a yard high and nearly as much through, unless we grow it ourselves.

Some years ago I made a fence with old bushy Quick, planting it on the turf bank common in the district; the tough bushes were placed close together and formed a fence at once, but as there were large bullocks nearly always in the pasture on one side, it was thought best to slip a single line of the slender and waste tops from a Larch plantation through the bushes at 2 feet from the ground. The fence made itself at once, and no bullock ever got through or injured it. The expense of fencing the Quick itself was wholly got rid of; an important point if we think of the trouble saved in this way. But to carry out this plan it is essential to put out young Quick and let them grow 3 feet or more high, and the stouter the better. They transplant easily and without risk at any time in autumn or winter.

Simplify the fencing. In planting rough corners of fields running into or near a wood we may often simplify the fencing by taking a short or easy line, so that the fences within the line become useless, and if among these useless fences there is one of Quick which is not very old, it is often well to move the plants to the new fence after cutting them down one-half their height. Having had occasion to move a bank and fence of not very old Quick, I levelled the bank and took the plants elsewhere for fencing. The following year the roots of the Quick left in the ground began to come up and make nice little plants, and in another year there was quite a strong line of Quick in the line of the old fence.

The best plants to use. There has been much talk of the Cherry Plum as a fence plant, but it is inferior to Quick in endurance, and in every way. I have much greater faith in some of the American Hawthorns, such as the Scarlet and Cockspur Thorns, which are well armed, tough, sturdy, and fine in colour in autumn. The difficulty is to get a stock of them, as nurserymen are not yet aware of their value, and they are mostly grown for pleasure grounds, and grafted, which means that the native Quick will in time kill the foreigner. I have used some thousands of the Sweet Brier for fencing, and with excellent effect. In one way it is better than Quick, as cattle will not touch it, and creatures of any kind give it a wide berth. A rough woodland fence made of Sweet Brier and Quick, or Cockspur Thorn, is the best possible protection against stock. Barbed wire is not half as fierce as old Sweet Brier, which is impassable to the boldest boy, who would laugh at the idea of barbed wire stopping him.

Let the woodland fence grow freely, and only cut it down every ten years or so; such bold fences are far better in their effect round the woodland than small trim fences, while they may be more effective against stock, and are often as pretty as any garden with wreaths of Honeysuckle, Clematis, and Wild Rose.

Woods without fencing. The needlessness of any kind of fencing in established woodlands is proved by the millions of acres of forest in many parts of Middle and Northern Europe, on mountain or plain, which are without fence of any kind, young or old trees as they come, boldly fringing river, rocky valley, or plain. No stiff or hard lines anywhere; the wood gracing the near land as the clouds grace the sky, while far away the hills massed and crested with Pines show, fold beyond fold, back into the delicate distance, in fine harmony in all lights, but loveliest when the sun bids the woods good-night in a sea of golden-purple air. If it be well to be free of living fences of Wild Rose, May, and Holly, how much more the costly iron or wire fence, so ugly in any place where we seek beauty of wood or landscape? This freedom from the ceaseless care and cost of fences is not only for those who plant for beauty, but the men who look to their woods for profit only in doing their work in the simplest way find the palm of beauty too. But this cannot be where the underwood plan is a never-ending nuisance, and the cutting up of woods and rides, the underwood when cut in recent years remaining in the woods for more than a year after the cutting—a nuisance for various reasons. If we wish to preserve some underwood it is easy to keep it near the centre of the wood, and so dispense with fencing from cattle, or we may even grow it as at present without sacrificing all our woodland scenery and any hope of profit from woodland. Our way in Britain of planting in skinny strips, instead of massing the wood naturally, very much adds to the cost and ugliness of the iron fence, both sides of the narrow strip being often fenced with iron, and on some estates the money spent on this rubbish of iron and wire would suffice to plant all the poor land of a parish.

No hard line. These words are written in a grassy glade of about a dozen acres set in the woods of the Bohemian hills. Falling gently to the west it is embosomed in close-set young trees—Spruce, Birch, Scotch and Silver Fir; there is no hard line to be seen; the glade is fringed as it might be in a natural forest. It is as easy to mow as it would be if fenced in the stiffest way, and it could be grazed without danger, as there is no underwood near. The work of the woodman around the glade (and there is a good deal of winter work in woods where tall trees are set close) is far more simple than where, as in many parts of Britain, access to every copse and wood is barred with fencing. For days we pass through such woodland and never see a fence, and when we leave the massed mountain woods, and go into the open plain, with smaller woods here and there, cresting a hill or making the best of a vein of poor land, it is just the same; there is no fence; cattle or men may take shelter or shade; and as the margin of the plantation is often free and varied, the effect is far better than when the wood is held tight with a fence. Certainly many of these are old woods; and when planting in an open country, with cattle grazing on all sides, we cannot hope to get free at once from a great evil; but if we plant only vigorous trees, a few years' good growth will make them safe, and tall trees do not tempt cattle as the shoots of the underwood do. If there be grazing creatures about, why should not the cool shade of the wood be free to them on hot days and its warm shelter on wintry ones if no harm come from it?

What to do with iron fencing. When our eyes are opened to the ugliness and danger of iron fencing, the question arises as to how it can be turned to account in other ways. The danger of wire fencing round pasture fields is evident, and its ugliness appalling in the foreground of fair landscapes. Live fences do away with the need of it in either case, but as there are miles of it in most districts to be got rid of, the best use for it is the protection of young plantations in woods. Most of our country is so infested with ground game that planting is impossible unless we protect the little trees. It is bad enough to lose Scotch Fir, Larch, and the commoner trees, after having had the trouble and cost of planting them, but when it is a question of the rarer trees, often difficult to procure, then we ought to protect thoroughly until they are large enough to take care of themselves. For common trees we may do what is needed with wire only, but there is the danger that with heavy snow it may be jumped by rabbits (or broken down by stock, gamekeepers, and others) and so fail us at a critical time. In choice planting the best way is to surround our plantations with spare iron fencing, and then wire. The most difficult spots to plant are patches in old woods, often of underwood which has ceased to be of any use. Planting choice little trees in such woods is out of the question, so I have fenced with iron an acre of such woodland which had nothing left in it but stubs and a few Birch and other trees of little value. The iron fence is wired $3\frac{1}{2}$ feet high, and within is a plantation of the Western Hemlock Spruce (*Abies Mertensiana*) and with it a sprinkling of Japanese Larch. This iron fencing is so placed as to be hardly visible from the rides near, and it is always safe against animals and other interlopers.

CHAPTER XXXII

ENGLISH NAMES FOR TREES

LORD ANNESLEY's lately published book on his collection of trees and shrubs presents us, as so many books have done, with a whole set of Latin names for each tree, no care being taken to find a good English name for any of them, not a difficult task. This is merely following the conventional way of botanists, who imagine that all men take the same interest in Latin names and synonyms as they do themselves. The facts are the other way. The majority of (even educated) people are interested solely in the beauty and the uses of things, and to them names in an unknown tongue are of no meaning and a source of ridicule. These names may even be used in such a way as to be a bar to knowledge, as is certainly the case in our country. In France and Germany it is otherwise, as their best books on garden and woodland work give the native name of each tree or plant, which, however, does not preclude the use of the Latin name in its right place. Names are artificial symbols merely adopted for convenience, and of far less importance than the things to which they relate, as is shown by the fact that many people forget names altogether, while retaining a clear memory of things. The multitude of Latin names is an unnecessary obstacle to women and children, and those occupied with outdoor work. On the other hand, good English names often tell a great deal to simple people, e.g. such names as Servian Spruce and Lebanon Cedar at once convey their own meaning. There is no more of science in the use of one language than of another. The Latin names are often hideous in structure, and often (so scholars tell us) invented by those whose learning is at fault. There are also numberless false names like *Glyptostrobus* and *Retinospora*—the unfortunate name for the Great Japanese Cypress (*C. obtusa*) which is still kept up in books and lists. If the true Latin names are confusing, how much more the false and needless ones. Then there is the endless multiplication of varieties with cumbrous Latin names, of which we see an outrageous example in the Kew List of Conifers, pages of which are given to variegated (i.e. diseased) and deformed sports, which are mere garden forms, valueless as trees. If these varieties are kept at all, they are quite unworthy of Latin names. Another evil resulting from this is that the general readers of catalogues and lists take all Latin names as equally important, until, even in the best conditions for growing trees, we see distorted and poor forms as often as the true trees, and a spotty and bad effect is given to collections, the very opposite of what growers of great trees should expect, and may easily obtain.

A good English name should have precedence of all others for general use. Trees covering vast regions and of great importance, like the Western Hemlock Spruce, deserve to be known by English names, which yet are the oftenest omitted in books and catalogues dealing with such trees. An Englishman, speaking to English people, should be able to find in his own tongue names for all things to which he needs to refer. As the Latin names are altered every decade or oftener (Mr. Sargent has now a new Latin name for the Western Hemlock Spruce) there is no keeping pace with them. There is no forest tree of Europe, Asia, or America for which a good English name might not be used, and, once generally adopted, we should not then care so much what each succeeding botanist might do towards inventing new Latin names or hunting up old ones.

INDEX

Abies amabilis, 324.
— concolor, 322.
— grandis, 319.
— nobilis, 319.
— Nordmanniana, 320.
— Parsonsiana, 323.
— sitchensis, 317.
Alleys, climber-covered, around play-lawns, 277.
— plashed, 83.
Alpine plants in groups, 102.
— rock, and wall gardens, 86.
Alton Towers, 2.
Arbor-vitae, the Giant, 318.
Arches over walks, light, 81.
Architecture and flower gardening, 36.
'Art and craft of garden making,' the, 12.
— talk of the day about, 18.
— the greatest and fairest things are done by nature, the lesser by, 19.
Artistic, the term, 21.
Artists in planting, 21.

Bamboo, Japanese, the, 333.
— palmate, 332.
Bambusa Metake, 333.
— palmata, 332.
Barberry, Evergreen, the, 329.
Batsford Park, 214.
Battersea Park, 208.

Beauty of form, 214.
— in the garden, 207.
Bedding-out, 26.
Berberis aquifolium, 329.
Berkeley, 40.
Bicton, 254.
Blair Athol, 28.
Bog and Water Gardens, Marsh, 316.
Border, flower, in the fruit or kitchen garden, 161.
Borders by grass walks in shade and sun, 158.
— flower, against walls and houses, 160.
— — to Shrubberies, 155.
— of hardy flowers, 150.
— — —, cost and endurance of, 150.
— — —, evergreen, 163.
Bristol House, 40.
Broom and Furze, 57, 144.
Bulwick, 234.

Camellia as a garden shrub, 68.
Carpet-bedding, 26.
— beds things of our own day, patterns of flowers and, 3.
Castle Ashby, 16.
— Howard, 2.
Cedar, Atlas, 314.
— Canoe, 316.

Cedar of Lebanon, 314.
— Red, the, 320.
Champs-Elysées, 48.
Chatsworth, 2, 18, 40.
Cherbuliez, M. Victor, 43.
Choice essential, 23.
Climber-covered alleys around play-lawns, 277.
Climbers and their artistic use, 72.
— annual and herbaceous, 82.
— evergreens as, 84.
— fragile, on shrubs, 76.
— of classic beauty and rarity, 75.
— on orchard trees, 274.
— — trees, vigorous, 74.
— Roses as, 77.
— trees supporting, 81.
Clipping back, no, 369.
Colour in the Rock Garden, 108.
Corot, 23.
Covert, evergreen, 327.
— from seed, 337.
— plant, a beautiful, 333.
Crewe Hall, 2.
Crome, 23.
Crystal Palace, 2, 18, 28, 30, 37, 38.
Cupressus Lawsoniana, 315.
— obtusa, 316.
Cypress, Great Japanese, 316.
— Lawsons, 315.

Design, garden, and recent writings upon it, 1.
— — Art in relation to flower-gardening and, 21.
— — Waterworks, 17.

Design in planting trees, 310.
— not formal only, 38.
Draining, 371.
Drayton, 2, 38.
Dulwich Park, 101.

Evergreens as climbers, 84.
— flowering, 55.
Evolution, 19.

Fencing for Woodland, 376.
— Iron, what to do with it, 382.
— simplify the, 378.
— to reduce the extent of, 376.
— Woods without, 379.
Fir, Cascade Mountains, 324.
— Columbian, 319.
— Crimean, 320.
— Douglas, 317.
— Puget Sound, 319.
— Silver, 318.
— White, 322.
Fisher, Mr. Mark, 29.
Flower border in fruit or kitchen garden, 161.
— borders against walls and houses, 160.
— — to Shrubberies, 155.
— garden, fine turf in and near the, 281.
— — in Autumn, 182.
— — — the house, 229.
— — — Winter, 193.
— — Rose to come back to the, 17.
— — shelter and wind screens in and near the, 250.
— — the true test of a, 11.

INDEX

Flower garden, Wild garden does not take the place of the, 5.
Flowers and carpet beds things of our day, patterns of, 3.
— annual, that bloom in the Spring, 141.
— degradation of, 25.
— hardy, borders of, 150.
— — — cost and endurance of, 160.
— — — evergreen, 163.
— Japanese ways of arranging, 233.
— of fruit trees, 267.
— Spring, 126.
— — in sun and shade and north and south aspects, 148.
Formal garden in Scotland, 7.
— — Percy Bysshe Shelley on the, 7.
— — Robert Southey on the, 8.
— — Victor Hugo on the, 8.
Fragrance, 222.
Fruit or kitchen garden, flower border in the, 161.
— trees, covered ways of, 83.
— — flowers of, 267.
— — kinds to plant, 266.
Fuel, 287.
Furze, Broom and, 57, 144.

Garden at Kensington, The R. H. S., 2.
— beauty of form in the, 207.
— design and recent writings upon it, 1.
— — art in relation to flower-gardening and, 21.
— — Waterworks, 17.

Garden, flower, fine turf in and near the, 281.
— — in Autumn, 182.
— — — the house, 229.
— — — Winter, 193.
— — the true test of a, 11.
— — Rose to come back to the, 171.
— — shelter and wind screens in and near the, 250.
— formal, in Scotland, 7.
— — Percy Bysshe Shelley on the, 7.
— — Robert Southey on the, 8.
— — Victor Hugo on the, 8.
— fruit or kitchen, flower border in, 161.
— Giusti, at Verona, 32.
— making, a fault in, 47.
— ornaments, on various pretended, 42.
— Rock, colour in the, 108.
— — planting the, 97.
— — position for the, 92.
— — soil for the, 96.
— Rose, the new, 167.
— shrub, Camellia as a, 68.
— ways, loss of, 4.
— who is to lay out the, 49.
— Wild, does not take the place of the flower garden, 5.
— — Narcissi in the, 117.
— — Orchard, the, 273.
— — reason for the, 116.
— — secret of the soil, 124.
— — the, 115.
— Winter, shrubs and trees in the, 200.
— Woodland, the, 303.
Gardenage, 9.

Gardening, flower, and garden design, Art in relation to, 21.
—— Architecture and, 36.
— Landscape, 9.
Gardens, Alpine, Rock and Wall, 86.
— cost and care of Stonework in, 38.
— formal made in our own day, 1.
— Landscape painting and, 27.
— Marsh, Bog and Water, 216.
— Rock, ill-formed, 98.
— Terraced, 32.
— Time and, 35.
— tracery, 26.
— variety the true source of beauty in the, 13.
— Wall, 104.
Gautheria Shallon, 331.
Goodwood, 254.
Grande Trianon, 29.
Grass, 112.
— walks in shade and sun, borders by, 158.
Greenlands, 40.
Grouping, beauty of, 110.
Groups, Yuccas in, 212.

Haddon, 40.
Ham House, 254.
Hedges and shelters of Holly, 335.
Hemlock Spruce, the, 320.
—— Western, 321.
Holly, 330.
— hedges and shelters of, 335.
Holmes, Oliver Wendell, 224.
Home Woods, 283.

House, flower garden in the, 229.
— Water Lilies and water-side plants for the, 236.

Idealism and realism, 22.
Ightham, 40.
Ilex, the, 253.
Iron fencing, what to do with it, 382.
Ivy, 331.

Juniper, 330.
Juniperus sabina, 330.
— Virginiana, 320.

Kew Gardens, 214.
Killerton, 254.
Kitchen garden, flower borders in the, fruit or, 161.
Knole, 40.

Land planting, poor, 285.
Landscape gardening, 9.
— painting and gardens, 27.
— planting, 9.
Laurel, 329.
— Cherry, 331.
— Portugal, 331.
Laurus nobilis, 329.
Lawns and playgrounds, 276.
— play, climber-covered alleys around, 277.
Leaves, 237.
Lilies, Water, and water-side plants for the house, 236.
Lincoln's Inn Fields, 63.
Line, no hard, 381.
London Parks, the, 209.
Longleat, 16.

Marnock, Robert, 50.
Marsh, Bog and Water Gardens, 216.
May bloom, 53.
Mentmore, 2.
Mosaic culture, 26.
Mount Usher, 17.

Narcissi, how to plant, 122.
— in the Wild Garden, 117.
Nature and the lesser by art, the greatest and fairest things are done by, 19.
'New Æsthetic,' 18
— Art,' 19.
Newick Park, 215.

Olmstead, F. L., 50.
Orchard Beautiful, fencing the, 265.
— — grafting the trees, 262.
— — poor soil should not hinder, 258.
— — root-pruning in the, 260.
— — the, 256.
— trees, climbers on, 274.
— — staking, 271.
— Wild Garden, the, 273.
Orchards, Cider, 261.
— Pear, for beauty, 268.
— starved, 263.
Ornaments, of various pretended, 42.
Owen, Sir Richard, 222.

Parks, London, the, 209.
Parthenon, the, 23.
Partridge Berry, the great, 331.
Pear orchards for beauty, 268.
Pears, Wild, 271.

Penjerrick, 17.
Pergola, 79.
Picea alba, 325.
— pungens, 317.
Pine, Austrian, 313.
— Cluster, 312.
— Corsican, 311.
— Himalayan, 324.
— Jefferys, 322.
— Monterey, 313.
— Scotch, 313.
— stem, the beauty of the, 299.
— White, 312.
— Yellow, 321.
Pinus canadensis, 325.
— excelsa, 324.
— insignis, 313.
— Jeffreyii, 322.
— Morinda, 323.
— orientalis, 323.
— pinaster, 312.
— polita, 323.
— ponderosa, 321.
— strobus, 312.
Planting, mixed, 357.
— near the sea, 252.
— waste in, 370.
Plants, coarse, 111.
— evergreen, 198.
— reap the stems of hardy, 197.
— to use, the best, 378.
Powis, 38, 40.

Realism, Idealism and, 22.
Repetition fatal to good effect, 112.
Rhododendrons at Weybridge Heath, 151.
Richmond Park, 39.

Rides, airy, 368.
— Woodland, 306, 364.
— — forming, 363.
Rock and Alpine plants, 128.
— — Wall Gardens, Alpine, 86.
— Garden, colour in the, 108.
— — planting the, 97.
— — position for the, 92.
— — soil for, 96.
— gardens, ill-formed, 98.
— misplaced artificial, 102.
Rockeries, refuse brick, 100.
Rockingham, 40.
Roehampton, 40.
Rose Garden, the new, 167.
— not a decorative plant, 169.
— ruin, September, 1905, 178.
— standard, the, 172.
— to come back to the flower garden, 171.
Rosebery, Lord, 44.
Roses as climbers, 77.

Savin, 330.
Sea, planting near the, 252.
Seed, covert from, 337.
Sequoia gigantea, 325.
Shade, Woodland, 367.
Shelter and wind screens in and near the flower garden, 250.
Shelters of Holly, hedges and, 335.
Shrub, nobler evergreen flowering, 247.
Shrubberies, flower borders to, 155.
Shrubland, 2.

Shrubs and trees and their artistic use, flowering, 53.
— — — Evergreen, 239.
— — — — ugly, 243.
— — — in the Winter Garden, 200.
— — — that bloom in the Spring, 141.
— fragile, climbers on, 76.
Site, any way good that best suits the, 16.
Soil-makers, trees as, 373.
Spring, annual flowers that bloom in the, 141.
— flowers in sun and shade and north and south aspects, 148.
— shrubs and trees that bloom in the, 141.
Spruce, Caucasian, 323.
— Hemlock, 320.
— — the Western, 321.
— Norway, 318.
— Rocky Mountain, 317.
— Sitka, the, 317.
— Tiger's tail, 323.
— White, the, 325.
St. Ann's, 254.
— James's Park, 47.
— — Square, 63.
— Leonard's Hill, Windsor, 70.
Statuomanie, 42.
Stonework in gardens, cost and care of, 38.
Styles and some common mistakes, of so-called, 30.
Sutton Place, 41.
Sweet Bay, the, 329.
Syon, 145.

INDEX

Talk of the day about Art, 18.
Taxus, 315.
Terms, misuse of, 7.
Thuja gigantea, 318.
Time and gardens, 35.
Trafalgar Square, 18.
Tree, Big, the, 325.
— colour, 289.
— Willows, 352.
Trees and shrubs and their artistic use, flowering, 53.
— — — Evergreen, 239.
— — — — ugly, 243.
— — — in the Winter Garden, 200.
— — — that bloom in the Spring, 141.
— as soil-makers, 373.
— design in planting, 310.
— English names for, 384.
— for beauty, 353.
— fruit, covered ways of, 83.
— — kinds to plant, 266.
— hardy flowers beneath, 125.
— native and European best, 349.
— — best for replanting old woodland, 344.
— nobler evergreen, 249.
— of the Northern Forest, the greater, 308.
— orchard, climbers on, 274.
— — staking, 271.
— supporting climbers, 81.
— time in planting, 297.
— to take their natural forms, 259.
— useless evergreen, 309.
— vigorous climbers on, 74.
Tregothnan, 71.

Trenching, 372.
Trentham, 2.
Tsuga canadensis, 320.
— Mertensiana, 321.
Turf, fine, in and near the flower garden, 281.
Turner, 23.

Underplanting, 368.
Underwoods and what to do with them, 342.
— — — an example, 243.

Variety essential, 15.
Venus of Milo, 23.
Versailles, 18, 30, 31, 37, 38.
Vines for their beauty of form, 78.

Walks, light arches over, 81.
— no formal, 94.
Wall Gardens, 104.
— — Alpine, Rock and, 86.
Water Gardens, Marsh, Bog and, 216.
— Lilies and water-side plants for the house, 236.
Waterlow Park, 101.
Weeds, evergreen, 245.
Wild Garden does not take the place of the flower garden, 5.
— — Narcissi in the, 117.
— — Orchard, the, 273.
— — reasons for the, 116.
— — Snowdrops in the, 121.
— — the secret of the soil, 124.
— — the, 115.
Willows, tree, 352.
Wilton, 16.
Windsor, 38.
Wind-waving, 344.

Winter Garden, shrubs and trees in the, 200.
Witley Court, 2.
Wood value, 350.
Woodland, fencing for, 376.
— Garden, the, 303.
— native trees best for replanting old, 344.
— rides, 306, 364.
— — forming, 363.
— shade, 367.
Woods, evergreen, for beauty, 284.
Woods from underwood growths, renewing, 346.
— home, 283.
— of mixed, 356.
— planting poor land, 285.
— quickness of growth, 286.
— shelter in, 285.
— sunny spots in, 365.
— without fencing, 379.
— — grubbing, replanting, 345.

Yew, Common, 315.
Yuccas in groups, 212.

OXFORD: HORACE HART
PRINTER TO THE UNIVERSITY

Lightning Source UK Ltd.
Milton Keynes UK
UKHW021852171119
353728UK00003B/33/P